THE LOG OF A COWBOY

THE LOG
OF A COWBOY

A Narrative of the Old Trail Days

By

ANDY ADAMS

ILLUSTRATED BY E. BOYD SMITH

"Our cattle also shall go with us."
—*Exodus* iv, 26.

UNIVERSITY OF NEBRASKA PRESS • LINCOLN/LONDON

Library of Congress Catalog card number 3-12817

The text of this book is reproduced from the edition pub-
lished in 1903 by Houghton Mifflin and Company, Boston.

Manufactured in the United States of America

ISBN 0-8032-5000-2 pbk.

First Bison Book printing March, 1964

Most recent printing shown by first digit below:
16   17   18   19   20   21   22

TO THE

COWMEN AND BOYS OF

THE OLD WESTERN TRAIL

THESE PAGES ARE

GRATEFULLY

DEDICATED

CONTENTS

LIST OF ILLUSTRATIONS

THE LOG OF A COWBOY

CHAPTER I

UP THE TRAIL

JUST why my father moved, at the close of the civil war, from Georgia to Texas, is to this good hour a mystery to me. While we did not exactly belong to the poor whites, we classed with them in poverty, being renters; but I am inclined to think my parents were intellectually superior to that common type of the South. Both were foreign born, my mother being Scotch and my father a north of Ireland man, — as I remember him, now, impulsive, hasty in action, and slow to confess a fault. It was his impulsiveness that led him to volunteer and serve four years in the Confederate army, — trying years to my mother, with a brood of seven children to feed, garb, and house. The war brought me my initiation as a cowboy, of which I have now, after the long lapse of years, the greater portion of which were spent with cattle, a distinct recollection. Sherman's army, in its march to the sea, passed through our county, devastating that section for miles in its passing.

Foraging parties scoured the country on either side of its path. My mother had warning in time and set her house in order. Our work stock consisted of two yoke of oxen, while our cattle numbered three cows, and for saving them from the foragers credit must be given to my mother's generalship. There was a wild canebrake, in which the cattle fed, several hundred acres in extent, about a mile from our little farm, and it was necessary to bell them in order to locate them when wanted. But the cows were in the habit of coming up to be milked, and a soldier can hear a bell as well as any one. I was a lad of eight at the time, and while my two older brothers worked our few fields, I was sent into the canebrake to herd the cattle. We had removed the bells from the oxen and cows, but one ox was belled after darkness each evening, to be unbelled again at daybreak. I always carried the bell with me, stuffed with grass, in order to have it at hand when wanted.

During the first few days of the raid, a number of mounted foraging parties passed our house, but its poverty was all too apparent, and nothing was molested. Several of these parties were driving herds of cattle and work stock of every description, while by day and by night gins and plantation houses were being given to the flames. Our one-roomed log cabin was spared, due to the ingenious tale told by my mother as to the whereabouts of my father ; and yet she taught her children to fear God and tell the truth. My vigil was trying to one of my years, for the days seemed like weeks, but the importance of hiding our cattle was thoroughly impressed upon my mind. Food was secretly brought to me, and under cover of darkness, my mother and eldest brother would come and milk the cows, when we would all return home together. Then, before daybreak, we would be in the cane listening for the first tinkle, to find the cattle and remove the bell. And my day's work commenced anew.

Only once did I come near betraying my trust. About the middle of the third day I grew very hungry, and as the cattle were lying down, I crept to the edge of the canebrake to see if my dinner was not forthcoming. Soldiers were in sight, which explained everything. Concealed in the rank cane I stood and watched them. Suddenly a squad of five or six turned a point of the brake and rode within fifty feet of me. I stood like a stone statue, my concealment being perfect. After they had passed, I took a step forward, the better to watch them as they rode away, when the grass dropped out of the bell and it clattered. A red-whiskered soldier heard the tinkle, and wheeling his horse, rode back. I grasped the clapper and lay flat on the ground, my heart beating like a trip-hammer. He rode within twenty feet of me, peering into the thicket of cane, and not seeing anything unusual, turned and galloped away after his companions. Then the lesson, taught me by my mother, of being " faithful over a

few things," flashed through my mind, and though
our cattle were spared to us, I felt very guilty.

Another vivid recollection of those boyhood days
in Georgia was the return of my father from the
army. The news of Lee's surrender had reached
us, and all of us watched for his coming. Though
he was long delayed, when at last he did come riding home on a swallow-marked brown mule, he was
a conquering hero to us children. We had never
owned a horse, and he assured us that the animal
was his own, and by turns set us on the tired mule's
back. He explained to mother and us children
how, though he was an infantryman, he came into
possession of the animal. Now, however, with my
mature years and knowledge of brands, I regret to
state that the mule had not been condemned and
was in the " U. S." brand. A story which Priest,
" The Rebel," once told me throws some light on the
matter; he asserted that all good soldiers would
steal. " Can you take the city of St. Louis ? " was
asked of General Price. " I don't know as I can
take it," replied the general to his consulting supe-
riors, " but if you will give me Louisiana troops,
I 'll agree to steal it."

Though my father had lost nothing by the war,
he was impatient to go to a new country. Many of
his former comrades were going to Texas, and, as
our worldly possessions were movable, to Texas we
started. Our four oxen were yoked to the wagon,
in which our few household effects were loaded and

in which mother and the smaller children rode, and with the cows, dogs, and elder boys bringing up the rear, our caravan started, my father riding the mule and driving the oxen. It was an entire summer's trip, full of incident, privation, and hardship. The stock fared well, but several times we were compelled to halt and secure work in order to supply our limited larder. Through certain sections, however, fish and game were abundant. I remember the enthusiasm we all felt when we reached the Sabine River, and for the first time viewed the promised land. It was at a ferry, and the sluggish river was deep. When my father informed the ferryman that he had no money with which to pay the ferriage, the latter turned on him remarking, sarcastically: "What, no money? My dear sir, it certainly can't make much difference to a man which side of the river he's on, when he has no money."

Nothing daunted by this rebuff, my father argued the point at some length, when the ferryman relented so far as to inform him that ten miles higher up, the river was fordable. We arrived at the ford the next day. My father rode across and back, testing the stage of the water and the river's bottom before driving the wagon in. Then taking one of the older boys behind him on the mule in order to lighten the wagon, he drove the oxen into the river. Near the middle the water was deep enough to reach the wagon box, but with shoutings and a free applica-

tion of the gad, we hurried through in safety. One
of the wheel oxen, a black steer which we called
" Pop-eye," could be ridden, and I straddled him
in fording, laving my sunburned feet in the cool
water. The cows were driven over next, the dogs
swimming, and at last, bag and baggage, we were
in Texas.

We reached the Colorado River early in the fall,
where we stopped and picked cotton for several
months, making quite a bit of money, and near
Christmas reached our final destination on the San
Antonio River, where we took up land and built a
house. That was a happy home; the country was
new and supplied our simple wants; we had milk
and honey, and, though the fig tree was absent,
along the river grew endless quantities of mustang
grapes.

At that time the San Antonio valley was principally a cattle country, and as the boys of our
family grew old enough the fascination of a horse
and saddle was too strong to be resisted. My two
older brothers went first, but my father and mother
made strenuous efforts to keep me at home, and
did so until I was sixteen. I suppose it is natural
for every country boy to be fascinated with some
other occupation than the one to which he is bred.
In my early teens, I always thought I should like
either to drive six horses to a stage or clerk in a
store, and if I could have attained either of those
lofty heights, at that age, I would have asked no

more.   So my father, rather than see me follow in
the footsteps of my older brothers, secured me a
situation in a village store some twenty miles distant.   The storekeeper was a fellow countryman
of my father — from the same county in Ireland,
in fact — and I was duly elated on getting away
from home to the life of the village.

But my elation was short-lived.   I was to receive
no wages for the first six months.   My father counseled the merchant to work me hard, and, if possible, cure me of the " foolish notion," as he termed
it.   The storekeeper cured me.   The first week I
was with him he kept me in a back warehouse shell-
ing corn.   The second week started out no better.
I was given a shovel and put on the street to work
out the poll-tax, not only of the merchant but of
two other clerks in the store.   Here was two weeks'
work in sight, but the third morning I took breakfast at home.   My mercantile career had ended,
and forthwith I took to the range as a preacher's
son takes to vice.   By the time I was twenty there
was no better cow-hand in the entire country.   I
could, besides, speak Spanish and play the fiddle,
and thought nothing of riding thirty miles to a
dance.   The vagabond temperament of the range
I easily assimilated.

Christmas in the South is always a season of fes-
tivity, and the magnet of mother and home yearly
drew us to the family hearthstone.   There we
brothers met and exchanged stories of our expe-

riences.   But one year both my brothers brought
home a new experience.   They had been up the
trail, and the wondrous stories they told about the
northern country set my blood on fire.   Until then
I thought I had had adventures, but mine paled into
insignificance beside theirs.   The following summer,
my eldest brother, Robert, himself was to boss a
herd up the trail, and I pleaded with him to give
me a berth, but he refused me, saying: "No,
Tommy; the trail is one place where a foreman
can have no favorites.   Hardship and privation
must be met, and the men must throw themselves
equally into the collar.   I don't doubt but you're
a good hand; still the fact that you're my brother
might cause other boys to think I would favor you.
A trail outfit has to work as a unit, and dissensions
would be ruinous."   I had seen favoritism shown
on ranches, and understood his position to be right.
Still I felt that I must make that trip if it were
possible.   Finally Robert, seeing that I was over-
anxious to go, came to me and said: "I've been
thinking that if I recommended you to Jim Flood,
my old foreman, he might take you with him next
year.   He is to have a herd that will take five
months from start to delivery, and that will be the
chance of your life.   I'll see him next week and
make a strong talk for you."

True to his word, he bespoke me a job with Flood
the next time he met him, and a week later a letter
from Flood reached me, terse and pointed, engaging

my services as a trail hand for the coming summer. The outfit would pass near our home on its way to receive the cattle which were to make up the trail herd. Time and place were appointed where I was to meet them in the middle of March, and I felt as if I were made. I remember my mother and sisters twitted me about the swagger that came into my walk, after the receipt of Flood's letter, and even asserted that I sat my horse as straight as a poker. Possibly! but wasn't I going up the trail with Jim Flood, the boss foreman of Don Lovell, the cowman and drover?

Our little ranch was near Cibollo Ford on the river, and as the outfit passed down the country, they crossed at that ford and picked me up. Flood was not with them, which was a disappointment to me, "Quince" Forrest acting as *segundo* at the time. They had four mules to the "chuck" wagon under Barney McCann as cook, while the *remuda*, under Billy Honeyman as horse wrangler, numbered a hundred and forty-two, ten horses to the man, with two extra for the foreman. Then, for the first time, I learned that we were going down to the mouth of the Rio Grande to receive the herd from across the river in Old Mexico; and that they were contracted for delivery on the Blackfoot Indian Reservation in the northwest corner of Montana. Lovell had several contracts with the Indian Department of the government that year, and had been granted the privilege of bringing in, free of duty, any cattle to be used in filling Indian contracts.

My worst trouble was getting away from home on the morning of starting. Mother and my sisters, of course, shed a few tears; but my father, stern and unbending in his manner, gave me his benediction in these words: "Thomas Moore, you're the third son to leave our roof, but your father's blessing goes with you. I left my own home beyond the sea before I was your age." And as they all stood at the gate, I climbed into my saddle and rode away, with a lump in my throat which left me speechless to reply.

CHAPTER II

IT was a nice ten days' trip from the San Antonio to the Rio Grande River. We made twenty-five to thirty miles a day, giving the saddle horses all the advantage of grazing on the way. Rather than hobble, Forrest night-herded them, using five guards, two men to the watch of two hours each. "As I have little hope of ever rising to the dignity of foreman," said our *segundo*, while arranging the guards, "I'll take this occasion to show you varmints what an iron will I possess. With the amount of help I have, I don't propose to even catch a night horse; and I'll give the cook orders to bring me a cup of coffee and a cigarette before I arise in the morning. I've been up the trail before and realize that this authority is short-lived, so I propose to make the most of it while it lasts. Now you all know your places, and see you don't incur your foreman's displeasure."

The outfit reached Brownsville on March 25th, where we picked up Flood and Lovell, and dropping down the river about six miles below Fort Brown, went into camp at a cattle ford known as Paso Ganado. The Rio Grande was two hundred yards wide at this point, and at its then stage was almost swimming from bank to bank. It had very little current, and when winds were favorable the tide from the Gulf ran in above the ford. Flood had spent the past two weeks across the river, receiving and road-branding the herd, so when the cattle should reach the river on the Mexican side we were in honor bound to accept everything bearing the "circle dot" ⊙ on the left hip. The contract called for a thousand she cattle, three and four years of age, and two thousand four and five year old beeves, estimated as sufficient to fill a million-pound beef contract. For fear of losses on the trail, our foreman had accepted fifty extra head of each class, and our herd at starting would number thirty-one hundred head. They were coming up from ranches in the interior, and we expected to cross them the first favorable day after their arrival. A number of different rancheros had turned in cattle in making up the herd, and Flood reported them in good, strong condition.

Lovell and Flood were a good team of cowmen. The former, as a youth, had carried a musket in the ranks of the Union army, and at the end of that struggle, cast his fortune with Texas. Where others had seen nothing but the desolation of war, Lovell saw opportunities of business, and had yearly forged ahead as a drover and beef contractor. He was well calculated to manage the cattle business, but was irritable and inclined to borrow trouble, therefore unqualified personally to oversee the actual management of a cow herd. In repose, Don Lovell was slow, almost dull, but in an emergency was astonishingly quick-witted and alert. He never insisted on temperance among his men, and though usually of a placid temperament, when out of tobacco — Lord !

Jim Flood, on the other hand, was in a hundred respects the antithesis of his employer. Born to the soil of Texas, he knew nothing but cattle, but he knew them thoroughly. Yet in their calling, the pair were a harmonious unit. He never crossed a bridge till he reached it, was indulgent with his men, and would overlook any fault, so long as they rendered faithful service. Priest told me this incident: Flood had hired a man at Red River the year before, when a self-appointed guardian present called Flood to one side and said, —

"Don't you know that that man you 've just hired is the worst drunkard in this country?"

"No, I did n't know it," replied Flood, "but I 'm glad to hear he is. I don't want to ruin an innocent man, and a trail outfit is not supposed to have any morals. Just so the herd don't count out shy on the day of delivery, I don't mind how many drinks the outfit takes."

The next morning after going into camp, the first thing was the allotment of our mounts for the trip. Flood had the first pick, and cut twelve bays and browns. His preference for solid colors, though

they were not the largest in the *remuda*, showed
his practical sense of horses.   When it came the
boys' turn to cut, we were only allowed to cut one
at a time by turns, even casting lots for first choice.
We had ridden the horses enough to have a fair
idea as to their merits, and every lad was his own
judge.   There were, as it happened, only three pinto
horses in the entire saddle stock, and these three
were the last left of the entire bunch.   Now a little
boy or girl, and many an older person, thinks that
a spotted horse is the real thing, but practical cattle men know that this freak of color in range-bred
horses is the result of in-and-in breeding, with consequent physical and mental deterioration.   It was
my good fortune that morning to get a good mount
of horses, — three sorrels, two grays, two coyotes, a
black, a brown, and a *grulla*.   The black was my
second pick, and though the color is not a hardy
one, his " bread-basket " indicated that he could
carry food for a long ride, and ought to be a good
swimmer.   My judgment of him was confirmed
throughout the trip, as I used him for my night
horse and when we had swimming rivers to ford.
I gave this black the name of " Nigger Boy."

For the trip each man was expected to furnish
his own accoutrements.   In saddles, we had the
ordinary Texas make, the housings of which covered our mounts from withers to hips, and would
weigh from thirty to forty pounds, bedecked with
the latest in the way of trimmings and trappings.

Our bridles were in keeping with the saddles, the reins as long as plough lines, while the bit was frequently ornamental and costly. The indispensable slicker, a greatcoat of oiled canvas, was ever at hand, securely tied to our cantle strings. Spurs were a matter of taste. If a rider carried a quirt, he usually dispensed with spurs, though, when used, those with large, dull rowels were the make commonly chosen. In the matter of leggings, not over half our outfit had any, as a trail herd always kept in the open, and except for night herding they were too warm in summer. Our craft never used a cattle whip, but if emergency required, the loose end of a rope served instead, and was more humane.

Either Flood or Lovell went into town every afternoon with some of the boys, expecting to hear from the cattle. On one trip they took along the wagon, laying in a month's supplies. The rest of us amused ourselves in various ways. One afternoon when the tide was in, we tried our swimming horses in the river, stripping to our underclothing, and, with nothing but a bridle on our horses, plunged into tidewater. My Nigger Boy swam from bank to bank like a duck. On the return I slid off behind, and taking his tail, let him tow me to our own side, where he arrived snorting like a tugboat.

One evening, on their return from Brownsville, Flood brought word that the herd would camp that night within fifteen miles of the river. At daybreak Lovell and the foreman, with "Fox" Quarternight and myself, started to meet the herd. The nearest ferry was at Brownsville, and it was eleven o'clock when we reached the cattle. Flood had dispensed with an interpreter and had taken Quarternight and me along to do the interpreting. The cattle were well shed and in good flesh for such an early season of the year, and in receiving, our foreman had been careful and had accepted only such as had strength for a long voyage. They were the long-legged, long-horned Southern cattle, pale-colored as a rule, possessed the running powers of a deer, and in an ordinary walk could travel with a horse. They had about thirty vaqueros under a corporal driving the herd, and the cattle were strung out in regular trailing manner. We rode with them until the noon hour, when, with the understanding that they were to bring the herd to Paso Ganado by ten o'clock the following day, we rode for Matamoros. Lovell had other herds to start on the trail that year, and was very anxious to cross the cattle the following day, so as to get the weekly steamer — the only mode of travel — which left Point Isabel for Galveston on the first of April.

The next morning was bright and clear, with an east wind, which insured a flood tide in the river. On first sighting the herd that morning, we made ready to cross them as soon as they reached the river. The wagon was moved up within a hundred yards of the ford, and a substantial corral of ropes was stretched. Then the entire saddle stock was driven in, so as to be at hand in case a hasty change of mounts was required. By this time Honeyman knew the horses of each man's mount, so all we had to do was to sing out our horse, and Billy would have a rope on one and have him at hand before you could unsaddle a tired one. On account of our linguistic accomplishments, Quarternight and I were to be sent across the river to put the cattle in and otherwise assume control. On the Mexican side there was a single string of high brush fence on the lower side of the ford, commencing well out in the water and running back about two hundred yards, thus giving us a half chute in forcing the cattle to take swimming water. This ford had been in use for years in crossing cattle, but I believe this was the first herd ever crossed that was intended for the trail, or for beyond the bounds of Texas.

When the herd was within a mile of the river, Fox and I shed our saddles, boots, and surplus clothing and started to meet it. The water was chilly, but we struck it with a shout, and with the cheers of our outfit behind us, swam like smugglers. A swimming horse needs freedom, and we scarcely touched the reins, but with one hand buried in a mane hold, and giving gentle slaps on the neck with the other, we guided our horses for the other shore. I was proving out my black, Fox had a gray of equal barrel displacement, — both good swimmers; and on reaching the Mexican shore, we dismounted and allowed them to roll in the warm sand.

Flood had given us general instructions, and we halted the herd about half a mile from the river. The Mexican corporal was only too glad to have us assume charge, and assured us that he and his outfit were ours to command. I at once proclaimed Fox Quarternight, whose years and experience outranked mine, the *gringo* corporal for the day, at which the vaqueros smiled, but I noticed they never used the word. On Fox's suggestion the Mexican corporal brought up his wagon and corralled his horses as we had done, when his cook, to our delight, invited all to have coffee before starting. That cook won our everlasting regards, for his coffee was delicious. We praised it highly, whereupon the corporal ordered the cook to have it at hand for the men in the intervals between crossing the different bunches of cattle. A March day on the Rio Grande with wet clothing is not summer, and the vaqueros hesitated a bit before following the example of Quarternight and myself and dispensing with saddles and boots. Five men were then detailed to hold the herd as compact as possible, and the remainder, twenty-seven all told, cut off about three hundred head and started for the river. I took the lead, for though cattle are less gregarious by nature than other animals, under pressure of excitement they will follow a leader. It was about noon and the herd were thirsty, so when we reached the brush chute, all hands started them on a run for the water. When the cattle were once inside the wing we went rapidly, four vaqueros riding outside the fence to keep the cattle from turning the chute on reaching swimming water. The leaders were crowding me close when Nigger breasted the water, and closely followed by several lead cattle, I struck straight for the American shore. The vaqueros forced every hoof into the river, following and shouting as far as the midstream, when they were swimming so nicely, Quarternight called off the men and all turned their horses back to the Mexican side. On landing opposite the exit from the ford, our men held the cattle as they came out, in order to bait the next bunch.

I rested my horse only a few minutes before taking the water again, but Lovell urged me to take an extra horse across, so as to have a change in case my black became fagged in swimming. Quarternight was a harsh *segundo*, for no sooner had I reached the other bank than he cut off the second bunch of about four hundred and started them. Turning Nigger Boy loose behind the brush fence, so as to be out of the way, I galloped out on my second horse, and meeting the cattle, turned and again took the lead for the river. My substitute did not swim with the freedom and ease of the black, and several times cattle swam so near me that I could lay my hand on their backs. When about halfway over, I heard shoutings behind me in English, and on looking back saw Nigger Boy swimming after us. A number of vaqueros attempted to catch him, but he outswam them and came out with the cattle; the excitement was too much for him to miss.

Each trip was a repetition of the former, with varying incident. Every hoof was over in less than two hours. On the last trip, in which there were about seven hundred head, the horse of one of the Mexican vaqueros took cramps, it was supposed, at about the middle of the river, and sank without a moment's warning. A number of us heard the man's terrified cry, only in time to see horse and rider sink. Every man within reach turned to the rescue, and a moment later the man rose to the surface. Fox caught him by the shirt, and, shaking the water out of him, turned him over to one of the other vaqueros, who towed him back to their own side. Strange as it may appear, the horse never came to the surface again, which supported the supposition of cramps.

After a change of clothes for Quarternight and myself, and rather late dinner for all hands, there yet remained the counting of the herd. The Mexican corporal and two of his men had come over for the purpose, and though Lovell and several wealthy rancheros, the sellers of the cattle, were present, it remained for Flood and the corporal to make the final count, as between buyer and seller. There was also present a river guard, — sent out by the

United States Custom House, as a matter of form
in the entry papers, — who also insisted on counting.   In order to have a second count on the herd,
Lovell ordered The Rebel to count opposite the government's man. We strung the cattle out, now logy
with water, and after making quite a circle, brought
the herd around where there was quite a bluff bank
of the river. The herd handled well, and for a
quarter of an hour we lined them between our four
mounted counters. The only difference in the
manner of counting between Flood and the Mexican corporal was that the American used a tally
string tied to the pommel of his saddle, on which
were ten knots, keeping count by slipping a knot
on each even hundred, while the Mexican used ten
small pebbles, shifting a pebble from one hand to
the other on hundreds.   "Just a mere difference
in nationality," Lovell had me interpret to the selling dons.

When the count ended only two of the men
agreed on numbers, The Rebel and the corporal
making the same thirty-one hundred and five, —
Flood being one under and the Custom House man
one over.   Lovell at once accepted the count of
Priest and the corporal; and the delivery, which,
as I learned during the interpreting that followed,
was to be sealed with a supper that night in
Brownsville, was consummated. Lovell was compelled to leave us, to make the final payment for
the herd, and we would not see him again for some

time. They were all seated in the vehicle ready
to start for town, when the cowman said to his
foreman, —

"Now, Jim, I can't give you any pointers on
handling a herd, but you have until the 10th day
of September to reach the Blackfoot Agency. An
average of fifteen miles a day will put you there
on time, so don't hurry. I'll try and see you at
Dodge and Ogalalla on the way. Now, live well,
for I like your outfit of men. Your credit letter is
good anywhere you need supplies, and if you want
more horses on the trail, buy them and draft on me
through your letter of credit. If any of your men
meet with accident or get sick, look out for them the
same as you would for yourself, and I'll honor all
bills. And don't be stingy over your expense account, for if that herd don't make money, you and
I had better quit cows."

I had been detained to do any interpreting need-
ful, and at parting Lovell beckoned to me. When
I rode alongside the carriage, he gave me his hand
and said, —

"Flood tells me to-day that you're a brother of
Bob Quirk. Bob is to be foreman of my herd that
I'm putting up in Nueces County. I'm glad you're
here with Jim, though, for it's a longer trip. Yes,
you'll get all the circus there is, and stay for the
concert besides. They say God is good to the poor
and the Irish; and if that's so, you'll pull through
all right. Good-by, son." And as he gave me a

hearty, ringing grip of the hand, I couldn't help feeling friendly toward him, Yankee that he was.

After Lovell and the dons had gone, Flood ordered McCann to move his wagon back from the river about a mile. It was now too late in the day to start the herd, and we wanted to graze them well, as it was our first night with them. About half our outfit grazed them around on a large circle, preparatory to bringing them up to the bed ground as it grew dusk. In the untrammeled freedom of the native range, a cow or steer will pick old dry grass on which to lie down, and if it is summer, will prefer an elevation sufficient to catch any passing breeze. Flood was familiar with the habits of cattle, and selected a nice elevation on which the old dry grass of the previous summer's growth lay matted like a carpet.

Our saddle horses by this time were fairly well broken to camp life, and, with the cattle on hand, night herding them had to be abandoned. Billy Honeyman, however, had noticed several horses that were inclined to stray on day herd, and these few leaders were so well marked in his memory that, as a matter of precaution, he insisted on putting a rope hobble on them. At every noon and night camp we strung a rope from the hind wheel of our wagon, and another from the end of the wagon tongue back to stakes driven in the ground or held by a man, forming a trianglar corral. Thus in a few minutes, under any conditions, we could construct a temporary corral for catching a change of mounts, or for the wrangler to hobble untrustworthy horses. On the trail all horses are free at night, except the regular night ones, which are used constantly during the entire trip, and under ordinary conditions keep strong and improve in flesh.

Before the herd was brought in for the night, and during the supper hour, Flood announced the guards for the trip. As the men usually bunked in pairs, the foreman chose them as they slept, but was under the necessity of splitting two berths of bedfellows. "Rod" Wheat, Joe Stallings, and Ash Borrowstone were assigned to the first guard, from eight to ten thirty P. M. Bob Blades, "Bull" Durham, and Fox Quarternight were given second guard, from ten thirty to one. Paul Priest, John Officer, and myself made up the third watch, from one to three thirty. The Rebel and I were bunkies, and this choice of guards, while not ideal, was much better than splitting bedfellows and having them annoy each other by going out and returning from guard separately. The only fault I ever found with Priest was that he could use the poorest judgment in selecting a bed ground for our blankets, and always talked and told stories to me until I fell asleep. He was a light sleeper himself, while I, being much younger, was the reverse. The fourth and last guard, from three thirty until relieved after daybreak, fell to Wyatt Roundtree, Quince Forrest, and "Moss" Strayhorn. Thus the only

men in the outfit not on night duty were Honeyman, our horse wrangler, Barney McCann, our
cook, and Flood, the foreman. The latter, however, made up by riding almost double as much as
any man in his outfit. He never left the herd
until it was bedded down for the night, and we
could always hear him quietly arousing the cook
and horse wrangler an hour before daybreak. He
always kept a horse on picket for the night, and
often took the herd as it left the bed ground at clear
dawn.

A half hour before dark, Flood and all the herd
men turned out to bed down the cattle for our first
night. They had been well grazed after counting,
and as they came up to the bed ground there was
not a hungry or thirsty animal in the lot. All
seemed anxious to lie down, and by circling around
slowly, while gradually closing in, in the course of
half an hour all were bedded nicely on possibly five
or six acres. I remember there were a number of
muleys among the cattle, and these would not ven-
ture into the compact herd until the others had lain
down. Being hornless, instinct taught them to be
on the defensive, and it was noticeable that they
were the first to arise in the morning, in advance of
their horned kin. When all had lain down, Flood
and the first guard remained, the others returning
to the wagon.

The guards ride in a circle about four rods outside the sleeping cattle, and by riding in opposite

directions make it impossible for any animal to make its escape without being noticed by the riders. The guards usually sing or whistle continuously, so that the sleeping herd may know that a friend and not an enemy is keeping vigil over their dreams. A sleeping herd of cattle make a pretty picture on a clear moonlight night, chewing their cuds and grunting and blowing over contented stomachs. The night horses soon learn their duty, and a rider may fall asleep or doze along in the saddle, but the horses will maintain their distance in their leisurely, sentinel rounds.

On returning to the wagon, Priest and I picketed our horses, saddled, where we could easily find them in the darkness, and unrolled our bed. We had two pairs of blankets each, which, with an ordinary wagon sheet doubled for a tarpaulin, and coats and boots for pillows, completed our couch. We slept otherwise in our clothing worn during the day, and if smooth, sandy ground was available on which to spread our bed, we had no trouble in sleeping the sleep that long hours in the saddle were certain to bring. With all his pardonable faults, The Rebel was a good bunkie and a hail companion, this being his sixth trip over the trail. He had been with Lovell over a year before the two made the discovery that they had been on opposite sides during the " late unpleasantness." On making this discovery, Lovell at once rechristened Priest " The Rebel," and that name he always bore. He was fifteen years my senior at this time, a wonderfully complex nature, hardened by unusual experiences into a character the gamut of whose moods ran from that of a good-natured fellow to a man of unrelenting severity in anger.

We were sleeping a nine knot gale when Fox Quarternight of the second guard called us on our watch. It was a clear, starry night, and our guard soon passed, the cattle sleeping like tired soldiers. When the last relief came on guard and we had returned to our blankets, I remember Priest telling me this little incident as I fell asleep.

" I was at a dance once in Live Oak County, and there was a stuttering fellow there by the name of Lem Todhunter. The girls, it seems, did n't care to dance with him, and pretended they could n't understand him. He had asked every girl at the party, and received the same answer from each — they could n't understand him. ' W-w-w-ell, g-g-g-go to hell, then. C-c-c-can y-y-you understand that?' he said to the last girl, and her brother threatened to mangle him horribly if he did n't apologize, to which he finally agreed. He went back into the house and said to the girl, ' Y-y-you n-n-n-need n't g-g-g-go to hell; y-y-your b-b-b-brother and I have m-m-made other 'r-r-r-rangements.' "

CHAPTER III

On the morning of April 1, 1882, our Circle Dot herd started on its long tramp to the Blackfoot Agency in Montana. With six men on each side, and the herd strung out for three quarters of a mile, it could only be compared to some mythical serpent or Chinese dragon, as it moved forward on its sinuous, snail-like course. Two riders, known as point men, rode out and well back from the lead cattle, and by riding forward and closing in as occasion required, directed the course of the herd. The main body of the herd trailed along behind the leaders like an army in loose marching order, guarded by outriders, known as swing men, who rode well out from the advancing column, warding off range cattle and seeing that none of the herd wandered away or dropped out. There was no driving to do ; the cattle moved of their own free will as in ordinary travel. Flood seldom gave orders ; but, as a number of us had never worked on the trail before, at breakfast on the morning of our start he gave in substance these general directions : —

"Boys, the secret of trailing cattle is never to let

your herd know that they are under restraint. Let everything that is done be done voluntarily by the cattle. From the moment you let them off the bed ground in the morning until they are bedded at night, never let a cow take a step, except in the direction of its destination. In this manner you can loaf away the day, and cover from fifteen to twenty miles, and the herd in the mean time will enjoy all the freedom of an open range. Of course, it's long, tiresome hours to the men; but the condition of the herd and saddle stock demands sacrifices on our part, if any have to be made. And I want to caution you younger boys about your horses; there is such a thing as having ten horses in your string, and at the same time being afoot. You are all well mounted, and on the condition of the *remuda* depends the success and safety of the herd. Accidents will happen to horses, but don't let it be your fault; keep your saddle blankets dry and clean, for no better word can be spoken of a man than that he is careful of his horses. Ordinarily a man might get along with six or eight horses, but in such emergencies as we are liable to meet, we have not a horse to spare, and a man afoot is useless."

And as all of us younger boys learned afterward, there was plenty of good, solid, horse-sense in Flood's advice; for before the trip ended there were men in our outfit who were as good as afoot, while others had their original mounts, every one fit for the saddle. Flood had insisted on a good

mount of horses, and Lovell was cowman enough
to know that what the mule is to the army the cow-
horse is to the herd.

The first and second day out there was no incident worth mentioning. We traveled slowly,
hardly making an average day's drive. The third
morning Flood left us, to look out a crossing on
the Arroyo Colorado. On coming down to receive
the herd, we had crossed this sluggish bayou about
thirty-six miles north of Brownsville. It was a
deceptive-looking stream, being over fifty feet deep
and between bluff banks. We ferried our wagon
and saddle horses over, swimming the loose ones.
But the herd was keeping near the coast line for
the sake of open country, and it was a question if
there was a ford for the wagon as near the coast
as our course was carrying us. The murmurings
of the Gulf had often reached our ears the day before, and herds had been known, in former years,
to cross from the mainland over to Padre Island,
the intervening Laguna Madre being fordable.

We were nooning when Flood returned with the
news that it would be impossible to cross our wagon
at any point on the bayou, and that we would have
to ford around the mouth of the stream. Where
the fresh and salt water met in the laguna, there
had formed a delta, or shallow bar; and by following its contour we would not have over twelve to
fourteen inches of water, though the half circle was
nearly two miles in length. As we would barely

have time to cross that day, the herd was at once started, veering for the mouth of the Arroyo Colorado. On reaching it, about the middle of the afternoon, the foreman led the way, having crossed in the morning and learned the ford. The wagon followed, the saddle horses came next, while the herd brought up the rear. It proved good footing on the sandbar, but the water in the laguna was too salty for the cattle, though the loose horses lay down and wallowed in it. We were about an hour in crossing, and on reaching the mainland met a vaquero, who directed us to a large fresh-water lake a few miles inland, where we camped for the night.

It proved an ideal camp, with wood, water, and grass in abundance, and very little range stock to annoy us. We had watered the herd just before noon, and before throwing them upon the bed ground for the night, watered them a second time. We had a splendid camp-fire that night, of dry live oak logs, and after supper was over and the first guard had taken the herd, smoking and story telling were the order of the evening. The camp-fire is to all outdoor life what the evening fireside is to domestic life. After the labors of the day are over, the men gather around the fire, and the social hour of the day is spent in yarning. The stories told may run from the sublime to the ridiculous, from a true incident to a base fabrication, or from a touching bit of pathos to the most vulgar vulgarity.

"Have I ever told this outfit my experience with the vigilantes when I was a kid?" inquired Bull Durham. There was a general negative response, and he proceeded. "Well, our folks were living on the Frio at the time, and there was a man in our neighborhood who had an outfit of four men out beyond Nueces Cañon hunting wild cattle for their hides. It was necessary to take them out supplies about every so often, and on one trip he begged my folks to let me go along for company. I was a slim slip of a colt about fourteen at the time, and as this man was a friend of ours, my folks consented to let me go along. We each had a good saddle horse, and two pack mules with provisions and ammunition for the hunting camp. The first night we made camp, a boy overtook us with the news that the brother of my companion had been accidentally killed by a horse, and of course he would have to return. Well, we were twenty miles on our way, and as it would take some little time to go back and return with the loaded mules, I volunteered, like a fool kid, to go on and take the packs through.

"The only question was, could I pack and unpack. I had helped him at this work, double-handed, but now that I was to try it alone, he showed me what he called a squaw hitch, with which you can lash a pack single-handed. After putting me through it once or twice, and satisfying himself that I could do the packing, he consented

to let me go on, he and the messenger returning
home during the night. The next morning I packed
without any trouble and started on my way. It
would take me two days yet, poking along with
heavy packs, to reach the hunters. Well, I had n't
made over eight or ten miles the first morning,
when, as I rounded a turn in the trail, a man
stepped out from behind a rock, threw a gun in my
face, and ordered me to hold up my hands. Then
another appeared from the opposite side with his
gun leveled on me. Inside of half a minute a dozen
men galloped up from every quarter, all armed to
the teeth. The man on leaving had given me his
gun for company, one of these old smoke-pole, cap-
and-ball six-shooters, but I must have forgotten
what guns were for, for I elevated my little hands
nicely. The leader of the party questioned me as
to who I was, and what I was doing there, and
what I had in those packs. That once, at least, I
told the truth. Every mother's son of them was
cursing and cross-questioning me in the same breath.
They ordered me off my horse, took my gun, and
proceeded to verify my tale by unpacking the
mules. So much ammunition aroused their suspi-
cions, but my story was as good as it was true, and
they never shook me from the truth of it. I soon
learned that robbery was not their motive, and the
leader explained the situation.

" A vigilance committee had been in force in that
county for some time, trying to rid the country of

lawless characters. But lawlessness got into the saddle, and had bench warrants issued and served on every member of this vigilance committee. As the vigilantes numbered several hundred, there was no jail large enough to hold such a number, so they were released on parole for appearance at court. When court met, every man served with a capias "—

"Hold on! hold your horses just a minute," interrupted Quince Forrest, "I want to get that word. I want to make a memorandum of it, for I may want to use it myself sometime. Capias? Now I have it; go ahead."

"When court met, every man served with a bench warrant from the judge presiding was present, and as soon as court was called to order, a squad of men arose in the court room, and the next moment the judge fell riddled with lead. Then the factions scattered to fight it out, and I was passing through the county while matters were active.

"They confiscated my gun and all the ammunition in the packs, but helped me to repack and started me on my way. A happy thought struck one of the men to give me a letter, which would carry me through without further trouble, but the leader stopped him, saying, 'Let the boy alone. Your letter would hang him as sure as hell's hot, before he went ten miles farther.' I declined the letter. Even then I did n't have sense enough to turn back, and inside of two hours I was rounded up by the other faction. I had learned my story perfectly by this time, but those packs had to come off again for everything to be examined. There was nothing in them now but flour and salt and such things — nothing that they might consider suspicious. One fellow in this second party took a fancy to my horse, and offered to help hang me on general principles, but kinder counsels prevailed. They also helped me to repack, and I started on once more. Before I reached my destination the following evening, I was held up seven different times. I got so used to it that I was happily disappointed every shelter I passed, if some man did not step out and throw a gun in my face.

" I had trouble to convince the cattle hunters of my experiences, but the absence of any ammunition, which they needed worst, at last led them to give credit to my tale. I was expected home within a week, as I was to go down on the Nueces on a cow hunt which was making up, and I only rested one day at the hunters' camp. On their advice, I took a different route on my way home, leaving the mules behind me. I never saw a man the next day returning, and was feeling quite gala on my good fortune. When evening came on, I sighted a little ranch house some distance off the trail, and concluded to ride to it and stay overnight. As I approached, I saw that some one lived there, as there were chickens and dogs about, but not a person in sight. I dismounted and knocked on the door, when, without a word, the door was thrown wide open and a half dozen guns were poked into my face. I was ordered into the house and given a chance to tell my story again. Whether my story was true or not, they took no chances on me, but kept me all night. One of the men took my horse to the stable and cared for him, and I was well fed and given a place to sleep, but not a man offered a word of explanation, from which I took it they did not belong to the vigilance faction. When it came time to go to bed, one man said to me, 'Now, sonny, don't make any attempt to get away, and don't move out of your bed without warning us, for you'll be shot as sure as you do. We won't harm a hair on your head if you're telling us the truth; only do as you're told, for we'll watch you.'

" By this time I had learned to obey orders while in that county, and got a fair night's sleep, though there were men going and coming all night. The next morning I was given my breakfast; my horse, well cuffed and saddled, was brought to the door, and with this parting advice I was given permission to go : ' Son, if you've told us the truth, don't look back when you ride away. You'll be watched for the first ten miles after leaving here, and if you've lied to us it will go hard with you. Now, remember, don't look back, for these are times when no one cares to be identified.' I never questioned that man's advice; it was ' die dog or eat the hatchet ' with me. I mounted my horse, waved the usual parting courtesies, and rode away. As I turned into the trail about a quarter mile from the house, I noticed two men ride out from behind the stable and follow me. I remembered the story about Lot's wife looking back, though it was lead and not miracles that I was afraid of that morning.

"For the first hour I could hear the men talking and the hoofbeats of their horses, as they rode along always the same distance behind me. After about two hours of this one-sided joke, as I rode over a little hill, I looked out of the corner of my eye back at my escort, still about a quarter of a mile behind me. One of them noticed me and raised his gun, but I instantly changed my view, and the moment the hill hid me, put spurs to my horse, so that when they reached the brow of the hill, I was half a mile in the lead, burning the earth like a canned dog. They threw lead close around me, but my horse lengthened the distance between us for the next five miles, when they dropped entirely out of sight. By noon I came into the old stage road, and by the middle of the afternoon reached home after over sixty miles in the saddle without a halt."

Just at the conclusion of Bull's story, Flood rode in from the herd, and after picketing his horse, joined the circle. In reply to an inquiry from one of the boys as to how the cattle were resting, he replied, —

"This herd is breaking into trail life nicely. If we'll just be careful with them now for the first

month, and no bad storms strike us in the night,
we may never have a run the entire trip. That
last drink of water they had this evening gave them
a night-cap that 'll last them until morning. No,
there's no danger of any trouble to-night."

For fully an hour after the return of our foreman, we lounged around the fire, during which
there was a full and free discussion of stampedes.
But finally, Flood, suiting the action to the word
by arising, suggested that all hands hunt their
blankets and turn in for the night. A quiet wink
from Bull to several of the boys held us for the
time being, and innocently turning to Forrest, Durham inquired, —

"Where was — when was — was it you that
was telling some one about a run you were in last
summer? I never heard you tell it. Where was
it?"

"You mean on the Cimarron last year when we
mixed two herds," said Quince, who had taken the
bait like a bass and was now fully embarked on a
yarn. "We were in rather close quarters, herds
ahead and behind us, when one night here came a
cow herd like a cyclone and swept right through
our camp. We tumbled out of our blankets and
ran for our horses, but before we could bridle " —

Bull had given us the wink, and every man in
the outfit fell back, and the snoring that checked
the storyteller was like a chorus of rip saws running through pine knots. Forrest took in the

situation at a glance, and as he arose to leave, looked back and remarked, —

" You must all think that's smart."

Before he was out of hearing, Durham said to the rest of us, —

" A few doses like that will cure him of sucking eggs and acting smart, interrupting folks."

CHAPTER IV

THE ATASCOSA

FOR the next few days we paralleled the coast, except when forced inland by various arms of the Laguna Madre. When about a week out from the Arroyo Colorado, we encountered the Salt Lagoon, which threw us at least fifty miles in from the coast. Here we had our last view of salt water, and the murmurings of the Gulf were heard no more. Our route now led northward through what were then the two largest ranches in Texas, the "Running W" and Laurel Leaf, which sent more cattle up the trail, bred in their own brand, than any other four ranches in the Lone Star State. We were nearly a week passing through their ranges, and on reaching Santa Gertruda ranch learned that three trail herds, of over three thousand head each, had already started in these two brands, while four more were to follow.

So far we had been having splendid luck in securing water for the herd, once a day at least, and often twice and three times. Our herd was becoming well trail-broken by this time, and for range cattle had quieted down and were docile and easy to handle. Flood's years of experience on the trail made him a believer in the theory that stampedes were generally due to negligence in not having the herd full of grass and water on reaching the bed ground at night. Barring accidents, which will happen, his view is the correct one, if care has been used for the first few weeks in properly breaking the herd to the trail. But though hunger and thirst are probably responsible for more stampedes than all other causes combined, it is the unexpected which cannot be guarded against. A stampede is the natural result of fear, and at night or in an uncertain light, this timidity might be imparted to an entire herd by a flash of lightning or a peal of thunder, while the stumbling of a night horse, or the scent of some wild animal, would in a moment's time, from frightening a few head, so infect a herd as to throw them into the wildest panic. Amongst the thousands of herds like ours which were driven over the trail during its brief existence, none ever made the trip without encountering more or less trouble from runs. Frequently a herd became so spoiled in this manner that it grew into a mania with them, so that they would stampede on the slightest provocation, — or no provocation at all.

A few days after leaving Santa Gertruda Ranch, we crossed the Nueces River, which we followed up for several days, keeping in touch with it for water for the herd. But the Nueces, after passing Oakville, makes an abrupt turn, doubling back to the southwest; and the Atascosa, one of its tributaries, became our source of water supply. We were beginning to feel a degree of overconfidence in the good behavior of our herd, when one night during the third week out, an incident occurred in which they displayed their running qualities to our complete satisfaction.

It occurred during our guard, and about two o'clock in the morning. The night was an unusually dark one and the atmosphere was very humid. After we had been on guard possibly an hour, John Officer and I riding in one direction on opposite sides of the herd, and The Rebel circling in the opposite, Officer's horse suddenly struck a gopher burrow with his front feet, and in a moment horse and rider were sprawling on the ground. The accident happened but a few rods from the sleeping herd, which instantly came to their feet as one steer, and were off like a flash. I was riding my Nigger Boy, and as the cattle headed toward me, away from the cause of their fright, I had to use both quirt and rowel to keep clear of the onrush. Fortunately we had a clear country near the bed ground, and while the terrified cattle pressed me close, my horse kept the lead. In the rumbling which ensued, all sounds were submerged by the general din; and I was only brought to the consciousness that I was not alone by seeing several distinct flashes from six-shooters on my left, and, realizing that I also had a gun, fired several times in the air in reply. I was soon joined by Priest and Officer, the latter having lost no time in regaining his seat in the saddle, and the three of us held together some little distance, for it would have been useless to attempt to check or turn this onslaught of cattle in their first mad rush.

The wagon was camped about two hundred yards from the bed ground, and the herd had given ample warning to the boys asleep, so that if we three could hold our position in the lead, help would come to us as soon as the men in camp could reach their horses. Realizing the wide front of the running cattle, Priest sent Officer to the left and myself to the right, to point in the leaders in order to keep the herd from splitting or scattering, while he remained in the centre and led the herd. I soon gained the outside of the leaders, and by dropping back and coming up the line, pointed them in to the best of my ability. I had repeated this a number of times, even quirting some cattle along the outside, or burning a little powder in the face of some obstinate leader, when across the herd and to the rear I saw a succession of flashes like fireflies, which told me the boys were coming to our assistance.

Running is not a natural gait with cattle, and if we could only hold them together and prevent splitting up, in time they would tire, while the rear cattle could be depended on to follow the leaders. All we could hope to do was to force them to run straight, and in this respect we were succeeding splendidly, though to a certain extent it was a guess

in the dark.   When they had run possibly a mile,
I noticed a horseman overtake Priest.   After they
had ridden together a moment, one of them came
over to my point, and the next minute our foreman
was racing along by my side.   In his impatience
to check the run, he took me with him, and circling
the leaders we reached the left point, by which time
the remainder of the outfit had come up.   Now
massing our numbers, we fell on the left point, and
amid the flash of guns deflected their course for a
few moments.   A dozen men, however, can cover
but a small space, and we soon realized that we had
turned only a few hundred head, for the momentum
of the main body bore steadily ahead.   Abandoning what few cattle we had turned, which, owing to
their running ability, soon resumed their places in
the lead, we attempted to turn them to the left.
Stretching out our line until there was a man about
every twenty feet, we threw our force against the
right point and lead in the hope of gradually devi-
ating their course.   For a few minutes the attempt
promised to be successful, but our cordon was too
weak and the cattle went through between the
riders, and we soon found a portion of our forces
on either side of the herd, while a few of the boys
were riding out of the rush in the lead.

On finding our forces thus divided, the five or
six of us who remained on the right contented ourselves by pointing in the leaders, for the cattle, so
far as we could tell, were running compactly.   Our

foreman, however, was determined to turn the run, and after a few minutes' time rejoined us on the right, when under his leadership we circled the front of the herd and collected on the left point, when, for a third time, we repeated the same tactics in our efforts to turn the stampede. But in this, which was our final effort, we were attempting to turn them slowly and on a much larger circle, and with a promise of success. Suddenly in the dark we encountered a mesquite thicket into which the lead cattle tore with a crashing of brush and a rattle of horns that sent a chill up and down my spine. But there was no time to hesitate, for our horses were in the thicket, and with the herd closing in on us there was no alternative but to go through it, every man for himself. I gave Nigger a free rein, shutting my eyes and clutching both cantle and pommel to hold my seat; the black responded to the rowel and tore through the thicket, in places higher than my head, and came out in an open space considerably in the lead of the cattle.

This thicket must have been eight or ten rods wide, and checked the run to a slight extent; but as they emerged from it, they came out in scattering files and resumed their running. Being alone, and not knowing which way to turn, I rode to the right and front and soon found myself in the lead of quite a string of cattle. Nigger and I were piloting them where they listed, when Joe Stallings, hatless himself and his horse heaving, overtook me,

and the two of us gave those lead cattle all the
trouble we knew how. But we did not attempt to
turn them, for they had caught their wind in forcing the thicket, and were running an easy stroke.
Several times we worried the leaders into a trot,
but as other cattle in the rear came up, we were
compelled to loosen out and allow them to resume
their running, or they would have scattered on us
like partridges. At this stage of the run, we had
no idea where the rest of the outfit were, but both
of us were satisfied the herd had scattered on leaving the mesquite thicket, and were possibly then
running in half a dozen bunches like the one we
were with.

Stallings's horse was badly winded, and on my
suggestion, he dropped out on one side to try to
get some idea how many cattle we were leading.
He was gone some little time, and as Nigger cantered along easily in the lead, I managed to eject
the shells from my six-shooter and refill the cylinder. On Joe's overtaking me again, he reported
that there was a slender column of cattle, half a
mile in length, following. As one man could easily
lead this string of the herd until daybreak, I left
Stallings with them and rode out to the left nearly
a quarter of a mile, listening to hear if there were
any cattle running to the left of those we were
leading. It took me but a few minutes to satisfy
myself that ours was the outside band on the left,
and after I rejoined Joe, we made an effort to
check our holding.

There were about fifty or sixty big steers in the lead of our bunch, and after worrying them into a trot, we opened in their front with our six-shooters, shooting into the ground in their very faces, and were rewarded by having them turn tail and head the other way. Taking advantage of the moment, we jumped our horses on the retreating leaders, and as fast as the rear cattle forged forward, easily turned them. Leaving Joe to turn the rear as they came up, I rode to the lead, unfastening my slicker as I went, and on reaching the turned leaders, who were running on an angle from their former course, flaunted my "fish" in their faces until they re-entered the rear guard of our string, and we soon had a mill going which kept them busy, and rested our horses. Once we had them milling, our trouble, as far as running was concerned, was over, for all two of us could hope to do was to let them exhaust themselves in this endless circle.

It then lacked an hour of daybreak, and all we could do was to ride around and wait for daylight. In the darkness preceding dawn, we had no idea of the number of our bunch, except as we could judge from the size and compactness of the milling cattle, which must have covered an acre or more. The humidity of the atmosphere, which had prevailed during the night, by dawn had changed until a heavy fog, cutting off our view on every hand, left us as much at sea as we had been previously. But with the break of day we rode through our holding a number of times, splitting and scattering the milling cattle, and as the light of day brightened, we saw them quiet down and go to grazing as though they had just arisen from the bed ground. It was over an hour before the fog lifted sufficiently to give us any idea as to our whereabouts, and during the interim both Stallings and myself rode to the nearest elevation, firing a number of shots in the hope of getting an answer from the outfit, but we had no response.

When the sun was sufficiently high to scatter the mists which hung in clouds, there was not an object in sight by which we could determine our location. Whether we had run east, west, or south during the night neither of us knew, though both Stallings and myself were satisfied that we had never crossed the trail, and all we did know for a certainty was that we had between six and seven hundred head of cattle. Stallings had lost his hat, and I had one sleeve missing and both outside pockets torn out of my coat, while the mesquite thorns had left their marks on the faces of both of us, one particularly ugly cut marking Joe's right temple. " I 've worn leggins for the last ten years," said Stallings to me, as we took an inventory of our disfigurements, " and for about ten seconds in forcing that mesquite thicket was the only time I ever drew interest on my investment. They 're a heap like a six-shooter — wear them all your life and never have any use for them."

With a cigarette for breakfast, I left Joe to look after our bunch, and after riding several miles to the right, cut the trail of quite a band of cattle. In following up this trail I could easily see that some one was in their lead, as they failed to hold their course in any one direction for any distance, as free cattle would. After following this trail about three miles, I sighted the band of cattle, and on overtaking them, found two of our boys holding about half as many as Stallings had. They reported that The Rebel and Bob Blades had been with them until daybreak, but having the freshest horses had left them with the dawn and ridden away to the right, where it was supposed the main body of the herd had run. As Stallings's bunch was some three or four miles to the rear and left of this band, Wyatt Roundtree suggested that he go and pilot in Joe's cattle, as he felt positive that the main body were somewhere to our right. On getting directions from me as to where he would find our holding, he rode away, and I again rode off to the right, leaving Rod Wheat with their catch.

The sun was now several hours high, and as my black's strength was standing the test bravely, I cross-cut the country and was soon on another trail of our stampeded cattle. But in following this trail, I soon noticed two other horsemen preceding me. Knowing that my services would be too late, I only followed far enough to satisfy myself of the

fact. The signs left by the running cattle were as
easy to follow as a public road, and in places where
the ground was sandy, the sod was cut up as if a
regiment of cavalry had charged across it. On
again bearing off to the right, I rode for an elevation which ought to give me a good view of the
country. Slight as this elevation was, on reaching
it, I made out a large band of cattle under herd,
and as I was on the point of riding to them, saw
our wagon and saddle horses heave in sight from a
northwest quarter. Supposing they were following up the largest trail, I rode for the herd, where
Flood and two of the boys had about twelve hundred cattle. From a comparison of notes, our foreman was able to account for all the men with the
exception of two, and as these proved to be Blades
and Priest, I could give him a satisfactory explanation as to their probable whereabouts. On my
report of having sighted the wagon and *remuda*,
Flood at once ordered me to meet and hurry them
in, as not only he, but Strayhorn and Officer, were
badly in need of a change of mounts.

I learned from McCann, who was doing the trailing from the wagon, that the regular trail was to
the west, the herd having crossed it within a quarter of a mile after leaving the bed ground. Joining Honeyman, I took the first horse which came
within reach of my rope, and with a fresh mount
under me, we rushed the saddle horses past the
wagon and shortly came up with our foreman.

There we rounded in the horses as best we could without the aid of the wagon, and before McCann arrived, all had fresh mounts and were ready for orders. This was my first trip on the trail, and I was hungry and thirsty enough to hope something would be said about eating, but that seemed to be the last idea in our foreman's mind. Instead, he ordered me to take the two other boys with me, and after putting them on the trail of the bunch which The Rebel and Blades were following, to drift in what cattle we had held on our left. But as we went, we managed to encounter the wagon and get a drink and a canteen of water from Mc-Cann before we galloped away on our mission. After riding a mile or so together, we separated, and on my arrival at the nearest bunch, I found Roundtree and Stallings coming up with the larger holding. Throwing the two bunches together, we drifted them a free clip towards camp. We soon sighted the main herd, and saw across to our right and about five miles distant two of our men bringing in another bunch. As soon as we turned our cattle into the herd, Flood ordered me, on account of my light weight, to meet this bunch, find out where the last cattle were, and go to their assistance.

With a hungry look in the direction of our wagon, I obeyed, and on meeting Durham and Borrowstone, learned that the outside bunch on the right, which had got into the regular trail, had not been checked until daybreak.   All they knew about their location was that the up stage from Oakville had seen two men with Circle Dot cattle about five miles below, and had sent up word by the driver that they had something like four hundred head.   With this meagre information, I rode away in the direction where one would naturally expect to find our absent men, and after scouring the country for an hour, sighted a single horseman on an elevation, whom from the gray mount I knew for Quince Forrest. He was evidently on the lookout for some one to pilot them in.   They had been drifting like lost sheep ever since dawn, but we soon had their cattle pointed in the right direction, and Forrest taking the lead, Quarternight and I put the necessary push behind them.   Both of them cursed me roundly for not bringing them a canteen of water, though they were well aware that in an emergency like the present, our foreman would never give a thought to anything but the recovery of the herd.   Our comfort was nothing; men were cheap, but cattle cost money.

We reached the camp about two o'clock, and found the outfit cutting out range cattle which had been absorbed into the herd during the run.   Throwing in our contingent, we joined in the work, and though Forrest and Quarternight were as good as afoot, there were no orders for a change of mounts, to say nothing of food and drink.   Several hundred mixed cattle were in the herd, and after they had been cut out, we lined our cattle out for a count. In the absence of Priest, Flood and John Officer did the counting, and as the hour of the day made the cattle sluggish, they lined through between the counters as though they had never done anything but walk in their lives. The count showed sixteen short of twenty-eight hundred, which left us yet over three hundred out. But good men were on their trail, and leaving two men on herd, the rest of us obeyed the most welcome orders of the day when Flood intimated that we would " eat a bite and go after the rest."

As we had been in our saddles since one or two o'clock the morning before, it is needless to add that our appetites were equal to the spread which our cook had waiting for us. Our foreman, as though fearful of the loss of a moment's time, sent Honeyman to rustle in the horses before we had finished our dinners. Once the *remuda* was corralled, under the rush of a tireless foreman, dinner was quickly over, and fresh horses became the order of the moment. The Atascosa, our nearest water, lay beyond the regular trail to the west, and leaving orders for the outfit to drift the herd into it and water, Flood and myself started in search of our absent men, not forgetting to take along two extra horses as a remount for Blades and Priest. The leading of these extra horses fell to me, but with the loose end of a rope in Jim Flood's hand as he followed, it took fast riding to keep clear of them.

After reaching the trail of the missing cattle, our foreman set a pace for five or six miles which would have carried us across the Nueces by nightfall, and we were only checked by Moss Strayhorn riding in on an angle and intercepting us in our headlong gait. The missing cattle were within a mile of us to the right, and we turned and rode to them. Strayhorn explained to us that the cattle had struck some recent fencing on their course, and after following down the fence several miles had encountered an offset, and the angle had held the squad until The Rebel and Blades overtook them. When Officer and he reached them, they were unable to make any accurate count, because of the range cattle amongst them, and they had considered it advisable to save horseflesh and not cut them until more help was available. When we came up with the cattle, my bunkie and Blades looked wistfully at our saddles, and anticipating their want, I untied my slicker, well remembering the reproof of Quarternight and Forrest, and produced a full canteen of water, — warm of course, but no less welcome.

No sooner were saddles shifted than we held up the bunch, cut out the range cattle, counted, and found we had some three hundred and thirty odd Circle Dots, — our number more than complete. With nothing now missing, Flood took the loose horses and two of the boys with him and returned to the herd, leaving three of us behind to bring in this last contingent of our stampeded cattle. This squad were nearly all large steers, and had run fully twenty miles, before, thanks to an angle in a fence, they had been checked. As our foreman galloped away, leaving us behind, Bob Blades said, —

"Has n't the boss got a wiggle on himself to-day! If he 'd made this old world, he 'd have made it in half a day, and gone fishing in the afternoon — if his horses had held out."

We reached the Atascosa shortly after the arrival of the herd, and after holding the cattle on the water for an hour, grazed them the remainder of the evening, for if there was any virtue in their having full stomachs, we wanted to benefit from it. While grazing that evening, we recrossed the trail on an angle, and camped in the most open country we could find, about ten miles below our camp of the night before. Every precaution was taken to prevent a repetition of the run; our best horses were chosen for night duty, as our regular ones were too exhausted; every advantage of elevation for a bed ground was secured, and thus fortified against accident, we went into camp for the night. But the expected never happens on the trail, and the sun arose the next morning over our herd grazing in peace and contentment on the flowery prairies which border on the Atascosa.

CHAPTER V

A DRY DRIVE

OUR cattle quieted down nicely after this run, and the next few weeks brought not an incident worth recording. There was no regular trail through the lower counties, so we simply kept to the open country. Spring had advanced until the prairies were swarded with grass and flowers, while water, though scarcer, was to be had at least once daily. We passed to the west of San Antonio — an outfitting point which all herds touched in passing northward — and Flood and our cook took the wagon and went in for supplies. But the outfit with the herd kept on, now launched on a broad, well-defined trail, in places seventy-five yards wide, where all local trails blent into the one common pathway, known in those days as the Old Western Trail. It is not in the province of this narrative to deal with the cause or origin of this cattle trail, though it marked the passage of many hundred thousand cattle which preceded our Circle Dots, and was destined to afford an outlet to several millions more to follow. The trail proper consisted of many scores of irregular cow paths, united into one broad passageway, narrowing and widening as conditions permitted, yet ever leading northward. After a few years of continued use, it became as well defined as the course of a river.

Several herds which had started farther up country were ahead of ours, and this we considered an advantage, for wherever one herd could go, it was reasonable that others could follow. Flood knew the trail as well as any of the other foremen, but there was one thing he had not taken into consideration : the drouth of the preceding summer. True, there had been local spring showers, sufficient to start the grass nicely, but water in such quantities as we needed was growing daily more difficult to find. The first week after leaving San Antonio, our foreman scouted in quest of water a full day in advance of the herd. One evening he returned to us with the news that we were in for a dry drive, for after passing the next chain of lakes it was sixty miles to the next water, and reports regarding the water supply even after crossing this arid stretch were very conflicting.

" While I know every foot of this trail through here," said the foreman, " there's several things that look scaly. There are only five herds ahead of us, and the first three went through the old route, but the last two, after passing Indian Lakes, for some reason or other turned and went westward. These last herds may be stock cattle, pushing out west to new ranges; but I don't like the outlook. It would take me two days to ride across and back,

and by that time we could be two thirds of the way
through. I 've made this drive before without a
drop of water on the way, and would n't dread it
now, if there was any certainty of water at the other
end. I reckon there 's nothing to do but tackle
her; but is n't this a hell of a country? I 've ridden fifty miles to-day and never saw a soul."

The Indian Lakes, some seven in number, were
natural reservoirs with rocky bottoms, and about a
mile apart. We watered at ten o'clock the next
day, and by night camped fifteen miles on our way.
There was plenty of good grazing for the cattle and
horses, and no trouble was experienced the first
night. McCann had filled an extra twenty gallon
keg for this trip. Water was too precious an
article to be lavish with, so we shook the dust from
our clothing and went unwashed. This was no
serious deprivation, and no one could be critical of
another, for we were all equally dusty and dirty.
The next morning by daybreak the cattle were
thrown off the bed ground and started grazing before the sun could dry out what little moisture the
grass had absorbed during the night. The heat of
the past week had been very oppressive, and in
order to avoid it as much as possible, we made late
and early drives. Before the wagon passed the
herd during the morning drive, what few canteens
we had were filled with water for the men. The
remuda was kept with the herd, and four changes
of mounts were made during the day, in order not

to exhaust any one horse. Several times for an hour or more, the herd was allowed to lie down and rest; but by the middle of the afternoon thirst made them impatient and restless, and the point men were compelled to ride steadily in the lead in order to hold the cattle to a walk. A number of times during the afternoon we attempted to graze them, but not until the twilight of evening was it possible.

After the fourth change of horses was made, Honeyman pushed on ahead with the saddle stock and overtook the wagon. Under Flood's orders he was to tie up all the night horses, for if the cattle could be induced to graze, we would not bed them down before ten that night, and all hands would be required with the herd. McCann had instructions to make camp on the divide, which was known to be twenty-five miles from our camp of the night before, or forty miles from the Indian Lakes. As we expected, the cattle grazed willingly after nightfall, and with a fair moon, we allowed them to scatter freely while grazing forward. The beacon of Mc-Cann's fire on the divide was in sight over an hour before the herd grazed up to camp, all hands remaining to bed the thirsty cattle. The herd was given triple the amount of space usually required for bedding, and even then for nearly an hour scarcely half of them lay down.

We were handling the cattle as humanely as possible under the circumstances. The guards for the

night were doubled, six men on the first half and
the same on the latter, Bob Blades being detailed
to assist Honeyman in night-herding the saddle
horses.   If any of us got more than an hour's sleep
that night, he was lucky.   Flood, McCann, and the
horse wranglers did not even try to rest.   To those
of us who could find time to eat, our cook kept
open house.   Our foreman knew that a well-fed
man can stand an incredible amount of hardship,
and appreciated the fact that on the trail a good
cook is a valuable asset.   Our outfit therefore was
cheerful to a man, and jokes and songs helped to
while away the weary hours of the night.

The second guard, under Flood, pushed the cattle
off their beds an hour before dawn, and before they
were relieved had urged the herd more than five
miles on the third day's drive over this waterless
mesa.   In spite of our economy of water, after
breakfast on this third morning there was scarcely
enough left to fill the canteens for the day.   In view
of this, we could promise ourselves no midday meal
— except a can of tomatoes to the man; so the
wagon was ordered to drive through to the expected
water ahead, while the saddle horses were held
available as on the day before for frequent changing of mounts.   The day turned out to be one of
torrid heat, and before the middle of the forenoon,
the cattle lolled their tongues in despair, while their
sullen lowing surged through from rear to lead and
back again in piteous yet ominous appeal.   The

HEAT AND THIRST

only relief we could offer was to travel them slowly, as they spurned every opportunity offered them either to graze or to lie down.

It was nearly noon when we reached the last divide, and sighted the scattering timber of the expected watercourse. The enforced order of the day before — to hold the herd in a walk and prevent exertion and heating — now required four men in the lead, while the rear followed over a mile behind, dogged and sullen. Near the middle of the afternoon, McCann returned on one of his mules with the word that it was a question if there was water enough to water even the horse stock. The preceding outfit, so he reported, had dug a shallow well in the bed of the creek, from which he had filled his kegs, but the stock water was a mere loblolly. On receipt of this news, we changed mounts for the fifth time that day; and Flood, taking Forrest, the cook, and the horse wrangler, pushed on ahead with the *remuda* to the waterless stream.

The outlook was anything but encouraging. Flood and Forrest scouted the creek up and down for ten miles in a fruitless search for water. The outfit held the herd back until the twilight of evening, when Flood returned and confirmed McCann's report. It was twenty miles yet to the next water ahead, and if the horse stock could only be watered thoroughly, Flood was determined to make the attempt to nurse the herd through to water. McCann was digging an extra well, and he expressed the belief that by hollowing out a number of holes, enough water could be secured for the saddle stock. Honeyman had corralled the horses and was letting only a few go to the water at a time, while the night horses were being thoroughly watered as fast as the water rose in the well.

Holding the herd this third night required all hands. Only a few men at a time were allowed to go into camp and eat, for the herd refused even to lie down. What few cattle attempted to rest were prevented by the more restless ones. By spells they would mill, until riders were sent through the herd at a break-neck pace to break up the groups. During these milling efforts of the herd, we drifted over a mile from camp; but by the light of moon and stars and the number of riders, scattering was prevented. As the horses were loose for the night, we could not start them on the trail until daybreak gave us a change of mounts, so we lost the early start of the morning before.

Good cloudy weather would have saved us, but in its stead was a sultry morning without a breath of air, which bespoke another day of sizzling heat. We had not been on the trail over two hours before the heat became almost unbearable to man and beast. Had it not been for the condition of the herd, all might yet have gone well; but over three days had now elapsed without water for the cattle, and they became feverish and ungovernable. The lead cattle turned back several times, wandering aimlessly in any direction, and it was with considerable difficulty that the herd could be held on the trail. The rear overtook the lead, and the cattle gradually lost all semblance of a trail herd. Our horses were fresh, however, and after about two hours' work, we once more got the herd strung out in trailing fashion; but before a mile had been covered, the leaders again turned, and the cattle congregated into a mass of unmanageable animals, milling and lowing in their fever and thirst. The milling only intensified their sufferings from the heat, and the outfit split and quartered them again and again, in the hope that this unfortunate outbreak might be checked. No sooner was the milling stopped than they would surge hither and yon, sometimes half a mile, as ungovernable as the waves of an ocean. After wasting several hours in this manner, they finally turned back over the trail, and the utmost efforts of every man in the outfit failed to check them. We threw our ropes in their faces, and when this failed, we resorted to shooting; but in defiance of the fusillade and the smoke they walked sullenly through the line of horsemen across their front. Six-shooters were discharged so close to the leaders' faces as to singe their hair, yet, under a noonday sun, they disregarded this and every other device to turn them, and passed wholly out of our control. In a number of instances wild steers deliberately walked against our horses, and then for the first time a fact dawned on us that chilled the marrow in our bones, — *the herd was going blind.*

The bones of men and animals that lie bleaching along the trails abundantly testify that this was not the first instance in which the plain had baffled the determination of man. It was now evident that nothing short of water would stop the herd, and we rode aside and let them pass. As the outfit turned back to the wagon, our foreman seemed dazed by the sudden and unexpected turn of affairs, but rallied and met the emergency.

" There 's but one thing left to do," said he, as we rode along, " and that is to hurry the outfit back to Indian Lakes. The herd will travel day and night, and instinct can be depended on to carry them to the only water they know. It 's too late to be of any use now, but it 's plain why those last two herds turned off at the lakes; some one had gone back and warned them of the very thing we 've met. We must beat them to the lakes, for water is the only thing that will check them now. It 's a good thing that they are strong, and five or six days without water will hardly kill any. It was no vague statement of the man who said if he owned hell and Texas, he 'd rent Texas and live in hell, for if this is n't Billy hell, I 'd like to know what you call it."

We spent an hour watering the horses from the wells of our camp of the night before, and about two o'clock started back over the trail for Indian Lakes. We overtook the abandoned herd during the afternoon. They were strung out nearly five miles in length, and were walking about a three-mile gait. Four men were given two extra horses apiece and left to throw in the stragglers in the rear, with instructions to follow them well into the night, and again in the morning as long as their canteens lasted. The remainder of the outfit pushed on without a halt, except to change mounts, and reached the lakes shortly after midnight. There we secured the first good sleep of any consequence for three days.

It was fortunate for us that there were no range cattle at these lakes, and we had only to cover a front of about six miles to catch the drifting herd. It was nearly noon the next day before the cattle began to arrive at the water holes in squads of from twenty to fifty. Pitiful objects as they were, it was a novelty to see them reach the water and slack their thirst. Wading out into the lakes until their sides were half covered, they would stand and low in a soft moaning voice, often for half an hour before attempting to drink. Contrary to our expectation, they drank very little at first, but stood in the water for hours. After coming out, they would lie down and rest for hours longer, and then drink again before attempting to graze, their thirst overpowering hunger. That they were blind there was no question, but with the causes that produced it once removed, it was probable their eyesight would gradually return.

By early evening, the rear guard of our outfit returned and reported the tail end of the herd some twenty miles behind when they left them. During the day not over a thousand head reached the lakes, and towards evening we put these under herd and easily held them during the night. All four of the men who constituted the rear guard were sent back the next morning to prod up the rear again, and during the night at least a thousand more came into the lakes, which held them better than a hundred men. With the recovery of the cattle our hopes grew, and with the gradual accessions to the herd, confidence was again completely restored. Our saddle stock, not having suffered as had the cattle, were in a serviceable condition, and while a few men were all that were necessary to hold the herd, the others scoured the country for miles in search of any possible stragglers which might have missed the water.

During the forenoon of the third day at the lakes, Nat Straw, the foreman of Ellison's first herd on the trail, rode up to our camp. He was scouting for water for his herd, and, when our situation was explained and he had been interrogated regarding loose cattle, gave us the good news that no stragglers in our road brand had been met by their outfit. This was welcome news, for we had made no count yet, and feared some of them, in their locoed condition, might have passed the water during the night. Our misfortune was an ill wind by which

Straw profited, for he had fully expected to keep on by the old route, but with our disaster staring him in the face, a similar experience was to be avoided. His herd reached the lakes during the middle of the afternoon, and after watering, turned and went westward over the new route taken by the two herds which preceded us. He had a herd of about three thousand steers, and was driving to the Dodge market. After the experience we had just gone through, his herd and outfit were a welcome sight. Flood made inquiries after Lovell's second herd, under my brother Bob as foreman, but Straw had seen or heard nothing of them, having come from Goliad County with his cattle.

After the Ellison herd had passed on and out of sight, our squad which had been working the country to the northward, over the route by which the abandoned herd had returned, came in with the information that that section was clear of cattle, and that they had only found three head dead from thirst. On the fourth morning, as the herd left the bed ground, a count was ordered, and to our surprise we counted out twenty-six head more than we had received on the banks of the Rio Grande a month before. As there had been but one previous occasion to count, the number of strays absorbed into our herd was easily accounted for by Priest: "If a steer herd could increase on the trail, why should n't ours, that had over a thousand cows in it?" The observation was hardly borne out when the ages of our herd were taken into consideration. But 1882 in Texas was a liberal day and generation, and " cattle stealing " was too drastic a term to use for the chance gain of a few cattle, when the foundations of princely fortunes were being laid with a rope and a branding iron.

In order to give the Ellison herd a good start of us, we only moved our wagon to the farthest lake and went into camp for the day. The herd had recovered its normal condition by this time, and of the troubles of the past week not a trace remained. Instead, our herd grazed in leisurely content over a thousand acres, while with the exception of a few men on herd, the outfit lounged around the wagon and beguiled the time with cards.

We had undergone an experience which my bunkie, The Rebel, termed " an interesting incident in his checkered career," but which not even he would have cared to repeat.   That night while on night herd together — the cattle resting in all contentment — we rode one round together, and as he rolled a cigarette he gave me an old war story : —

" They used to tell the story in the army, that during one of the winter retreats, a cavalryman, riding along in the wake of the column at night, saw a hat apparently floating in the mud and water.   In the hope that it might be a better hat than the one he was wearing, he dismounted to get it.   Feeling his way carefully through the ooze until he reached the hat, he was surprised to find a man underneath and wearing it. 'Hello, comrade,' he sang out, 'can I lend you a hand?'

" 'No, no,' replied the fellow, 'I 'm all right; I 've got a good mule yet under me.' "

CHAPTER VI

A REMINISCENT NIGHT

On the ninth morning we made our second start
from the Indian Lakes. An amusing incident
occurred during the last night of our camp at these
water holes. Coyotes had been hanging around
our camp for several days, and during the quiet
hours of the night these scavengers of the plain
had often ventured in near the wagon in search of
scraps of meat or anything edible. Rod Wheat
and Ash Borrowstone had made their beds down
some distance from the wagon; the coyotes as they
circled round the camp came near their bed, and
in sniffing about awoke Borrowstone. There was
no more danger of attack from these cowards than
from field mice, but their presence annoyed Ash,
and as he dared not shoot, he threw his boots at the
varmints. Imagine his chagrin the next morning
to find that one boot had landed among the banked
embers of the camp-fire, and was burned to a crisp.
It was looked upon as a capital joke by the outfit,
as there was no telling when we would reach a store
where he could secure another pair.

The new trail, after bearing to the westward for
several days, turned northward, paralleling the old

one, and a week later we came into the old trail
over a hundred miles north of the Indian Lakes.
With the exception of one thirty-mile drive without
water, no fault could be found with the new trail.
A few days after coming into the old trail, we passed
Mason, a point where trail herds usually put in for
supplies. As we passed during the middle of the
afternoon, the wagon and a number of the boys
went into the burg. Quince Forrest and Billy
Honeyman were the only two in the outfit for whom
there were any letters, with the exception of a letter
from Lovell, which was common property. Never
having been over the trail before, and not even
knowing that it was possible to hear from home, I
was n't expecting any letter; but I felt a little
twinge of homesickness that night when Honeyman
read us certain portions of his letter, which was
from his sister. Forrest's letter was from a sweet-
heart, and after reading it a few times, he burnt it,
and that was all we ever knew of its contents, for
he was too foxy to say anything, even if it had not
been unfavorable. Borrowstone swaggered around
camp that evening in a new pair of boots, which
had the Lone Star set in filigree-work in their red
tops.

At our last camp at the lakes, The Rebel and I,
as partners, had been shamefully beaten in a game
of seven-up by Bull Durham and John Officer, and
had demanded satisfaction in another trial around
the fire that night. We borrowed McCann's lan-

tern, and by the aid of it and the camp-fire had an abundance of light for our game. In the absence of a table, we unrolled a bed and sat down Indian fashion over a game of cards in which all friendship ceased.

The outfit, with the exception of myself, had come from the same neighborhood, and an item in Honeyman's letter causing considerable comment was a wedding which had occurred since the outfit had left. It seemed that a number of the boys had sparked the bride in times past, and now that she was married, their minds naturally became reminiscent over old sweethearts.

"The way I make it out," said Honeyman, in commenting on the news, "is that the girl had met this fellow over in the next county while visiting her cousins the year before. My sister gives it as a horseback opinion that she'd been engaged to this fellow nearly eight months; girls, you know, sabe each other that way. Well, it won't affect my appetite any if all the girls I know get married while I'm gone."

"You certainly have never experienced the tender passion," said Fox Quarternight to our horse wrangler, as he lighted his pipe with a brand from the fire. "Now I have. That's the reason why I sympathize with these old beaus of the bride. Of course I was too old to stand any show on her string, and I reckon the fellow who got her ain't so powerful much, except his veneering and being a stranger, which was a big advantage. To be sure, if she took a smile to this stranger, no other fellow could check her with a three-quarter rope and a snubbing post. I've seen girls walk right by a dozen good fellows and fawn over some scrub. My experience teaches me that when there's a woman in it, it's haphazard pot luck with no telling which way the cat will hop. You can't play any system, and merit cuts little figure in general results."

"Fox," said Durham, while Officer was shuffling the cards, "your auger seems well oiled and working keen to-night. Suppose you give us that little experience of yours in love affairs. It will be a treat to those of us who have never been in love, and won't interrupt the game a particle. Cut loose, won't you?"

"It's a long time back," said Quarternight, meditatively, "and the scars have all healed, so I don't mind telling it. I was born and raised on the border of the Blue Grass Region in Kentucky. I had the misfortune to be born of poor but honest parents, as they do in stories; no hero ever had the advantage of me in that respect. In love affairs, however, it's a high card in your hand to be born rich. The country around my old home had good schools, so we had the advantage of a good education. When I was about nineteen, I went away from home one winter to teach school — a little country school about fifteen miles from home. But in the old States fifteen miles from home makes you a dead rank stranger. The trustee of the township was shucking corn when I went to apply for the school. I simply whipped out my peg and helped him shuck out a shock or two while we talked over school matters. The dinner bell rang, and he insisted on my staying for dinner with him. Well, he gave me a better school than I had asked for — better neighborhood, he said — and told me to board with a certain family who had no children; he gave his reasons, but that's immaterial. They were friends of his, so I learned afterwards. They proved to be fine people. The woman was one of those kindly souls who never know where to stop. She planned and schemed to marry me off in spite of myself. The first month that I was with them she told me all about the girls in that immediate neighborhood. In fact, she rather got me unduly excited, being a youth and somewhat verdant. She dwelt powerful heavy on a girl who lived in a big brick house which stood back of the road some distance. This girl had gone to school at a seminary for young ladies near Lexington,— studied music and painting and was 'way up on everything. She described her to me as black-eyed with raven tresses, just like you read about in novels.

"Things were rocking along nicely, when a few days before Christmas a little girl who belonged to the family who lived in the brick house brought me a note one morning. It was an invitation to take supper with them the following evening. The note

was written in a pretty hand, and the name signed
to it — I'm satisfied now it was a forgery. My
landlady agreed with me on that point; in fact, she
may have mentioned it first. I never ought to have
taken her into my confidence like I did. But I
wanted to consult her, showed her the invitation,
and asked her advice. She was in the seventh
heaven of delight; had me answer it at once, accept
the invitation with pleasure and a lot of stuff that
I never used before — she had been young once
herself. I used up five or six sheets of paper in
writing the answer, spoilt one after another, and
the one I did send was a flat failure compared to
the one I received. Well, the next evening when
it was time to start, I was nervous and uneasy. It
was nearly dark when I reached the house, but I
wanted it that way. Say, but when I knocked on
the front door of that house it was with fear and
trembling. 'Is this Mr. Quarternight?' inquired
a very affable lady who received me. I knew I was
one of old man Quarternight's seven boys, and
admitted that that was my name, though it was the
first time any one had ever called me *mister*. I was
welcomed, ushered in, and introduced all around.
There were a few small children whom I knew, so
I managed to talk to them. The girl whom I was
being braced against was not a particle overrated,
but sustained the Kentucky reputation for beauty.
She made herself so pleasant and agreeable that my
fears soon subsided. When the man of the house

came in I was cured entirely. He was gruff and hearty, opened his mouth and laughed deep. I built right up to him. We talked about cattle and horses until supper was announced. He was really sorry I had n't come earlier, so as to look at a three year old colt that he set a heap of store by. He showed him to me after supper with a lantern. Fine colt, too. I don't remember much about the supper, except that it was fine and I came near spilling my coffee several times, my hands were so large and my coat sleeves so short. When we returned from looking at the colt, we went into the parlor. Say, fellows, it was a little the nicest thing that ever I went against. Carpet that made you think you were going to bog down every step, springy like marsh land, and I was glad I came. Then the younger children were ordered to retire, and shortly afterward the man and his wife followed suit.

" When I heard the old man throw his heavy boots on the floor in the next room, I realized that I was left all alone with their charming daughter. All my fears of the early part of the evening tried to crowd on me again, but were calmed by the girl, who sang and played on the piano with no audience but me. Then she interested me by telling her school experiences, and how glad she was that they were over. Finally she lugged out a great big family album, and sat down aside of me on one of these horsehair sofas. That album had a clasp on it, a buckle of pure silver, same as these eighteen dollar bridles. While we were looking at the pictures — some of the old varmints had fought in the Revolutionary war, so she said — I noticed how close we were sitting together. Then we sat farther apart after we had gone through the album, one on each end of the sofa, and talked about the neighborhood, until I suddenly remembered that I had to go. While she was getting my hat and I was getting away, somehow she had me promise to take dinner with them on Christmas.

" For the next two or three months it was hard to tell if I lived at my boarding house or at the brick. If I failed to go, my landlady would hatch up some errand and send me over. If she had n't been such a good woman, I 'd never forgive her for leading me to the sacrifice like she did. Well, about two weeks before school was out, I went home over Saturday and Sunday. Those were fatal days in my life. When I returned on Monday morning, there was a letter waiting for me. It was from the girl's mamma. There had been a quilting in the neighborhood on Saturday, and at this meet of the local gossips, some one had hinted that there was liable to be a wedding as soon as school was out. Mamma was present, and neither admitted nor denied the charge. But there was a woman at this quilting who had once lived over in our neighborhood and felt it her duty to enlighten the company as to who I was. I got all this later from my landlady. ' Law me,' said this woman, ' folks round here in this section think our teacher is the son of that big farmer who raises so many cattle and horses. Why, I 've known both families of those Quarternights for nigh on to thirty year. Our teacher is one of old John Fox's boys, the Irish Quarternights, who live up near the salt licks on Doe Run. They were always so poor that the children never had enough to eat and hardly half enough to wear.'

" This plain statement of facts fell like a bombshell on mamma. She started a private investigation of her own, and her verdict was in that letter. It was a centre shot. That evening when I locked the schoolhouse door it was for the last time, for I never unlocked it again. My landlady, dear old womanly soul, tried hard to have me teach the school out at least, but I did n't see it that way. The cause of education in Kentucky might have gone straight to eternal hell, before I 'd have stayed another day in that neighborhood. I had money enough to get to Texas with, and here I am. When a fellow gets it burnt into him like a brand that way once, it lasts him quite a while. He 'll feel his way next time."

" That was rather a raw deal to give a fellow," said Officer, who had been listening while playing cards. " Did n't you never see the girl again ? "

" No, nor you would n't want to either if that letter had been written to you. And some folks claim that seven is a lucky number; there were seven boys in our family and nary one ever married."

"That experience of Fox's," remarked Honeyman, after a short silence, "is almost similar to one I had. Before Lovell and Flood adopted me, I worked for a horse man down on the Nueces. Every year he drove up the trail a large herd of horse stock. We drove to the same point on the trail each year, and I happened to get acquainted up there with a family that had several girls in it. The youngest girl in the family and I seemed to understand each other fairly well. I had to stay at the horse camp most of the time, and in one way and another did not get to see her as much as I would have liked. When we sold out the herd, I hung around for a week or so, and spent a month's wages showing her the cloud with the silver lining. She stood it all easy, too. When the outfit went home, of course I went with them. I was banking plenty strong, however, that next year, if there was a good market in horses, I'd take her home with me. I had saved my wages and rustled around, and when we started up the trail next year, I had forty horses of my own in the herd. I had figured they would bring me a thousand dollars, and there was my wages besides.

"When we reached this place, we held the herd out twenty miles, so it was some time before I got into town to see the girl. But the first time I did get to see her I learned that an older sister of hers,

who had run away with some renegade from Texas
a year or so before, had drifted back home lately
with tears in her eyes and a big fat baby boy in
her arms.   She warned me to keep away from the
house, for men from Texas were at a slight discount
right then in that family.   The girl seemed to regret it and talked reasonable, and I thought I could
see encouragement.   I did n't crowd matters, nor
did her folks forget me when they heard that Byler
had come in with a horse herd from the Nueces.   I
met the girl away from home several times during
the summer, and learned that they kept hot water
on tap to scald me if I ever dared to show up.   One
son-in-law from Texas had simply surfeited that
family — there was no other vacancy.   About the
time we closed out and were again ready to go
home, there was a cattleman's ball given in this little
trail town.   We stayed over several days to take
in this ball, as I had some plans of my own.   My
girl was at the ball all easy enough, but she warned
me that her brother was watching me.   I paid no
attention to him, and danced with her right along,
begging her to run away with me.   It was obviously
the only play to make.   But the more I 'd 'suade
her the more she 'd 'fuse.   The family was on the
prod bigger than a wolf, and there was no use reasoning with them.   After I had had every dance
with her for an hour or so, her brother coolly
stepped in and took her home.   The next morning
he felt it his duty, as his sister's protector, to hunt

me up and inform me that if I even spoke to his sister again, he 'd shoot me like a dog.

" ' Is that a bluff, or do you mean it for a real play ? ' I inquired, politely.

" ' You 'll find that it will be real enough,' he answered, angrily.

" ' Well, now, that 's too bad,' I answered ; ' I 'm really sorry that I can't promise to respect your request. But this much I can assure you : any time that you have the leisure and want to shoot me, just cut loose your dog. But remember this one thing — that it will be my second shot.' "

" Are you sure you wasn't running a blazer yourself, or is the wind merely rising ? " inquired Durham, while I was shuffling the cards for the next deal.

" Well, if I was, I hung up my gentle honk before his eyes and ears and gave him free license to call it. The truth is, I did n't pay any more attention to him than I would to an empty bottle. I reckon the girl was all right, but the family were these razor-backed, barnyard savages. It makes me hot under the collar yet when I think of it. They 'd have lawed me if I had, but I ought to have shot him and checked the breed."

" Why did n't you run off with her ? " inquired Fox, dryly.

" Well, of course a man of your nerve is always capable of advising others. But you see, I 'm strong on the breed. Now a girl can't show her true colors like the girl's brother did, but get her in the harness once, and then she 'll show you the white of her eye, balk, and possibly kick over the wagon tongue. No, I believe in the breed — blood 'll tell."

" I worked for a cowman once," said Bull, irrelevantly, " and they told it on him that he lost twenty thousand dollars the night he was married."

" How, gambling? " I inquired.

" No. The woman he married claimed to be worth twenty thousand dollars and she never had a cent. Spades trump? "

" No; hearts," replied The Rebel. " I used to know a foreman up in DeWitt County, — ' Honest ' John Glen they called him. He claimed the only chance he ever had to marry was a widow, and the reason he did n't marry her was, he was too honest to take advantage of a dead man."

While we paid little attention to wind or weather, this was an ideal night, and we were laggard in seeking our blankets. Yarn followed yarn; for nearly every one of us, either from observation or from practical experience, had a slight acquaintance with the great mastering passion. But the poetical had not been developed in us to an appreciative degree, so we discussed the topic under consideration much as we would have done horses or cattle.

Finally the game ended. A general yawn went

the round of the loungers about the fire. The second guard had gone on, and when the first rode in, Joe Stallings, halting his horse in passing the fire, called out sociably, "That muley steer, the white four year old, did n't like to bed down amongst the others, so I let him come out and lay down by himself. You 'll find him over on the far side of the herd. You all remember how wild he was when we first started ? Well, you can ride within three feet of him to-night, and he 'll grunt and act sociable and never offer to get up. I promised him that he might sleep alone as long as he was good ; I just love a good steer. Make down our bed, pardner ; I 'll be back as soon as I picket my horse."

CHAPTER VII

THE COLORADO

THE month of May found our Circle Dot herd, in spite of all drawbacks, nearly five hundred miles on its way. For the past week we had been traveling over that immense tableland which skirts the arid portion of western Texas. A few days before, while passing the blue mountains which stand as a southern sentinel in the chain marking the head-waters of the Concho River, we had our first glimpse of the hills. In its almost primitive condition, the country was generous, supplying every want for sustenance of horses and cattle. The grass at this stage of the season was well matured, the herd taking on flesh in a very gratifying manner, and, while we had crossed some rocky country, lame and sore-footed cattle had as yet caused us no serious trouble.

One morning when within one day's drive of the Colorado River, as our herd was leaving the bed ground, the last guard encountered a bunch of cattle drifting back down the trail. There were nearly fifty head of the stragglers ; and as one of our men on guard turned them to throw them away from our herd, the road brand caught his eye, and

he recognized the strays as belonging to the Ellison herd which had passed us at the Indian
Lakes some ten days before. Flood's attention
once drawn to the brand, he ordered them thrown
into our herd. It was evident that some trouble
had occurred with the Ellison cattle, possibly a
stampede; and it was but a neighborly act to lend
any assistance in our power. As soon as the outfit
could breakfast, mount, and take the herd, Flood
sent Priest and me to scout the country to the
westward of the trail, while Bob Blades and Ash
Borrowstone started on a similar errand to the
eastward, with orders to throw in any drifting cattle in the Ellison road brand. Within an hour
after starting, the herd encountered several straggling bands, and as Priest and I were on the point
of returning to the herd, we almost overrode a
bunch of eighty odd head lying down in some
broken country. They were gaunt and tired, and
The Rebel at once pronounced their stiffened movements the result of a stampede.

We were drifting them back towards the trail,
when Nat Straw and two of his men rode out from
our herd and met us. "I always did claim that it
was better to be born lucky than handsome," said
Straw as he rode up. "One week Flood saves me
from a dry drive, and the very next one, he's just
the right distance behind to catch my drift from
a nasty stampede. Not only that, but my peelers
and I are riding Circle Dot horses, as well as

reaching the wagon in time for breakfast and lining our flues with Lovell's good chuck. It's too good luck to last, I'm afraid.

"I'm not hankering for the dramatic in life, but we had a run last night that would curl your hair. Just about midnight a bunch of range cattle ran into us, and before you could say Jack Robinson, our dogies had vamoosed the ranch and were running in half a dozen different directions. We rounded them up the best we could in the dark, and then I took a couple of men and came back down the trail about twenty miles to catch any drift when day dawned. But you see there's nothing like being lucky and having good neighbors, — cattle caught, fresh horses, and a warm breakfast all waiting for you. I'm such a lucky dog, it's a wonder some one didn't steal me when I was little. I can't help it, but some day I'll marry a banker's daughter, or fall heir to a ranch as big as old McCulloch County."

Before meeting us, Straw had confided to our foreman that he could assign no other plausible excuse for the stampede than that it was the work of cattle rustlers. He claimed to know the country along the Colorado, and unless it had changed recently, those hills to the westward harbored a good many of the worst rustlers in the State. He admitted it might have been wolves chasing the range cattle, but thought it had the earmarks of being done by human wolves. He maintained that few herds had ever passed that river without loss of cattle, unless the rustlers were too busy elsewhere to give the passing herd their attention. Straw had ordered his herd to drop back down the trail about ten miles from their camp of the night previous, and about noon the two herds met on a branch of Brady Creek. By that time our herd had nearly three hundred head of the Ellison cattle, so we held it up and cut theirs out. Straw urged our foreman, whatever he did, not to make camp in the Colorado bottoms or anywhere near the river, if he did n't want a repetition of his experience. After starting our herd in the afternoon, about half a dozen of us turned back and lent a hand in counting Straw's herd, which proved to be over a hundred head short, and nearly half his outfit were still out hunting cattle. Acting on Straw's advice, we camped that night some five or six miles back from the river on the last divide. From the time the second guard went on until the third was relieved, we took the precaution of keeping a scout outriding from a half to three quarters of a mile distant from the herd, Flood and Honeyman serving in that capacity. Every precaution was taken to prevent a surprise; and in case anything did happen, our night horses tied to the wagon wheels stood ready saddled and bridled for any emergency. But the night passed without incident.

An hour or two after the herd had started the next morning, four well mounted, strange men

rode up from the westward, and representing themselves as trail cutters, asked for our foreman.
Flood met them, in his usual quiet manner, and
after admitting that we had been troubled more or
less with range cattle, assured our callers that if
there was anything in the herd in the brands they
represented, he would gladly hold it up and give
them every opportunity to cut their cattle out.
As he was anxious to cross the river before noon,
he invited the visitors to stay for dinner, assuring
them that before starting the herd in the afternoon, he would throw the cattle together for their
inspection. Flood made himself very agreeable,
inquiring into cattle and range matters in general
as well as the stage of water in the river ahead.
The spokesman of the trail cutters met Flood's invitation to dinner with excuses about the pressing demands on his time, and urged, if it did not
seriously interfere with our plans, that he be allowed to inspect the herd before crossing the river.
His reasons seemed trivial and our foreman was
not convinced.

"You see, gentlemen," he said, "in handling
these southern cattle, we must take advantage of
occasions. We have timed our morning's drive so
as to reach the river during the warmest hour of
the day, or as near noon as possible. You can
hardly imagine what a difference there is, in fording
this herd, between a cool, cloudy day and a clear,
hot one. You see the herd is strung out nearly a

mile in length now, and to hold them up and waste an hour or more for your inspection would seriously disturb our plans. And then our wagon and *remuda* have gone on with orders to noon at the first good camp beyond the river. I perfectly understand your reasons, and you equally understand mine ; but I will send a man or two back to help you re-cross any cattle you may find in our herd. Now, if a couple of you gentlemen will ride around on the far side with me, and the others will ride up near the lead, we will trail the cattle across when we reach the river without cutting the herd into blocks."

Flood's affability, coupled with the fact that the lead cattle were nearly up to the river, won his point. Our visitors could only yield, and rode forward with our lead swing men to assist in forcing the lead cattle into the river. It was swift water, but otherwise an easy crossing, and we allowed the herd, after coming out on the farther side, to spread out and graze forward at its pleasure. The wagon and saddle stock were in sight about a mile ahead, and leaving two men on herd to drift the cattle in the right direction, the rest of us rode leisurely on to the wagon, where dinner was waiting. Flood treated our callers with marked courtesy during dinner, and casually inquired if any of their number had seen any cattle that day or the day previous in the Ellison road brand. They had not, they said, explaining that their range lay on both sides of the Concho, and that during the trail season they kept all their cattle between that river and the main Colorado. Their work had kept them on their own range recently, except when trail herds were passing and needed to be looked through for strays. It sounded as though our trail cutters could also use diplomacy on occasion.

When dinner was over and we had caught horses for the afternoon and were ready to mount, Flood asked our guests for their credentials as duly authorized trail cutters. They replied that they had none, but offered in explanation the statement that they were merely cutting in the interest of the immediate locality, which required no written authority.

Then the previous affability of our foreman turned to iron. "Well, men," said he, "if you have no authority to cut this trail, then you don't cut this herd. I must have inspection papers before I can move a brand out of the county in which it is bred, and I'll certainly let no other man, local or duly appointed, cut an animal out of this herd without written and certified authority. You know that without being told, or ought to. I respect the rights of every man posted on a trail to cut it. If you want to see my inspection papers, you have a right to demand them, and in turn I demand of you your credentials, showing who you work for and the list of brands you represent; otherwise no harm's done; nor do you cut any herd that I'm driving."

" Well," said one of the men, " I saw a couple of head in my own individual brand as we rode up the herd. I 'd like to see the man who says that I have n't the right to claim my own brand, anywhere I find it."

" If there 's anything in our herd in your individual brand," said Flood, " all you have to do is to give me the brand, and I 'll cut it for you. What 's your brand? "

" The ' Window Sash.' "

" Have any of you boys seen such a brand in our herd? " inquired Flood, turning to us as we all stood by our horses ready to start.

"I did n't recognize it by that name," replied Quince Forrest, who rode in the swing on the branded side of the cattle and belonged to the last guard, "but I remember seeing such a brand, though I would have given it a different name. Yes, come to think, I 'm sure I saw it, and I 'll tell you where: yesterday morning when I rode out to throw those drifting cattle away from our herd, I saw that brand among the Ellison cattle which had stampeded the night before. When Straw's outfit cut theirs out yesterday, they must have left the ' Window Sash ' cattle with us; those were the range cattle which stampeded his herd. It looked to me a little blotched, but if I 'd been called on to name it, I 'd called it a thief's brand. If these gentlemen claim them, though, it 'll only take a minute to cut them out."

"This outfit need n't get personal and fling out their insults," retorted the claimant of the " Window Sash " brand, " for I 'll claim my own if there were a hundred of you. And you can depend that any animal I claim, I 'll take, if I have to go back to the ranch and bring twenty men to help me do it."

" You won't need any help to get all that 's coming to you," replied our foreman, as he mounted his horse. " Let 's throw the herd together, boys, and cut these ' Window Sash ' cattle out. We don't want any cattle in our herd that stampede on an open range at midnight ; they must certainly be terrible wild."

As we rode out together, our trail cutters dropped behind and kept a respectable distance from the herd while we threw the cattle together. When the herd had closed to the required compactness, Flood called our trail cutters up and said, " Now, men, each one of you can take one of my outfit with you and inspect this herd to your satisfaction. If you see anything there you claim, we 'll cut it out for you, but don't attempt to cut anything yourselves."

We rode in by pairs, a man of ours with each stranger, and after riding leisurely through the herd for half an hour, cut out three head in the blotched brand called the " Window Sash." Before leaving the herd, one of the strangers laid claim to a red cow, but Fox Quarternight refused to cut the animal.

When the pair rode out the stranger accosted Flood. " I notice a cow of mine in there," said he, "not in your road brand, which I claim. Your man here refuses to cut her for me, so I appeal to you."

" What's her brand, Fox ? " asked Flood.

" She's a ' Q ' cow, but the colonel here thinks it's an ' O.' I happen to know the cow and the brand both ; she came into the herd four hundred miles south of here while we were watering the herd in the Nueces River. The ' Q ' is a little dim, but it's plenty plain to hold her for the present."

" If she's a ' Q ' cow I have no claim on her," protested the stranger, " but if the brand is an ' O,' then I claim her as a stray from our range, and I don't care if she came into your herd when you were watering in the San Fernando River in Old Mexico, I'll claim her just the same. I'm going to ask you to throw her."

" I'll throw her for you," coolly replied Fox, "and bet you my saddle and six-shooter on the side that it isn't an ' O,' and even if it was, you and all the thieves on the Concho can't take her. I know a few of the simple principles of rustling myself. Do you want her thrown ? "

"That's what I asked for."

" Throw her, then," said Flood, "and don't let's parley."

Fox rode back into the herd, and after some little delay, located the cow and worked her out to the edge of the cattle. Dropping his rope, he cut her out clear of the herd, and as she circled around in an endeavor to reënter, he rode close and made an easy cast of the rope about her horns. As he threw his horse back to check the cow, I rode to his assistance, my rope in hand, and as the cow turned ends, I heeled her. A number of the outfit rode up and dismounted, and one of the boys taking her by the tail, we threw the animal as humanely as possible. In order to get at the brand, which was on the side, we turned the cow over, when Flood took out his knife and cut the hair away, leaving the brand easily traceable.

" What is she, Jim ? " inquired Fox, as he sat his horse holding the rope taut.

" I 'll let this man who claims her answer that question," replied Flood, as her claimant critically examined the brand to his satisfaction.

" I claim her as an ' O ' cow," said the stranger, facing Flood.

" Well, you claim more than you 'll ever get," replied our foreman. " Turn her loose, boys."

The cow was freed and turned back into the herd, but the claimant tried to argue the matter with Flood, claiming the branding iron had simply slipped, giving it the appearance of a " Q " instead of an " O " as it was intended to be. Our foreman paid little attention to the stranger, but when his persistence became annoying checked his argument by saying, —

" My Christian friend, there's no use arguing this matter. You asked to have the cow thrown, and we threw her. You might as well try to tell me that the cow is white as to claim her in any other brand than a ' Q.' You may read brands as well as I do, but you're wasting time arguing against the facts. You'd better take your ' Window Sash ' cattle and ride on, for you've cut all you're going to cut here to-day. But before you go, for fear I may never see you again, I 'll take this occasion to say that I think you're common cow thieves."

By his straight talk, our foreman stood several inches higher in our estimation as we sat our horses, grinning at the discomfiture of the trail cutters, while a dozen six-shooters slouched languidly at our hips to give emphasis to his words.

" Before going, I 'll take this occasion to say to you that you will see me again," replied the leader, riding up and confronting Flood. " You have n't got near enough men to bluff me. As to calling me a cow thief, that 's altogether too common a name to offend any one; and from what I can gather, the name would n't miss you or your outfit over a thousand miles. Now in taking my leave, I want to tell you that you 'll see me before another day passes, and what 's more, I 'll bring an outfit with me and we 'll cut your herd clean to your road brand, if for no better reasons, just to learn you not to be so insolent."

After hanging up this threat, Flood said to him as he turned to ride away, " Well, now, my young friend, you 're bargaining for a whole lot of fun. I notice you carry a gun and quite naturally suppose you shoot a little as occasion requires. Suppose when you and your outfit come back, you come a-shooting, so we 'll know who you are ; for I 'll promise you there 's liable to be some powder burnt when you cut this herd."

Amid jeers of derision from our outfit, the trail cutters drove off their three lonely " Window Sash " cattle. We had gained the point we wanted, and now in case of any trouble, during inspection or at night, we had the river behind us to catch our herd. We paid little attention to the threat of our disappointed callers, but several times Straw's remarks as to the character of the residents of those hills to the westward recurred to my mind. I was young, but knew enough, instead of asking foolish questions, to keep mum, though my eyes and ears drank in everything. Before we had been on the trail over an hour, we met two men riding down the trail towards the river. Meeting us, they turned and rode along with our foreman, some distance apart from the herd, for nearly an hour, and curiosity ran freely among us boys around the herd as to who they might be. Finally Flood rode forward to the point men and gave the order to throw off the trail and make a short drive that afternoon. Then in company with the two strangers, he rode forward to overtake our wagon, and we saw nothing more of him until we reached camp that evening. This much, however, our point man was able to get from our foreman : that the two men were members of a detachment of Rangers who had been sent as a result of information given by the first herd over the trail that year. This herd, which had passed some twenty days ahead of us, had met with a stampede below the river, and on reaching Abilene had reported the presence of rustlers preying on through herds at the crossing of the Colorado.

On reaching camp that evening with the herd, we found ten of the Rangers as our guests for the night. The detachment was under a corporal named Joe Hames, who had detailed the two men we had met during the afternoon to scout this crossing. Upon the information afforded by our foreman about the would-be trail cutters, these scouts, accompanied by Flood, had turned back to advise the Ranger squad, encamped in a secluded spot about ten miles northeast of the Colorado crossing. They had only arrived late the day before, and this was their first meeting with any trail herd to secure any definite information.

Hames at once assumed charge of the herd, Flood gladly rendering every assistance possible. We night herded as usual, but during the two middle guards, Hames sent out four of his Rangers to scout the immediate outlying country, though, as we expected, they met with no adventure. At daybreak the Rangers threw their packs into our wagon and their loose stock into our *remuda*, and riding up the trail a mile or more, left us, keeping well out of sight. We were all hopeful now that the trail cutters of the day before would make good their word and return. In this hope we killed time for several hours that morning, grazing the cattle and holding the wagon in the rear. Sending the wagon ahead of the herd had been agreed on as the signal between our foreman and the Ranger corporal, at first sight of any posse behind us. We were beginning to despair of their coming, when a dust cloud appeared several miles back down the trail. We at once hurried the wagon and *remuda* ahead to warn the Rangers, and allowed the cattle to string out nearly a mile in length.

A fortunate rise in the trail gave us a glimpse of the cavalcade in our rear, which was entirely too large to be any portion of Straw's outfit; and shortly we were overtaken by our trail cutters of the day before, now increased to twenty-two mounted men. Flood was intentionally in the lead of the herd, and the entire outfit galloped forward to stop the cattle. When they had nearly reached the lead, Flood turned back and met the rustlers.

"Well, I'm as good as my word," said the leader, "and I'm here to trim your herd as I promised you I would. Throw off and hold up your cattle, or I'll do it for you."

Several of our outfit rode up at this juncture in

time to hear Flood's reply: " If you think you 're
equal to the occasion, hold them up yourself. If
I had as big an outfit as you have, I would n't ask
any man to help me. I want to watch a Colorado
River outfit work a herd, — I might learn something. My outfit will take a rest, or perhaps hold
the cut or otherwise clerk for you. But be careful and don't claim anything that you are not certain is your own, for I reserve the right to look
over your cut before you drive it away."

The rustlers rode in a body to the lead, and when
they had thrown the herd off the trail, about half
of them rode back and drifted forward the rear
cattle. Flood called our outfit to one side and gave
us our instructions, the herd being entirely turned
over to the rustlers. After they began cutting,
we rode around and pretended to assist in holding
the cut as the strays in our herd were being cut
out. When the red " Q " cow came out, Fox cut
her back, which nearly precipitated a row, for she
was promptly recut to the strays by the man who
claimed her the day before. Not a man of us even
cast a glance up the trail, or in the direction of the
Rangers; but when the work was over, Flood protested with the leader of the rustlers over some five
or six head of dim-branded cattle which actually
belonged to our herd. But he was exultant and
would listen to no protests, and attempted to drive
away the cut, now numbering nearly fifty head.
Then we rode across their front and stopped them.

In the parley which ensued, harsh words were passing, when one of our outfit blurted out in well
feigned surprise, —

"Hello, who's that, coming over there?"

A squad of men were riding leisurely through
our abandoned herd, coming over to where the
two outfits were disputing.

"What's the trouble here, gents?" inquired
Hames as he rode up.

"Who are you and what might be your business,
may I ask?" inquired the leader of the rustlers.

"Personally I'm nobody, but officially I'm Corporal in Company B, Texas Rangers — well, if
there isn't smiling Ed Winters, the biggest cattle
thief ever born in Medina County. Why, I've got
papers for you; for altering the brands on over
fifty head of 'C' cattle into a 'G' brand. Come
here, dear, and give me that gun of yours. Come
on, and no false moves or funny work or I'll shoot
the white out of your eye. Surround this layout,
lads, and let's examine them more closely."

At this command, every man in our outfit whipped
out his six-shooter, the Rangers leveled their car-
bines on the rustlers, and in less than a minute's
time they were disarmed and as crestfallen a group
of men as ever walked into a trap of their own setting. Hames got out a "black book," and after
looking the crowd over concluded to hold the entire
covey, as the descriptions of the "wanted" seemed
to include most of them. Some of the rustlers

attempted to explain their presence, but Hames decided to hold the entire party, "just to learn them to be more careful of their company the next time," as he put it.

The cut had drifted away into the herd again during the arrest, and about half our outfit took the cattle on to where the wagon camped for noon. McCann had anticipated an extra crowd for dinner and was prepared for the emergency. When dinner was over and the Rangers had packed and were ready to leave, Hames said to Flood, —

"Well, Flood, I'm powerful glad I met you and your outfit. This has been one of the biggest round-ups for me in a long time. You don't know how proud I am over this bunch of beauties. Why, there's liable to be enough rewards out for this crowd to buy my girl a new pair of shoes. And say, when your wagon comes into Abilene, if I ain't there, just drive around to the sheriff's office and leave those captured guns. I'm sorry to load your wagon down that way, but I'm short on pack mules and it will be a great favor to me; besides, these fellows are not liable to need any guns for some little time. I like your company and your chuck, Flood, but you see how it is; the best of friends must part; and then I have an invitation to take dinner in Abilene by to-morrow noon, so I must be a-riding. Adios, everybody."

CHAPTER VIII

ON THE BRAZOS AND WICHITA

As we neared Buffalo Gap a few days later, a deputy sheriff of Taylor County, who resided at the Gap, rode out and met us. He brought an urgent request from Hames to Flood to appear as a witness against the rustlers, who were to be given a preliminary trial at Abilene the following day. Much as he regretted to leave the herd for even a single night, our foreman finally consented to go. To further his convenience we made a long evening drive, camping for the night well above Buffalo Gap, which at that time was little more than a landmark on the trail. The next day we made an easy drive and passed Abilene early in the afternoon, where Flood rejoined us, but refused any one permission to go into town, with the exception of McCann with the wagon, which was a matter of necessity. It was probably for the best, for this cow town had the reputation of setting a pace that left the wayfarer purseless and breathless, to say nothing about headaches. Though our foreman had not reached those mature years in life when the pleasures and frivolities of dissipation no longer allure, yet it was but natural that he should wish to keep his men from the temptation of the cup that cheers and the wiles of the siren. But when the wagon returned that evening, it was evident that our foreman was human, for with a box of cigars which were promised us were several bottles of Old Crow.

After crossing the Clear Fork of the Brazos a few days later, we entered a well-watered, open country, through which the herd made splendid progress. At Abilene, we were surprised to learn that our herd was the twentieth that had passed that point. The weather so far on our trip had been exceptionally good; only a few showers had fallen, and those during the daytime. But we were now nearing a country in which rain was more frequent, and the swollen condition of several small streams which have their headwaters in the Staked Plains was an intimation to us of recent rains to the westward of our route. Before reaching the main Brazos, we passed two other herds of yearling cattle, and were warned of the impassable condition of that river for the past week. Nothing daunted, we made our usual drive; and when the herd camped that night, Flood, after scouting ahead to the river, returned with the word that the Brazos had been unfordable for over a week, five herds being waterbound.

As we were then nearly twenty miles south of the river, the next morning we threw off the trail and turned the herd to the northeast, hoping to strike the Brazos a few miles above Round Timber ferry. Once the herd was started and their course for the day outlined to our point men by definite landmarks, Flood and Quince Forrest set out to locate the ferry and look up a crossing. Had it not been for our wagon, we would have kept the trail, but as there was no ferry on the Brazos at the crossing of the western trail, it was a question either of waiting or of making this detour. Then all the grazing for several miles about the crossing was already taken by the waterbound herds, and to crowd up and trespass on range already occupied would have been a violation of an unwritten law. Again, no herd took kindly to another attempting to pass them when in traveling condition the herds were on an equality. Our foreman had conceived the scheme of getting past these waterbound herds, if possible, which would give us a clear field until the next large watercourse was reached.

Flood and Forrest returned during the noon hour, the former having found, by swimming, a passable ford near the mouth of Monday Creek, while the latter reported the ferry in " apple-pie order." No sooner, then, was dinner over than the wagon set out for the ferry under Forrest as pilot, though we were to return to the herd once the ferry was sighted. The mouth of Monday Creek was not over ten miles below the regular trail crossing on the Brazos, and much nearer our noon camp than the regular one; but the wagon was compelled to make a direct elbow, first turning to the eastward, then doubling back after the river was crossed. We held the cattle off water during the day, so as to have them thirsty when they reached the river. Flood had swum it during the morning, and warned us to be prepared for fifty or sixty yards of swimming water in crossing. When within a mile, we held up the herd and changed horses, every man picking out one with a tested ability to swim. Those of us who were expected to take the water as the herd entered the river divested ourselves of boots and clothing, which we intrusted to riders in the rear. The approach to crossing was gradual, but the opposite bank was abrupt, with only a narrow passageway leading out from the channel. As the current was certain to carry the swimming cattle downstream, we must, to make due allowance, take the water nearly a hundred yards above the outlet on the other shore. All this was planned out in advance by our foreman, who now took the position of point man on the right hand or down the riverside; and with our saddle horses in the immediate lead, we breasted the angry Brazos.

The water was shallow as we entered, and we reached nearly the middle of the river before the loose saddle horses struck swimming water. Honeyman was on their lee, and with the cattle crowding in their rear, there was no alternative but to swim. A loose horse swims easily, however, and our *remuda* readily faced the current, though it was swift enough to carry them below the passageway on the opposite side. By this time the lead cattle were adrift, and half a dozen of us were on their lower side, for the footing under the cutbank was narrow, and should the cattle become congested on landing, some were likely to drown. For a quarter of an hour it required cool heads to keep the trail of cattle moving into the water and the passageway clear on the opposite landing. While they were crossing, the herd represented a large letter " U," caused by the force of the current drifting the cattle downstream, or until a foothold was secured on the farther side. Those of us fortunate enough to have good swimming horses swam the river a dozen times, and then after the herd was safely over, swam back to get our clothing. It was a thrilling experience to us younger lads of the outfit, and rather attractive; but the elder and more experienced men always dreaded swimming rivers. Their reasons were made clear enough when, a fortnight later, we crossed Red River, where a newly made grave was pointed out to us, amongst others of men who had lost their lives while swimming cattle.

Once the bulk of the cattle were safely over, with no danger of congestion on the farther bank, they were allowed to loiter along under the cutbank and drink to their hearts' content. Quite a number strayed above the passageway, and in order to rout them out, Bob Blades, Moss Strayhorn, and I rode out through the outlet and up the river, where we found some of them in a passageway down a dry arroyo. The steers had found a soft, damp place in the bank, and were so busy horning the waxy, red mud, that they hardly noticed our approach until we were within a rod of them. We halted our horses and watched their antics. The kneeling cattle were cutting the bank viciously with their horns and matting their heads with the red mud, but on discovering our presence, they curved their tails and stampeded out as playfully as young lambs on a hillside.

" Can you sabe where the fun comes in to a steer, to get down on his knees in the mud and dirt, and horn the bank and muss up his curls and enjoy it like that ? " inquired Strayhorn of Blades and me.

" Because it 's healthy and funny besides," replied Bob, giving me a cautious wink. " Did you never hear of people taking mud baths ? You 've seen dogs eat grass, have n't you ? Well, it 's something on the same order. Now, if I was a student of the nature of animals, like you are, I 'd get off my horse and imagine I had horns, and scar and otherwise mangle that mud bank shamefully. I 'll hold your horse if you want to try it — some of the secrets of the humor of cattle might be revealed to you."

The banter, though given in jest, was too much

for this member of a craft that can always be depended on to do foolish things; and when we rejoined the outfit, Strayhorn presented a sight no sane man save a member of our tribe ever would have conceived of.

The herd had scattered over several thousand acres after leaving the river, grazing freely, and so remained during the rest of the evening. Forrest changed horses and set out down the river to find the wagon and pilot it in, for with the long distance that McCann had to cover, it was a question if he would reach us before dark. Flood selected a bed ground and camp about a mile out from the river, and those of the outfit not on herd dragged up an abundance of wood for the night, and built a roaring fire as a beacon to our absent commissary. Darkness soon settled over camp, and the prospect of a supperless night was confronting us; the first guard had taken the herd, and yet there was no sign of the wagon. Several of us youngsters then mounted our night horses and rode down the river a mile or over in the hope of meeting McCann. We came to a steep bank, caused by the shifting of the first bottom of the river across to the north bank, rode up this bluff some little distance, dismounted, and fired several shots; then with our ears to the earth patiently awaited a response. It did not come, and we rode back again. "Hell's fire and little fishes!" said Joe Stallings, as we clambered into our saddles to return, "it's not supper or breakfast that's troubling me, but will we get any dinner to-morrow? That's a more pregnant question."

It must have been after midnight when I was awakened by the braying of mules and the rattle of the wagon, to hear the voices of Forrest and McCann, mingled with the rattle of chains as they unharnessed, condemning to eternal perdition the broken country on the north side of the Brazos, between Round Timber ferry and the mouth of Monday Creek.

"I think that when the Almighty made this country on the north side of the Brazos," said McCann the next morning at breakfast, "the Creator must have grown careless or else made it out of odds and ends. There's just a hundred and one of these dry arroyos that you can't see until you are right onto them. They wouldn't bother a man on horseback, but with a loaded wagon it's different. And I'll promise you all right now that if Forrest hadn't come out and piloted me in, you might have tightened up your belts for breakfast and drank out of cow tracks and smoked cigarettes for nourishment. Well, it'll do you good; this high living was liable to spoil some of you, but I notice that you are all on your feed this morning. The black strap? Honeyman, get that molasses jug out of the wagon — it sits right in front of the chuck box. It does me good to see this outfit's tastes once more going back to the good old staples of life."

We made our usual early start, keeping well out from the river on a course almost due northward. The next river on our way was the Wichita, still several days' drive from the mouth of Monday Creek. Flood's intention was to parallel the old trail until near the river, when, if its stage of water was not fordable, we would again seek a lower crossing in the hope of avoiding any waterbound herds on that watercourse. The second day out from the Brazos it rained heavily during the day and drizzled during the entire night. Not a hoof would bed down, requiring the guards to be doubled into two watches for the night. The next morning, as was usual when off the trail, Flood scouted in advance, and near the middle of the afternoon's drive we came into the old trail. The weather in the mean time had faired off, which revived life and spirit in the outfit, for in trail work there is nothing that depresses the spirits of men like falling weather. On coming into the trail, we noticed that no herds had passed since the rain began. Shortly afterward our rear guard was overtaken by a horseman who belonged to a mixed herd which was encamped some four or five miles below the point where we came into the old trail. He reported the Wichita as having been unfordable for the past week, but at that time falling; and said that if the rain of the past few days had not extended as far west as the Staked Plains, the river would be fordable in a day or two.

Before the stranger left us, Flood returned and confirmed this information, and reported further that there were two herds lying over at the Wichita ford expecting to cross the following day. With this outlook, we grazed our herd up to within five miles of the river and camped for the night, and our visitor returned to his outfit with Flood's report of our expectation of crossing on the morrow. But with the fair weather and the prospects of an easy night, we encamped entirely too close to the trail, as we experienced to our sorrow. The grazing was good everywhere, the recent rains having washed away the dust, and we should have camped farther away. We were all sleepy that night, and no sooner was supper over than every mother's son of us was in his blankets. We slept so soundly that the guards were compelled to dismount when calling the relief, and shake the next guards on duty out of their slumber and see that they got up, for men would unconsciously answer in their sleep. The cattle were likewise tired, and slept as willingly as the men.

About midnight, however, Fox Quarternight dashed into camp, firing his six-shooter and yelling like a demon. We tumbled out of our blankets in a dazed condition to hear that one of the herds camped near the river had stampeded, the heavy rumbling of the running herd and the shooting of their outfit now being distinctly audible. We lost no time getting our horses, and in less than a minute were riding for our cattle, which had already got up and were timidly listening to the approaching noise. Although we were a good quarter mile from the trail, before we could drift our herd to a point of safety, the stampeding cattle swept down the trail like a cyclone and our herd was absorbed into the maelstrom of the onrush like leaves in a whirlwind. It was then that our long-legged Mexican steers set us a pace that required a good horse to equal, for they easily took the lead, the other herd having run between three and four miles before striking us, and being already well winded. The other herd were Central Texas cattle, and numbered over thirty-five hundred, but in running capacity were never any match for ours.

Before they had run a mile past our camp, our outfit, bunched well together on the left point, made the first effort to throw them out and off the trail, and try to turn them. But the waves of an angry ocean could as easily have been brought under subjection as our terrorized herd during this first mad dash. Once we turned a few hundred of the leaders, and about the time we thought success was in reach, another contingent of double the number had taken the lead ; then we had to abandon what few we had, and again ride to the front. When we reached the lead, there, within half a mile ahead, burned the camp-fire of the herd of mixed cattle which had moved up the trail that evening. They had had ample warning of impending trouble, just as we had; and before the running cattle reached them about half a dozen of their outfit rode to our assistance, when we made another effort to turn or hold the herds from mixing. None of the outfit of the first herd had kept in the lead with us, their horses fagging, and when the foreman of this mixed herd met us, not knowing that we were as innocent of the trouble as himself, he made some slighting remarks about our outfit and cattle. But it was no time to be sensitive, and with his outfit to help we threw our whole weight against the left point a second time, but only turned a few hundred; and before we could get into the lead again their camp-fire had been passed and their herd of over three thousand cattle more were in the run. As cows and calves predominated in this mixed herd, our own southerners were still leaders in the stampede.

It is questionable if we would have turned this stampede before daybreak, had not the nature of the country come to our assistance. Something over two miles below the camp of the last herd was a deep creek, the banks of which were steep and the passages few and narrow. Here we succeeded in turning the leaders, and about half the outfit of the mixed herd remained, guarding the crossing and turning the lagging cattle in the run as they came up. With the leaders once turned and no chance for the others to take a new lead, we had the entire run of cattle turned back within an hour and safely under control. The first outfit joined us

during the interim, and when day broke we had
over forty men drifting about ten thousand cattle
back up the trail. The different outfits were un-
fortunately at loggerheads, no one being willing to
assume any blame. Flood hunted up the foreman
of the mixed herd and demanded an apology for
his remarks on our abrupt meeting with him the
night before; and while it was granted, it was plain
that it was begrudged. The first herd disclaimed
all responsibility, holding that the stampede was
due to an unavoidable accident, their cattle having grown restless during their enforced lay-over.
The indifferent attitude of their foreman, whose
name was Wilson, won the friendly regard of our
outfit, and before the wagon of the mixed cattle
was reached, there was a compact, at least tacit,
between their outfit and ours. Our foreman was
not blameless, for had we taken the usual precaution and camped at least a mile off the trail,
which was our custom when in close proximity to
other herds, we might and probably would have
missed this mix-up, for our herd was inclined to be
very tractable. Flood, with all his experience, well
knew that if stampeded cattle ever got into a
known trail, they were certain to turn backward
over their course ; and we were now paying the
fiddler for lack of proper precaution.

Within an hour after daybreak, and before the
cattle had reached the camp of the mixed herd,
our saddle horses were sighted coming over a slight

divide about two miles up the trail, and a minute later McCann's mules hove in sight, bringing up the rear. They had made a start with the first dawn, rightly reasoning, as there was no time to leave orders on our departure, that it was advisable for Mahomet to go to the mountain. Flood complimented our cook and horse wrangler on their foresight, for the wagon was our base of sustenance; and there was little loss of time before Barney McCann was calling us to a hastily prepared breakfast. Flood asked Wilson to bring his outfit to our wagon for breakfast, and as fast as they were relieved from herd, they also did ample justice to McCann's cooking. During breakfast, I remember Wilson explaining to Flood what he believed was the cause of the stampede. It seems that there were a few remaining buffalo ranging north of the Wichita, and at night when they came into the river to drink they had scented the cattle on the south side. The bellowing of buffalo bulls had been distinctly heard by his men on night herd for several nights past. The foreman stated it as his belief that a number of bulls had swum the river and had by stealth approached near the sleeping cattle, — then, on discovering the presence of the herders, had themselves stampeded, throwing his herd into a panic.

We had got a change of mounts during the breakfast hour, and when all was ready Flood and Wilson rode over to the wagon of the mixed herd,

the two outfits following, when Flood inquired of
their foreman, —

" Have you any suggestions to make in the cutting of these herds ? "

" No suggestions," was the reply, " but I intend
to cut mine first and cut them northward on the
trail."

" You intend to cut them northward, you mean,
provided there are no objections, which I 'm positive there will be," said Flood. " It takes me
some little time to size a man up, and the more I
see of you during our brief acquaintance, the more
I think there 's two or three things that you might
learn to your advantage.   I 'll not enumerate them
now, but when these herds are separated, if you
insist, it will cost you nothing but the asking for
my opinion of you.   This much you can depend on:
when the cutting 's over, you 'll occupy the same
position on the trail that you did before this accident happened.   Wilson, here, has nothing but
jaded horses, and his outfit will hold the herd while
yours and mine cut their cattle.   And instead of
you cutting north, you can either cut south where
you belong on the trail or sulk in your camp, your
own will and pleasure to govern.   But if you are a
cowman, willing to do your part, you 'll have your
outfit ready to work by the time we throw the cattle together."

Not waiting for any reply, Flood turned away,
and the double outfit circled around the grazing

herd and began throwing the sea of cattle into a compact body ready to work. Rod Wheat and Ash Borrowstone were detailed to hold our cut, and the remainder of us, including Honeyman, entered the herd and began cutting. Shortly after we had commenced the work, the mixed outfit, finding themselves in a lonesome minority, joined us and began cutting out their cattle to the westward. When we had worked about half an hour, Flood called us out, and with the larger portion of Wilson's men, we rode over and drifted the mixed cut around to the southward, where they belonged. The mixed outfit pretended they meant no harm, and were politely informed that if they were sincere, they could show it more plainly. For nearly three hours we sent a steady stream of cattle out of the main herd into our cut, while our horses dripped with sweat. With our advantage in the start, as well as that of having the smallest herd, we finished our work first. While the mixed outfit were finishing their cutting, we changed mounts, and then were ready to work the separated herds. Wilson took about half his outfit, and after giving our herd a trimming, during which he recut about twenty, the mixed outfit were given a similar chance, and found about half a dozen of their brand. These cattle of Wilson's and the other herd amongst ours were not to be wondered at, for we cut by a liberal rule. Often we would find a number of ours on the outside of the main herd, when two men would cut the squad in a bunch, and if there was a wrong brand amongst them, it was no matter, — we knew our herd would have to be retrimmed anyhow, and the other outfits might be disappointed if they found none of their cattle amongst ours.

The mixed outfit were yet working our herd when Wilson's wagon and saddle horses arrived, and while they were changing mounts, we cut the mixed herd of our brand and picked up a number of strays which we had been nursing along, though when we first entered the main herd, strays had received our attention, being well known to us by ranch brands as well as flesh marks. In gathering up this very natural flotsam of the trail, we cut nothing but what our herd had absorbed in its travels, showing due regard to a similar right of the other herds. Our work was finished first, and after Wilson had recut the mixed herd, we gave his herd one more looking over in a farewell parting. Flood asked him if he wanted the lead, but Wilson waived his right in his open, frank manner, saying, "If I had as long-legged cattle as you have, I would n't ask no man for the privilege of passing. Why, you ought to out-travel horses. I 'm glad to have met you and your outfit, personally, but regret the incident which has given you so much trouble. As I don't expect to go farther than Dodge or Ogalalla at the most, you are more than welcome to the lead. And if you or any of these rascals in your outfit are ever in Coryell County, hunt up Frank Wilson of the Block Bar Ranch, and I'll promise you a drink of milk or something stronger if possible."

We crossed the Wichita late that afternoon, there being not over fifty feet of swimming water for the cattle. Our wagon gave us the only trouble, for the load could not well be lightened, and it was an imperative necessity to cross it the same day. Once the cattle were safely over and a few men left to graze them forward, the remainder of the outfit collected all the ropes and went back after the wagon. As mules are always unreliable in the water, Flood concluded to swim them loose. We lashed the wagon box securely to the gearing with ropes, arranged our bedding in the wagon where it would be on top, and ran the wagon by hand into the water as far as we dared without flooding the wagon box. Two men, with guy ropes fore and aft, were then left to swim with the wagon in order to keep it from toppling over, while the remainder of us recrossed to the farther side of the swimming channel, and fastened our lariats to two long ropes from the end of the tongue. We took a wrap on the pommels of our saddles with the loose end, and when the word was given our eight horses furnished abundant motive power, and the wagon floated across, landing high and dry amid the shoutings of the outfit.

CHAPTER IX

DOAN'S CROSSING

It was a nice open country between the Wichita and Pease rivers. On reaching the latter, we found an easy stage of water for crossing, though there was every evidence that the river had been on a recent rise, the débris of a late freshet littering the cutbank, while high-water mark could be easily noticed on the trees along the river bottom. Summer had advanced until the June freshets were to be expected, and for the next month we should be fortunate if our advance was not checked by floods and falling weather. The fortunate stage of the Pease encouraged us, however, to hope that possibly Red River, two days' drive ahead, would be fordable. The day on which we expected to reach it, Flood set out early to look up the ford which had then been in use but a few years, and which in later days was known as Doan's Crossing on Red River. Our foreman returned before noon and reported a favorable stage of water for the herd, and a new ferry that had been established for wagons. With this good news, we were determined to put that river behind us in as few hours as possible, for it was a common occurrence that a river which was fordable at night was the reverse by daybreak. McCann was sent ahead with the wagon, but we held the saddle horses with us to serve as leaders in taking the water at the ford.

The cattle were strung out in trailing manner nearly a mile, and on reaching the river near the middle of the afternoon, we took the water without a halt or even a change of horses. This boundary river on the northern border of Texas was a terror to trail drovers, but on our reaching it, it had shallowed down, the flow of water following several small channels. One of these was swimming, with shallow bars intervening between the channels. But the majestic grandeur of the river was apparent on every hand, — with its red, bluff banks, the sediment of its red waters marking the timber along its course, while the driftwood, lodged in trees and high on the banks, indicated what might be expected when she became sportive or angry. That she was merciless was evident, for although this crossing had been in use only a year or two when we forded, yet five graves, one of which was less than ten days made, attested her disregard for human life. It can safely be asserted that at this and lower trail crossings on Red River, the lives of more trail men were lost by drowning than on all other rivers together. Just as we were nearing the river, an unknown horseman from the south overtook our herd. It was evident that he belonged to some through herd and was looking out

the crossing. He made himself useful by lending
a hand while our herd was fording, and in a brief
conversation with Flood, informed him that he
was one of the hands with a " Running W " herd,
gave the name of Bill Mann as their foreman,
the number of cattle they were driving, and reported the herd as due to reach the river the next
morning. He wasted little time with us, but recrossed the river, returning to his herd, while we
grazed out four or five miles and camped for the
night.

I shall never forget the impression left in my
mind of that first morning after we crossed Red
River into the Indian lands. The country was as
primitive as in the first day of its creation. The
trail led up a divide between the Salt and North
forks of Red River. To the eastward of the latter
stream lay the reservation of the Apaches, Kiowas,
and Comanches, the latter having been a terror
to the inhabitants of western Texas. They were a
warlike tribe, as the records of the Texas Rangers
and government troops will verify, but their last
effective dressing down was given them in a fight
at Adobe Walls by a party of buffalo hunters whom
they hoped to surprise. As we wormed our way up
this narrow divide, there was revealed to us a pano-
rama of green-swarded plain and timber-fringed
watercourse, with not a visible evidence that it had
ever been invaded by civilized man, save cattlemen
with their herds. Antelope came up in bands and

gratified their curiosity as to who these invaders might be, while old solitary buffalo bulls turned tail at our approach and lumbered away to points of safety. Very few herds had ever passed over this route, but buffalo trails leading downstream, deep worn by generations of travel, were to be seen by hundreds on every hand. We were not there for a change of scenery or for our health, so we may have overlooked some of the beauties of the landscape. But we had a keen eye for the things of our craft. We could see almost back to the river, and several times that morning noticed clouds of dust on the horizon. Flood noticed them first. After some little time the dust clouds arose clear and distinct, and we were satisfied that the " Running W " herd had forded and were behind us, not more than ten or twelve miles away.

At dinner that noon, Flood said he had a notion to go back and pay Mann a visit. " Why, I 've not seen ' Little-foot ' Bill Mann," said our foreman, as he helped himself to a third piece of " fried chicken " (bacon), " since we separated two years ago up at Ogalalla on the Platte. I 'd just like the best in the world to drop back and sleep in his blankets one night and complain of his chuck. Then I 'd like to tell him how we had passed them, starting ten days' drive farther south. He must have been amongst those herds laying over on the Brazos."

" Why don't you go, then ? " said Fox Quarter-

night. " Half the outfit could hold the cattle now
with the grass and water we 're in at present."

" I 'll go you one for luck," said our foreman.
" Wrangler, rustle in your horses the minute
you 're through eating. I 'm going visiting."

We all knew what horse he would ride, and when
he dropped his rope on " Alazanito," he had not only
picked his own mount of twelve, but the top horse
of the entire *remuda*, — a chestnut sorrel, fifteen
hands and an inch in height, that drew his first
breath on the prairies of Texas. No man who sat
him once could ever forget him. Now, when the
trail is a lost occupation, and reverie and reminis-
cence carry the mind back to that day, there are
friends and faces that may be forgotten, but there
are horses that never will be. There were emergencies in which the horse was everything, his rider
merely the accessory. But together, man and horse,
they were the force that made it possible to move
the millions of cattle which passed up and over the
various trails of the West.

When we had caught our horses for the afternoon,
and Flood had saddled and was ready to start, he
said to us, " You fellows just mosey along up the
trail. I 'll not be gone long, but when I get back
I shall expect to find everything running smooth.
An outfit that can't run itself without a boss ought
to stay at home and do the milking. So long, fellows ! "

The country was well watered, and when we

rounded the cattle into the bed ground that night, they were actually suffering from stomachs gorged with grass and water. They went down and to sleep like tired children ; one man could have held them that night. We all felt good, and McCann got up an extra spread for supper. We even had dried apples for dessert. McCann had talked the storekeeper at Doan's, where we got our last supplies, out of some extras as a *pelon*. Among them was a can of jam. He sprung this on us as a surprise. Bob Blades toyed with the empty can in mingled admiration and disgust over a picture on the paper label. It was a supper scene, every figure wearing full dress. " Now, that 's General Grant," said he, pointing with his finger, " and this is Tom Ochiltree. I can't quite make out this other duck, but I reckon he 's some big auger — a senator or governor, maybe. Them old girls have got their gall with them. That style of dress is what you call *lo* and *behold*. The whole passel ought to be ashamed. And they seem to be enjoying themselves, too."

Though it was a lovely summer night, we had a fire, and supper over, the conversation ranged wide and free. As the wagon on the trail is home, naturally the fire is the hearthstone, so we gathered and lounged around it.

" The only way to enjoy such a fine night as this," remarked Ash, " is to sit up smoking until you fall asleep with your boots on. Between too much sleep and just enough, there's a happy medium which suits me."

" Officer," inquired Wyatt Roundtree, trailing into the conversation very innocently, " why is it that people who live up among those Yankees always say ' be ' the remainder of their lives ? "

" What 's the matter with the word ? " countered Officer.

" Oh, nothing, I reckon, only it sounds a little odd, and there 's a tale to it."

" A story, you mean," said Officer, reprovingly.

" Well, I 'll tell it to you," said Roundtree, " and then you can call it to suit yourself. It was out in New Mexico where this happened. There was a fellow drifted into the ranch where I was working, dead broke. To make matters worse, he could do nothing ; he would n't fit anywhere. Still, he was a nice fellow and we all liked him. Must have had a good education, for he had good letters from people up North. He had worked in stores and had once clerked in a bank, at least the letters said so. Well, we put up a job to get him a place in a little town out on the railroad. You all know how clannish Kentuckians are. Let two meet who never saw each other before, and inside of half an hour they 'll be chewing tobacco from the same plug and trying to loan each other money."

" That 's just like them," interposed Fox Quarternight.

" Well, there was an old man lived in this town,

who was the genuine blend of bluegrass and Bourbon. If another Kentuckian came within twenty miles of him, and he found it out, he 'd hunt him up and they 'd hold a two-handed reunion. We put up the job that this young man should play that he was a Kentuckian, hoping that the old man would take him to his bosom and give him something to do. So we took him into town one day, coached and fully posted how to act and play his part. We met the old man in front of his place of business, and, after the usual comment on the news over our way, weather, and other small talk, we were on the point of passing on, when one of our own crowd turned back and inquired, ' Uncle Henry, have you met the young Kentuckian who 's in the country ? '

" ' No,' said the old man, brightening with interest, ' who is he and where is he ? '

" ' He 's in town somewhere,' volunteered one of the boys. We pretended to survey the street from where we stood, when one of the boys blurted out, ' Yonder he stands now. That fellow in front of the drug store over there, with the hard-boiled hat on.'

" The old man started for him, angling across the street, in disregard of sidewalks. We watched the meeting, thinking it was working all right. We were mistaken. We saw them shake hands, when the old man turned and walked away very haughtily. Something had gone wrong. He took

the sidewalk on his return, and when he came near
enough to us, we could see that he was angry and
on the prod. When he came near enough to speak,
he said, 'You think you're smart, don't you?
He's a Kentuckian, is he? Hell's full of such
Kentuckians!' And as he passed beyond hearing
he was muttering imprecations on us. The young
fellow joined us a minute later with the question,
'What kind of a crank is that you ran me up
against?'

"'He's as nice a man as there is in this country,' said one of the crowd. 'What did you say
to him?'

"'Nothing; he came up to me, extended his
hand, saying, "My young friend, I understand
that you're from Kentucky." "I be, sir," I replied, when he looked me in the eye and said,
"You're a G— d— liar," and turned and walked
away. Why, he must have wanted to insult me.'
And then we all knew why our little scheme had
failed. There was food and raiment in it for him,
but he would use that little word 'be.'"

"Did any of you notice my saddle horse lie down
just after we crossed this last creek this afternoon?" inquired Rod Wheat.

"No; what made him lie down?" asked several
of the boys.

"Oh, he just found a gopher hole and stuck his
forefeet into it one at a time, and then tried to
pull them both out at once, and when he couldn't

do it, he simply shut his eyes like a dying sheep and lay down."

" Then you 've seen sheep die," said the horse wrangler.

" Of course I have ; a sheep can die any time he makes up his mind to by simply shutting both eyes — then he 's a goner."

Quince Forrest, who had brought in his horse to go out with the second watch, he and Bob Blades having taken advantage of the foreman's absence to change places on guard for the night, had been listening to the latter part of Wyatt's yarn very attentively. We all hoped that he would mount and ride out to the herd, for though he was a good story-teller and meaty with personal experiences, where he thought they would pass muster he was inclined to overcolor his statements. We usually gave him respectful attention, but were frequently compelled to regard him as a cheerful, harmless liar. So when he showed no disposition to go, we knew we were in for one from him.

" When I was boss bull-whacker," he began, "for a big army sutler at Fort Concho, I used to make two round trips a month with my train. It was a hundred miles to wagon from the freight point where we got our supplies. I had ten teams, six and seven yoke to the team, and trail wagons to each. I was furnished a night herder and a cook, saddle horses for both night herder and myself. You hear me, it was a slam up fine layout. We could handle three or four tons to the team, and with the whole train we could chamber two car loads of anything. One day we were nearing the fort with a mixed cargo of freight, when a messenger came out and met us with an order from the sutler. He wanted us to make the fort that night and unload. The mail buckboard had reported us to the sutler as camped out back on a little creek about ten miles. We were always entitled to a day to unload and drive back to camp, which gave us good grass for the oxen, but under the orders the whips popped merrily that afternoon, and when they all got well strung out, I rode in ahead, to see what was up. Well, it seems that four companies of infantry from Fort McKavett, which were out for field practice, were going to be brought into this post to be paid three months' wages. This, with the troops stationed at Concho, would turn loose quite a wad of money. The sutler called me into his office when I reached the fort, and when he had produced a black bottle used for cutting the alkali in your drinking water, he said, ' Jack,' — he called me Jack; my full name is John Quincy Forrest, — ' Jack, can you make the round trip, and bring in two cars of bottled beer that will be on the track waiting for you, and get back by pay day, the 10th? '

"I figured the time in my mind; it was twelve days.

"'There's five extra in it for each man for the

trip, and I 'll make it right with you,' he added, as he noticed my hesitation, though I was only making a mental calculation.

" ' Why, certainly, Captain,' I said. ' What's that fable about the jack rabbit and the land tarrapin? ' He did n't know and I did n't either, so I said to illustrate the point : ' Put your freight on a bull train, and it always goes through on time. A race horse can't beat an ox on a hundred miles and repeat to a freight wagon.' Well, we unloaded before night, and it was pitch dark before we made camp. I explained the situation to the men. We planned to go in empty in five days, which would give us seven to come back loaded. We made every camp on time like clockwork. The fifth morning we were anxious to get a daybreak start, so we could load at night. The night herder had his orders to bring in the oxen the first sign of day, and I called the cook an hour before light. When the oxen were brought in, the men were up and ready to go to yoking. But the nigh wheeler in Joe Jenk's team, a big brindle, muley ox, a regular pet steer, was missing. I saw him myself, Joe saw him, and the night herder swore he came in with the rest. Well, we looked high and low for that Mr. Ox, but he had vanished. While the men were eating their breakfast, I got on my horse and the night herder and I scoured and circled that country for miles around, but no ox. The country was so bare and level that a jack rabbit needed to carry a fly for shade. I was worried, for we needed every ox and every moment of time. I ordered Joe to tie his mate behind the trail wagon and pull out one ox shy.

" Well, fellows, that thing worried me powerful. Half the teamsters, good, honest, truthful men as ever popped a whip, swore they saw that ox when they came in. Well, it served a strong argument that a man can be positive and yet be mistaken. We nooned ten miles from our night camp that day. Jerry Wilkens happened to mention it at dinner that he believed his trail needed greasing. ' Why,' said Jerry, ' you 'd think that I was loaded, the way my team kept their chains taut.' I noticed Joe get up from dinner before he had finished, as if an idea had struck him. He went over and opened the sheet in Jerry's trail wagon, and a smile spread over his countenance. ' Come here, fellows,' was all he said.

" We ran over to the wagon and there " —

The boys turned their backs with indistinct mutterings of disgust.

" You all don't need to believe this if you don't want to, but there was the missing ox, coiled up and sleeping like a bear in the wagon. He even had Jerry's roll of bedding for a pillow. You see, the wagon sheet was open in front, and he had hopped up on the trail tongue and crept in there to steal a ride. Joe climbed into the wagon, and gave him a few swift kicks in the short ribs, when he opened his eyes, yawned, got up, and jumped out."

Bull was rolling a cigarette before starting, while Fox's night horse was hard to bridle, which hindered them. With this slight delay, Forrest turned his horse back and continued : "That same ox on the next trip, one night when we had the wagons parked into a corral, got away from the herder, tip-toed over the men's beds in the gate, stood on his hind legs long enough to eat four fifty-pound sacks of flour out of the rear end of a wagon, got down on his side, and wormed his way under the wagon back into the herd, without being detected or waking a man."

As they rode away to relieve the first guard, McCann said, " Is n't he a muzzle-loading daisy ? If I loved a liar I 'd hug that man to death."

The absence of our foreman made no difference. We all knew our places on guard. Experience told us there would be no trouble that night. After Wyatt Roundtree and Moss Strayhorn had made down their bed and got into it, Wyatt remarked, —

"Did you ever notice, old sidey, how hard this ground is ? "

"Oh, yes," said Moss, as he turned over, hunting for a soft spot, " it is hard, but we 'll forget all that when this trip ends. Brother, dear, just think of those long slings with red cherries floating around in them that we 'll be drinking, and picture us smoking cigars in a blaze. That thought alone ought to make a hard bed both soft and warm. Then to think we 'll ride all the way home on the cars."

McCann banked his fire, and the first guard, Wheat, Stallings, and Borrowstone, rode in from the herd, all singing an old chorus that had been composed, with little regard for music or sense, about a hotel where they had stopped the year before : —

"Sure it 's one cent for coffee and two cents for bread,
Three for a steak and five for a bed,
Sea breeze from the gutter wafts a salt water smell,
To the festive cowboy in the Southwestern hotel."

CHAPTER X

FLOOD overtook us the next morning, and as a number of us gathered round him to hear the news, told us of a letter that Mann had got at Doan's, stating that the first herd to pass Camp Supply had been harassed by Indians. The " Running W " people, Mann's employers, had a representative at Dodge, who was authority for the statement. Flood had read the letter, which intimated that an appeal would be made to the government to send troops from either Camp Supply or Fort Sill to give trail herds a safe escort in passing the western border of this Indian reservation. The letter, therefore, admonished Mann, if he thought the Indians would give any trouble, to go up the south side of Red River as far as the Pan-handle of Texas, and then turn north to the government trail at Fort Elliot.

"I told Mann," said our foreman, " that before I'd take one step backward, or go off on a wild goose chase through that Pan-handle country, I'd go back home and start over next year on the Chisholm trail. It's the easiest thing in the world for some big auger to sit in a hotel somewhere and

direct the management of a herd.   I don't look for
no soldiers to furnish an escort ; it would take the
government six months to get a move on her, even
in an emergency.   I left Billy Mann in a quandary ;
he does n't know what to do.   That big auger at
Dodge is troubling him, for if he don't act on his
advice, and loses cattle as the result — well, he 'll
never boss any more herds for King and Kennedy.
So, boys, if we 're ever to see the Blackfoot Agency,
there 's but one course for us to take, and that 's
straight ahead.   As old Oliver Loving, the first
Texas cowman that ever drove a herd, used to say,
' Never borrow trouble, or cross a river before you
reach it.'   So when the cattle are through grazing,
let them hit the trail north.   It 's entirely too late
for us to veer away from any Indians."

We were following the regular trail, which had
been slightly used for a year or two, though none of
our outfit had ever been over it, when late on the
third afternoon, about forty miles out from Doan's,
about a hundred mounted bucks and squaws sighted
our herd and crossed the North Fork from their
encampment.   They did not ride direct to the herd,
but came into the trail nearly a mile above the
cattle, so it was some little time from our first sighting them before we met.   We did not check the
herd or turn out of the trail, but when the lead
came within a few hundred yards of the Indians,
one buck, evidently the chief of the band, rode
forward a few rods and held up one hand, as if

commanding a halt. At the sight of this gaudily bedecked apparition, the cattle turned out of the trail, and Flood and I rode up to the chief, extending our hands in friendly greeting. The chief could not speak a word of English, but made signs with his hands; when I turned loose on him in Spanish, however, he instantly turned his horse and signed back to his band. Two young bucks rode forward and greeted Flood and myself in good Spanish.

On thus opening up an intelligible conversation, I called Fox Quarternight, who spoke Spanish, and he rode up from his position of third man in the swing and joined in the council. The two young Indians through whom we carried on the conversation were Apaches, no doubt renegades of that tribe, and while we understood each other in Spanish, they spoke in a heavy guttural peculiar to the Indian. Flood opened the powwow by demanding to know the meaning of this visit. When the question had been properly interpreted to the chief, the latter dropped his blanket from his shoulders and dismounted from his horse. He was a fine specimen of the Plains Indian, fully six feet in height, perfectly proportioned, and in years well past middle life. He looked every inch a chief, and was a natural born orator. There was a certain easy grace to his gestures, only to be seen in people who use the sign language, and often when he was speaking to the Apache interpreters, I could anticipate his requests before they were translated to us, although I did not know a word of Comanche.

Before the powwow had progressed far it was evident that begging was its object. In his prelude, the chief laid claim to all the country in sight as the hunting grounds of the Comanche tribe, — an intimation that we were intruders. He spoke of the great slaughter of the buffalo by the white hide-hunters, and the consequent hunger and poverty amongst his people. He dwelt on the fact that he had ever counseled peace with the whites, until now his band numbered but a few squaws and papooses, the younger men having deserted him for other chiefs of the tribe who advocated war on the pale-faces. When he had fully stated his position, he offered to allow us to pass through his country in consideration of ten beeves. On receiving this proposition, all of us dismounted, including the two Apaches, the latter seating themselves in their own fashion, while we whites lounged on the ground in truly American laziness, rolling cigarettes. In dealing with people who know not the value of time, the civilized man is taken at a disadvantage, and unless he can show an equal composure in wasting time, results will be against him. Flood had had years of experience in dealing with Mexicans in the land of *mañana*, where all maxims regarding the value of time are religiously discarded. So in dealing with this Indian chief he showed no desire to

MEETING WITH INDIANS

hasten matters, and carefully avoided all reference to the demand for beeves.

His first question, instead, was to know the distance to Fort Sill and Fort Elliot. The next was how many days it would take for cavalry to reach him. He then had us narrate the fact that when the first herd of cattle passed through the country less than a month before, some bad Indians had shown a very unfriendly spirit. They had taken many of the cattle and had killed and eaten them, and now the great white man's chief at Washington was very much displeased. If another single ox were taken and killed by bad Indians, he would send his soldiers from the forts to protect the cattle, even though their owners drove the herds through the reservation of the Indians — over the grass where their ponies grazed. He had us inform the chief that our entire herd was intended by the great white man's chief at Washington as a present to the Blackfeet Indians who lived in Montana, because they were good Indians, and welcomed priests and teachers amongst them to teach them the ways of the white man. At our foreman's request we then informed the chief that he was under no obligation to give him even a single beef for any privilege of passing through his country, but as the squaws and little papooses were hungry, he would give him two beeves.

The old chief seemed not the least disconcerted, but begged for five beeves, as many of the squaws were in the encampment across the North Fork, those present being not quite half of his village. It was now getting late in the day and the band seemed to be getting tired of the parleying, a number of squaws having already set out on their return to the village. After some further talk, Flood agreed to add another beef, on condition they be taken to the encampment before being killed. This was accepted, and at once the entire band set up a chattering in view of the coming feast. The cattle had in the mean time grazed off nearly a mile, the outfit, however, holding them under a close herd during the powwowing. All the bucks in the band, numbering about forty, now joined us, and we rode away to the herd. I noticed, by the way, that quite a number of the younger braves had arms, and no doubt they would have made a display of force had Flood's diplomacy been of a more warlike character. While drifting the herd back to the trail we cut out a big lame steer and two stray cows for the Indians, who now left us and followed the beeves which were being driven to their village.

Flood had instructed Quarternight and me to invite the two Apaches to our camp for the night, on the promise of sugar, coffee, and tobacco. They consulted with the old chief, and gaining his consent came with us. We extended the hospitality of our wagon to our guests, and when supper was over, promised them an extra beef if they would give us particulars of the trail until it crossed the North Fork, after that river turned west towards the Pan-handle. It was evident that they were familiar with the country, for one of them accepted our offer, and with his finger sketched a rude map on the ground where there had formerly been a camp-fire. He outlined the two rivers between which we were then encamped, and traced the trail until it crossed the North Fork or beyond the Indian reservation. We discussed the outline of the trail in detail for an hour, asking hundreds of unimportant questions, but occasionally getting in a leading one, always resulting in the information wanted. We learned that the big summer encampment of the Comanches and Kiowas was one day's ride for a pony or two days' with cattle up the trail, at the point where the divide between Salt and North Fork narrows to about ten miles in width. We leeched out of them very cautiously the information that the encampment was a large one, and that all herds this year had given up cattle, some as many as twenty-five head.

Having secured the information we wanted, Flood gave to each Apache a package of Arbuckle coffee, a small sack of sugar, and both smoking and chewing tobacco. Quarternight informed them that as the cattle were bedded for the night, they had better remain until morning, when he would pick them out a nice fat beef. On their consenting, Fox stripped the wagon sheet off the wagon and made them a good bed, in which, with their body blankets, they were as comfortable as any of us. Neither of them was armed, so we felt no fear of them, and after they had lain down on their couch, Flood called Quarternight and me, and we strolled out into the darkness and reviewed the information. We agreed that the topography of the country they had given was most likely correct, because we could verify much of it by maps in our possession. Another thing on which we agreed was, that there was some means of communication between this small and seemingly peaceable band and the main encampment of the tribe ; and that more than likely our approach would be known in the large encampment before sunrise. In spite of the good opinion we entertained of our guests, we were also satisfied they had lied to us when they denied they had been in the large camp since the trail herds began to pass. This was the last question we had asked, and the artful manner in which they had parried it showed our guests to be no mean diplomats themselves.

Our camp was astir by daybreak, and after breakfast, as we were catching our mounts for the day, one of the Apaches offered to take a certain pinto horse in our *remuda* in lieu of the promised beef, but Flood declined the offer. On overtaking the herd after breakfast, Quarternight cut out a fat two year old stray heifer, and he and I assisted our guests to drive their beef several miles toward their village. Finally bidding them farewell, we returned to the herd, when the outfit informed us that Flood and The Rebel had ridden on ahead to look out a crossing on the Salt Fork. From this move it was evident that if a passable ford could be found, our foreman intended to abandon the established route and avoid the big Indian encampment.

On the return of Priest and Flood about noon, they reported having found an easy ford of the Salt Fork, which, from the indications of their old trails centring from every quarter at this crossing, must have been used by buffalo for generations. After dinner we put our wagon in the lead, and following close at hand with the cattle, turned off the trail about a mile above our noon camp and struck to the westward for the crossing. This we reached and crossed early that evening, camping out nearly five miles to the west of the river. Rain was always to be dreaded in trail work, and when bedding down the herd that night, we had one of the heaviest downpours which we had experienced since leaving the Rio Grande. It lasted several hours, but we stood it uncomplainingly, for this fortunate drenching had obliterated every trace left by our wagon and herd since abandoning the trail, as well as the sign left at the old buffalo crossing on the Salt Fork. The rain ceased about ten o'clock, when the cattle bedded down easily, and the second guard took them for their watch. Wood was too scarce to afford a fire, and while our slickers had partially protected us from the rain, many of us went to bed in wet clothing that night. After another half day's drive to the west, we turned northward and traveled in that direction through a nice country, more or less broken with small hills, but well watered. On the morning of the first day after turning north, Honeyman reported a number of our saddle horses had strayed from camp. This gave Flood some little uneasiness, and a number of us got on our night horses without loss of time and turned out to look up the missing saddle stock. The Rebel and I set out together to the southward, while others of the outfit set off to the other points of the compass.

I was always a good trailer, was in fact acknowledged to be one of the best, with the exception of my brother Zack, on the San Antonio River, where we grew up as boys. In circling about that morning, I struck the trail of about twenty horses — the missing number — and at once signaled to Priest, who was about a mile distant, to join me. The ground was fortunately fresh from the recent rain and left an easy trail. We galloped along it easily for some little distance, when the trail suddenly turned and we could see that the horses had been running, having evidently received a sudden scare. On following up the trail nearly a mile, we noticed where they had quieted down and had evidently grazed for several hours, but in looking up the trail by which they had left these parts, Priest

made the discovery of signs of cattle. We located
the trail of the horses soon, and were again surprised to find that they had been running as before, though the trail was much fresher, having
possibly been made about dawn. We ran the trail
out until it passed over a slight divide, when there
before us stood the missing horses. They never
noticed us, but were standing at attention, cautiously sniffing the early morning air, on which was
borne to them the scent of something they feared.
On reaching them, their fear seemed not the least
appeased, and my partner and I had our curiosity
sufficiently aroused to ride forward to the cause of
their alarm. As we rounded the spur of the hill,
there in plain view grazed a band of about twenty
buffalo. We were almost as excited as the horses
over the discovery. By dropping back and keeping the hill between us and them, then dismounting and leaving our horses, we thought we could
reach the apex of the hill. It was but a small elevation, and from its summit we secured a splendid
view of the animals, now less than three hundred
yards distant. Flattening ourselves out, we spent
several minutes watching the shaggy animals as
they grazed leisurely forward, while several calves
in the bunch gamboled around their mothers. A
buffalo calf, I had always heard, made delicious
veal, and as we had had no fresh meat since we
had started, I proposed to Priest that we get one.

He suggested trying our ropes, for if we could

ever get within effective six-shooter range, a rope
was much the surest. Certainly such cumbrous,
awkward looking animals, he said, could be no
match for our Texas horses. We accordingly
dropped back off the hill to our saddle stock, when
Priest said that if he only had a certain horse of
his out of the band we had been trailing he would
promise me buffalo veal if he had to follow them
to the Pan-handle. It took us but a few minutes
to return to our horses, round them in, and secure
the particular horse he wanted. I was riding my
Nigger Boy, my regular night horse, and as only one
of my mount was in this bunch, — a good horse, but
sluggish, — I concluded to give my black a trial,
not depending on his speed so much as his staying
qualities. It took but a minute for The Rebel to
shift his saddle from one horse to another, when
he started around to the south, while I turned to the
north, so as to approach the buffalo simultaneously.
I came in sight of the band first, my partner having a farther ride to make, but had only a few
moments to wait, before I noticed the quarry take
alarm, and the next instant Priest dashed out from
behind a spur of the hill and was after them, I
following suit. They turned westward, and when
The Rebel and I came together on the angle of
their course, we were several hundred yards in
their rear. My bunkie had the best horse in speed
by all odds, and was soon crowding the band so
close that they began to scatter, and though I

passed several old bulls and cows, it was all I could
do to keep in sight of the calves. After the chase
had continued over a mile, the staying qualities of
my horse began to shine, but while I was nearing
the lead, The Rebel tied to the largest calf in the
bunch. The calf he had on his rope was a beauty,
and on overtaking him, I reined in my horse, for
to have killed a second one would have been sheer
waste. Priest wanted me to shoot the calf, but I
refused, so he shifted the rope to the pommel of
my saddle, and, dismounting, dropped the calf at
the first shot. We skinned him, cut off his head,
and after disemboweling him, lashed the carcass
across my saddle. Then both of us mounted
Priest's horse, and started on our return.

On reaching the horse stock, we succeeded in
catching a sleepy old horse belonging to Rod
Wheat's mount, and I rode him bridleless and
bareback to camp. We received an ovation on
our arrival, the recovery of the saddle horses being
a secondary matter compared to the buffalo veal.
" So it was buffalo that scared our horses, was it,
and ran them out of camp?" said McCann, as he
helped to unlash the calf. " Well, it 's an ill wind
that blows nobody good." There was no particular
loss of time, for the herd had grazed away on our
course several miles, and after changing our mounts
we overtook the herd with the news that not only
the horses had been found, but that there was fresh
meat in camp — and buffalo veal at that! The

other men out horse hunting, seeing the cattle strung out in traveling shape, soon returned to their places beside the trailing herd.

We held a due northward course, which we figured ought to carry us past and at least thirty miles to the westward of the big Indian encampment. The worst thing with which we had now to contend was the weather, it having rained more or less during the past day and night, or ever since we had crossed the Salt Fork. The weather had thrown the outfit into such a gloomy mood that they would scarcely speak to or answer each other. This gloomy feeling had been growing on us for several days, and it was even believed secretly that our foreman didn't know where he was; that the outfit was drifting and as good as lost. About noon of the third day, the weather continuing wet with cold nights, and with no abatement of the general gloom, our men on point noticed smoke arising directly ahead on our course, in a little valley through which ran a nice stream of water. When Flood's attention was directed to the smoke, he rode forward to ascertain the cause, and returned worse baffled than I ever saw him.

It was an Indian camp, and had evidently been abandoned only that morning, for the fires were still smouldering. Ordering the wagon to camp on the creek and the cattle to graze forward till noon, Flood returned to the Indian camp, taking two of the boys and myself with him. It had not been a permanent camp, yet showed evidence of having been occupied several days at least, and had contained nearly a hundred lean-tos, wickyups, and tepees — altogether too large an encampment to suit our tastes. The foreman had us hunt up the trail leaving, and once we had found it, all four of us ran it out five or six miles, when, from the freshness of it, fearing that we might be seen, we turned back. The Indians had many ponies and possibly some cattle, though the sign of the latter was hard to distinguish from buffalo. Before quitting their trail, we concluded they were from one of the reservations, and were heading for their old stamping ground, the Pan-handle country, — peaceable probably; but whether peaceable or not, we had no desire to meet with them. We lost little time, then, in returning to the herd and making late and early drives until we were out of that section.

But one cannot foresee impending trouble on the cattle trail, any more than elsewhere, and although we encamped that night a long distance to the north of the abandoned Indian camp, the next morning we came near having a stampede. It happened just at dawn. Flood had called the cook an hour before daybreak, and he had started out with Honeyman to drive in the *remuda*, which had scattered badly the morning before. They had the horses rounded up and were driving them towards camp when, about half a mile from the wagon, four old buffalo bulls ran quartering past the horses. This was tinder among 'stubble, and in their panic the horses outstripped the wranglers and came thundering for camp. Luckily we had been called to breakfast, and those of us who could see what was up ran and secured our night horses. Before half of the horses were thus secured, however, one hundred and thirty loose saddle stock dashed through camp, and every horse on picket went with them, saddles and all, and dragging the picket ropes. Then the cattle jumped from the bed ground and were off like a shot, the fourth guard, who had them in charge, with them. Just for the time being it was an open question which way to ride, our saddle horses going in one direction and the herd in another. Priest was an early riser and had hustled me out early, so fortunately we reached our horses, though over half the outfit in camp could only look on and curse their luck at being left afoot. The Rebel was first in the saddle, and turned after the horses, but I rode for the herd. The cattle were not badly scared, and as the morning grew clearer, five of us quieted them down before they had run more than a short mile.

The horses, however, gave us a long, hard run, and since a horse has a splendid memory, the effects of this scare were noticeable for nearly a month after. Honeyman at once urged our foreman to hobble at night, but Flood knew the im-

portance of keeping the *remuda* strong, and refused. But his decision was forced, for just as it
was growing dusk that evening, we heard the
horses running, and all hands had to turn out, to
surround them and bring them into camp. We
hobbled every horse and side-lined certain leaders,
and for fully a week following, one scare or another seemed to hold our saddle stock in constant
terror. During this week we turned out our night
horses, and taking the worst of the leaders in their
stead, tied them solidly to the wagon wheels all
night, not being willing to trust to picket ropes.
They would even run from a mounted man during
the twilight of evening or early dawn, or from any
object not distinguishable in uncertain light; but
the wrangler now never went near them until after
sunrise, and their nervousness gradually subsided.

Trouble never comes singly, however, and when
we struck the Salt Fork, we found it raging, and
impassable nearly from bank to bank. But get
across we must. The swimming of it was nothing,
but it was necessary to get our wagon over, and
there came the rub. We swam the cattle in twenty
minutes' time, but it took us a full half day to get
the wagon over. The river was at least a hundred yards wide, three quarters of which was swimming to a horse. But we hunted up and down the
river until we found an eddy, where the banks
had a gradual approach to deep water, and started
to raft the wagon over — a thing none of the out-

fit had ever seen done, though we had often heard of it around camp-fires in Texas. The first thing was to get the necessary timber to make the raft. We scouted along the Salt Fork for a mile either way before we found sufficient dry, dead cotton-wood to form our raft. Then we set about cutting it, but we had only one axe, and were the poorest set of axemen that were ever called upon to perform a similar task; when we cut a tree it looked as though a beaver had gnawed it down. On horse-back the Texan shines at the head of his class, but in any occupation which must be performed on foot he is never a competitor. There was scarcely a man in our outfit who could not swing a rope and tie down a steer in a given space of time, but when it came to swinging an axe to cut logs for the raft, our lustre faded. " Cutting these logs," said Joe Stallings, as he mopped the sweat from his brow, " reminds me of what the Tennessee girl who married a Texan wrote home to her sister. ' Texas,' so she wrote, ' is a good place for men and dogs, but it 's hell on women and oxen.' "

Dragging the logs up to the place selected for the ford was an easy matter. They were light, and we did it with ropes from the pommels of our saddles, two to four horses being sufficient to handle any of the trees. When everything was ready, we ran the wagon out into two-foot water and built the raft under it. We had cut the dry logs from eighteen to twenty feet long, and now ran a tier of these under the wagon between the wheels. These we lashed securely to the axle, and even lashed one large log on the underside of the hub on the outside of the wheel. Then we cross-timbered under these, lashing everything securely to this outside guard log. Before we had finished the cross-timbering, it was necessary to take an anchor rope ashore for fear our wagon would float away. By the time we had succeeded in getting twenty-five dry cottonwood logs under our wagon, it was afloat. Half a dozen of us then swam the river on our horses, taking across the heaviest rope we had for a tow line. We threw the wagon tongue back and lashed it, and making fast to the wagon with one end of the tow rope, fastened our lariats to the other. With the remainder of our unused rope, we took a guy line from the wagon and snubbed it to a tree on the south bank. Everything being in readiness, the word was given, and as those on the south bank eased away, those on horseback on the other side gave the rowel to their horses, and our commissary floated across. The wagon floated so easily that McCann was ordered on to the raft to trim the weight when it struck the current. The current carried it slightly downstream, and when it lodged on the other side, those on the south bank fastened lariats to the guy rope; and with them pulling from that side and us from ours, it was soon brought opposite the landing and hauled into shallow water. Once the raft timber was unlashed and removed, the tongue was lowered, and from the pommels of six saddles the wagon was set high and dry on the north bank. There now only remained to bring up the cattle and swim them, which was an easy task and soon accomplished.

After putting the Salt Fork behind us, our spirits were again dampened, for it rained all the latter part of the night and until noon the next day. It was with considerable difficulty that McCann could keep his fire from drowning out while he was getting breakfast, and several of the outfit refused to eat at all. Flood knew it was useless to rally the boys, for a wet, hungry man is not to be jollied or reasoned with. Five days had now elapsed since we turned off the established trail, and half the time rain had been falling. Besides, our doubt as to where we were had been growing, so before we started that morning, Bull Durham very good-naturedly asked Flood if he had any idea where he was.

"No, I have n't. No more than you have," replied our foreman. "But this much I do know, or will just as soon as the sun comes out: I know north from south. We have been traveling north by a little west, and if we hold that course we 're bound to strike the North Fork, and within a day or two afterwards we will come into the government trail, running from Fort Elliot to Camp Supply, which will lead us into our own trail. Or if we were certain that we had cleared the Indian reservation, we could bear to our right, and in time we would reënter the trail that way. I can't help the weather, boys, and as long as I have chuck, I'd as lief be lost as found."

If there was any recovery in the feelings of the outfit after this talk of Flood's, it was not noticeable, and it is safe to say that two thirds of the boys believed we were in the Pan-handle of Texas. One man's opinion is as good as another's in a strange country, and while there was n't a man in the outfit who cared to suggest it, I know the majority of us would have indorsed turning northeast. But the fates smiled on us at last. About the middle of the forenoon, on the following day, we cut an Indian trail, about three days old, of probably fifty horses. A number of us followed the trail several miles on its westward course, and among other things discovered that they had been driving a small bunch of cattle, evidently making for the sand hills which we could see about twenty miles to our left. How they had come by the cattle was a mystery, — perhaps by forced levy, perhaps from a stampede. One thing was certain: the trail must have contributed them, for there were none but trail cattle in the country. This was reassuring and gave some hint of guidance. We were all tickled, therefore, after nooning that day and on starting the herd in the afternoon, to hear our foreman give orders to point the herd a little east of north. The next few days we made long drives, our saddle horses recovered from their scare, and the outfit fast regained its spirits.

On the morning of the tenth day after leaving the trail, we loitered up a long slope to a divide in our lead from which we sighted timber to the north. This we supposed from its size must be the North Fork.   Our route lay up this divide some distance, and before we left it, some one in the rear sighted a dust cloud to the right and far behind us.   As dust would hardly rise on a still morning without a cause, we turned the herd off the divide and pushed on, for we suspected Indians.   Flood and Priest hung back on the divide, watching the dust signals, and after the herd had left them several miles in the rear, they turned and rode towards it, — a move which the outfit could hardly make out.   It was nearly noon when we saw them returning in a long lope, and when they came in sight of the herd, Priest waved his hat in the air and gave the long yell.   When he explained that there was a herd of cattle on the trail in the rear and to our right, the yell went around the herd, and was reëchoed by our wrangler and cook in the rear.   The spirits of the outfit instantly rose.   We halted the herd and camped for noon, and McCann set out his best in celebrating the occasion.   It was the most enjoyable meal we had had in the past ten days.   After a good noonday rest, we set out, and having entered the trail during the afternoon, crossed the North Fork late that evening.   As we were going into camp, we noticed a horseman coming up the trail, who turned out to be smiling Nat Straw, whom we had left on the Colorado River. "Well, girls," said Nat, dismounting, "I did n't know who you were, but I just thought I'd ride ahead and over-take whoever it was and stay all night. Indians? Yes; I would n't drive on a trail that had n't any excitement on it. I gave the last big encampment ten strays, and won them all back and four ponies besides on a horse race. Oh, yes, got some running stock with us. How soon will supper be ready, cusi? Get up something extra, for you've got company."

CHAPTER XI

A BOGGY FORD

THAT night we learned from Straw our location on the trail. We were far above the Indian reservation, and instead of having been astray our foreman had held a due northward course, and we were probably as far on the trail as if we had followed the regular route. So in spite of all our good maxims, we had been borrowing trouble; we were never over thirty miles to the westward of what was then the new Western Cattle Trail. We concluded that the " Running W " herd had turned back, as Straw brought the report that some herd had recrossed Red River the day before his arrival, giving for reasons the wet season and the danger of getting waterbound.

About noon of the second day after leaving the North Fork of Red River, we crossed the Washita, a deep stream, the slippery banks of which gave every indication of a recent rise. We had no trouble in crossing either wagon or herd, it being hardly a check in our onward course. The abandonment of the regular trail the past ten days had been a noticeable benefit to our herd, for the cattle had had an abundance of fresh country to graze over as well as plenty of rest. But now that we were back on the trail, we gave them their freedom and frequently covered twenty miles a day, until we reached the South Canadian, which proved to be the most delusive stream we had yet encountered. It also showed, like the Washita, every evidence of having been on a recent rampage. On our arrival there was no volume of water to interfere, but it had a quicksand bottom that would bog a saddle blanket. Our foreman had been on ahead and examined the regular crossing, and when he returned, freely expressed his opinion that we would be unable to trail the herd across, but might hope to effect it by cutting it into small bunches. When we came, therefore, within three miles of the river, we turned off the trail to a near-by creek and thoroughly watered the herd. This was contrary to our practice, for we usually wanted the herd thirsty when reaching a large river. But any cow brute that halted in fording the Canadian that day was doomed to sink into quicksands from which escape was doubtful.

We held the wagon and saddle horses in the rear, and when we were half a mile away from the trail ford, cut off about two hundred head of the leaders and started for the crossing, leaving only the horse wrangler and one man with the herd. On reaching the river we gave them an extra push, and the cattle plunged into the muddy water. Before the cattle had advanced fifty feet, instinct warned them of the treacherous footing, and the leaders tried to turn back; but by that time we had the entire bunch in the water and were urging them forward. They had halted but a moment and begun milling, when several heavy steers sank; then we gave way and allowed the rest to come back. We did not realize fully the treachery of this river until we saw that twenty cattle were caught in the merciless grasp of the quicksand. They sank slowly to the level of their bodies, which gave sufficient resistance to support their weight, but they were hopelessly bogged. We allowed the free cattle to return to the herd, and immediately turned our attention to those that were bogged, some of whom were nearly submerged by water. We dispatched some of the boys to the wagon for our heavy corral ropes and a bundle of horse-hobbles; and the remainder of us, stripped to the belt, waded out and surveyed the situation at close quarters. We were all experienced in handling bogged cattle, though this quicksand was the most deceptive that I, at least, had ever witnessed. The bottom of the river as we waded through it was solid under our feet, and as long as we kept moving it felt so, but the moment we stopped we sank as in a quagmire. The "pull" of this quicksand was so strong that four of us were unable to lift a steer's tail out, once it was imbedded in the sand. And when we had released a tail by burrowing around it to arm's length and freed it, it would sink of its own weight in a minute's time until it would have to be burrowed out again. To avoid this we had to coil up the tails and tie them with a soft rope hobble.

Fortunately none of the cattle were over forty feet from the bank, and when our heavy rope arrived we divided into two gangs and began the work of rescue. We first took a heavy rope from the animal's horns to solid footing on the river bank, and tied to this five or six of our lariats. Meanwhile others rolled a steer over as far as possible and began burrowing with their hands down alongside a fore and hind leg simultaneously until they could pass a small rope around the pastern above the cloof, or better yet through the cloven in the hoof, when the leg could be readily lifted by two men. We could not stop burrowing, however, for a moment, or the space would fill and solidify. Once a leg was freed, we doubled it back short and securely tied it with a hobble, and when the fore and hind leg were thus secured, we turned the animal over on that side and released the other legs in a similar manner. Then we hastened out of the water and into our saddles, and wrapped the loose end of our ropes to the pommels, having already tied the lariats to the heavy corral rope from the animal's horns. When the word was given, we took a good swinging start, and unless something gave way there was one steer less in the bog. After we had landed the animal high and dry on the bank, it was but a minute's work to free the rope and untie the hobbles. Then it was advisable to get into the saddle with little loss of time and give him a wide berth, for he generally arose angry and sullen.

It was dark before we got the last of the bogged cattle out and retraced our way to camp from the first river on the trip that had turned us. But we were not the least discouraged, for we felt certain there was a ford that had a bottom somewhere within a few miles, and we could hunt it up on the morrow. The next one, however, we would try before we put the cattle in. There was no question that the treacherous condition of the river was due to the recent freshet, which had brought down new deposits of sediment and had agitated the old, even to changing the channel of the river, so that it had not as yet had sufficient time to settle and solidify.

The next morning after breakfast, Flood and two or three of the boys set out up the river, while an equal number of us started, under the leadership of The Rebel, down the river on a similar errand, — to prospect for a crossing. Our party scouted for about five miles, and the only safe footing we could find was a swift, narrow channel between the bank and an island in the river, while beyond the island was a much wider channel with water deep enough in several places to swim our saddle horses. The footing seemed quite secure to our horses, but the cattle were much heavier; and if an animal ever bogged in the river, there was water enough to drown him before help could be rendered. We stopped our horses a number of times, however, to try the footing, and in none of our experiments was there any indication of quicksand, so we counted the crossing safe. On our return we found the herd already in motion, headed up the river where our foreman had located a crossing. As it was then useless to make any mention of the island crossing which we had located, at least until a trial had been given to the upper ford, we said nothing. When we came within half a mile of the new ford, we held up the herd and allowed them to graze, and brought up the *remuda* and crossed and recrossed them without bogging a single horse. Encouraged at this, we cut off about a hundred head of heavy lead cattle and started for the ford. We had a good push on them when we struck the water, for there were ten riders around them and Flood was in the lead. We called to him several times that the cattle were bogging, but he never halted until he pulled out on the opposite bank, leaving twelve of the heaviest steers in the quicksand.

"Well, in all my experience in trail work," said Flood, as he gazed back at the dozen animals struggling in the quicksand, "I never saw as deceptive a bottom in any river. We used to fear the Cimarron and Platte, but the old South Canadian is the girl that can lay it over them both. Still, there ain't any use crying over spilt milk, and we have n't got men enough to hold two herds, so surround them, boys, and we 'll recross them if we leave twenty-four more in the river. Take them back a good quarter, fellows, and bring them up on a run, and I 'll take the lead when they strike the water; and give them no show to halt until they get across."

As the little bunch of cattle had already grazed out nearly a quarter, we rounded them into a compact body and started for the river to recross them. The nearer we came to the river, the faster we went, till we struck the water. In several places where there were channels, we could neither force the cattle nor ride ourselves faster than a walk on account of the depth of the water, but when we struck the shallows, which were the really dangerous places, we forced the cattle with horse and quirt. Near the middle of the river, in shoal water, Rod Wheat was quirting up the cattle, when a big dun steer, trying to get out of his reach, sank in the quicksand, and Rod's horse stumbled across the animal and was thrown. He floundered in attempting to rise, and his hind feet sank to the haunches. His ineffectual struggles caused him to sink farther to the flanks in the loblolly which the tramping of the cattle had caused, and there horse and steer lay, side by side, like two in a bed. Wheat loosened the cinches of the saddle on either side, and stripping the bridle off, brought up the rear, carrying saddle, bridle, and blankets on his

back. The river was at least three hundred yards
wide, and when we got to the farther bank, our
horses were so exhausted that we dismounted and
let them blow. A survey showed we had left a
total of fifteen cattle and the horse in the quicksands. But we congratulated ourselves that we had
bogged down only three head in recrossing. Getting these cattle out was a much harder task than
the twenty head gave us the day before, for many
of these were bogged more than a hundred yards
from the bank. But no time was to be lost; the
wagon was brought up in a hurry, fresh horses were
caught, and we stripped for the fray. While Mc-
Cann got dinner we got out the horse, even saving
the cinches that were abandoned in freeing him of
the saddle.

During the afternoon we were compelled to
adopt a new mode of procedure, for with the limited amount of rope at hand, we could only use one
rope for drawing the cattle out to solid footing,
after they were freed from the quagmire. But we
had four good mules to our chuck wagon, and instead of dragging the cattle ashore from the pommels of saddles, we tied one end of the rope to the
hind axle and used the mules in snaking the cattle
out. This worked splendidly, but every time we
freed a steer we had to drive the wagon well out
of reach, for fear he might charge the wagon and
team. But with three crews working in the water,
tying up tails and legs, the work progressed more

rapidly than it had done the day before, and two hours before sunset the last animal had been freed. We had several exciting incidents during the operation, for several steers showed fight, and when released went on the prod for the first thing in sight. The herd was grazing nearly a mile away during the afternoon, and as fast as a steer was pulled out, some one would take a horse and give the freed animal a start for the herd. One big black steer turned on Flood, who generally attended to this, and gave him a spirited chase. In getting out of the angry steer's way, he passed near the wagon, when the maddened beef turned from Flood and charged the commissary. McCann was riding the nigh wheel mule, and when he saw the steer coming, he poured the whip into the mules and circled around like a battery in field practice, trying to get out of the way. Flood made several attempts to cut off the steer from the wagon, but he followed it like a mover's dog, until a number of us, fearing our mules would be gored, ran out of the water, mounted our horses, and joined in the chase. When we came up with the circus, our foreman called to us to rope the beef, and Fox Quarternight, getting in the first cast, caught him by the two front feet and threw him heavily. Before he could rise, several of us had dismounted and were sitting on him like buzzards on carrion. McCann then drove the team around behind a sand dune, out of sight; we released the beef, and he was glad to return to the herd, quite sobered by the throwing.

Another incident occurred near the middle of the afternoon. From some cause or other, the hind leg of a steer, after having been tied up, became loosened. No one noticed this; but when, after several successive trials, during which Barney McCann exhausted a large vocabulary of profanity, the mule team was unable to move the steer, six of us fastened our lariats to the main rope, and dragged the beef ashore with great *éclat*. But when one of the boys dismounted to unloose the hobbles and rope, a sight met our eyes that sent a sickening sensation through us, for the steer had left one hind leg in the river, neatly disjointed at the knee. Then we knew why the mules had failed to move him, having previously supposed his size was the difficulty, for he was one of the largest steers in the herd. No doubt the steer's leg had been unjointed in swinging him around, but it had taken six extra horses to sever the ligaments and skin, while the merciless quicksands of the Canadian held the limb. A friendly shot ended the steer's sufferings, and before we finished our work for the day, a flight of buzzards were circling around in anticipation of the coming feast.

Another day had been lost, and still the South Canadian defied us. We drifted the cattle back to the previous night camp, using the same bed ground for our herd. It was then that The Rebel

broached the subject of a crossing at the island
which we had examined that morning, and offered
to show it to our foreman by daybreak. We put
two extra horses on picket that night, and the next
morning, before the sun was half an hour high, the
foreman and The Rebel had returned from the island
down the river with word that we were to give the
ford a trial, though we could not cross the wagon
there. Accordingly we grazed the herd down the
river and came opposite the island near the middle
of the forenoon. As usual, we cut off about one
hundred of the lead cattle, the leaders naturally
being the heaviest, and started them into the water.
We reached the island and scaled the farther bank
without a single animal losing his footing. We
brought up a second bunch of double, and a third
of triple the number of the first, and crossed them
with safety, but as yet the Canadian was dallying
with us. As we crossed each successive bunch,
the tramping of the cattle increasingly agitated the
sands, and when we had the herd about half over,
we bogged our first steer on the farther landing.
As the water was so shallow that drowning was
out of the question, we went back and trailed in
the remainder of the herd, knowing the bogged
steer would be there when we were ready for him.

The island was about two hundred yards long
by twenty wide, lying up and down the river,
and in leaving it for the farther bank, we always
pushed off at the upper end. But now, in trailing

the remainder of the cattle over, we attempted to force them into the water at the lower end, as the footing at that point of this middle ground had not, as yet, been trampled up as had the upper end. Everything worked nicely until the rear guard of the last five or six hundred congested on the island, the outfit being scattered on both sides of the river as well as in the middle, leaving a scarcity of men at all points. When the final rear guard had reached the river the cattle were striking out for the farther shore from every quarter of the island at their own sweet will, stopping to drink and loitering on the farther side, for there was no one to hustle them out.

All were over at last, and we were on the point of congratulating ourselves, — for, although the herd had scattered badly, we had less than a dozen bogged cattle, and those near the shore, — when suddenly up the river over a mile, there began a rapid shooting. Satisfied that it was by our own men, we separated, and, circling right and left, began to throw the herd together. Some of us rode up the river bank and soon located the trouble. We had not ridden a quarter of a mile before we passed a number of our herd bogged, these having reëntered the river for their noonday drink, and on coming up with the men who had done the shooting, we found them throwing the herd out from the water. They reported that a large number of cattle were bogged farther up the river.

All hands rounded in the herd, and drifting them out nearly a mile from the river, left them under two herders, when the remainder of us returned to the bogged cattle. There were by actual count, including those down at the crossing, over eighty bogged cattle that required our attention, extending over a space of a mile or more above the island ford.

The outlook was anything but pleasing. Flood was almost speechless over the situation, for it might have been guarded against. But realizing the task before us, we recrossed the river for dinner, well knowing the inner man needed fortifying for the work before us. No sooner had we disposed of the meal and secured a change of mounts all round, than we sent two men to relieve the men on herd. When they were off, Flood divided up our forces for the afternoon work.

"It will never do," said he, "to get separated from our commissary. So, Priest, you take the wagon and *remuda* and go back up to the regular crossing and get our wagon over somehow. There will be the cook and wrangler besides yourself, and you may have two other men. You will have to lighten your load; and don't attempt to cross those mules hitched to the wagon; rely on your saddle horses for getting the wagon over. Forrest, you and Bull, with the two men on herd, take the cattle to the nearest creek and water them well. After watering, drift them back, so they will be within a mile of these bogged cattle. Then leave two men with them and return to the river. I 'll take the remainder of the outfit and begin at the ford and work up the river. Get the ropes and hobbles, boys, and come on."

John Officer and I were left with The Rebel to get the wagon across, and while waiting for the men on herd to get in, we hooked up the mules. Honeyman had the *remuda* in hand to start the minute our herders returned, their change of mounts being already tied to the wagon wheels. The need of haste was very imperative, for the river might rise without an hour's notice, and a two-foot rise would drown every hoof in the river as well as cut us off from our wagon. The South Canadian has its source in the Staked Plains and the mountains of New Mexico, and freshets there would cause a rise here, local conditions never affecting a river of such width. Several of us had seen these Plains rivers,—when the mountain was sportive and dallying with the plain, — under a clear sky and without any warning of falling weather, rise with a rush of water like a tidal wave or the stream from a broken dam. So when our men from herd galloped in, we stripped their saddles from tired horses and cinched them to fresh ones, while they, that there might be no loss of time, bolted their dinners. It took us less than an hour to reach the ford, where we unloaded the wagon of everything but the chuck-box, which was ironed fast. We had an extra saddle

in the wagon, and McCann was mounted on a good
horse, for he could ride as well as cook.   Priest
and I rode the river, selecting a route; and on our
return, all five of us tied our lariats to the tongue
and sides of the wagon.   We took a running start,
and until we struck the farther bank we gave the
wagon no time to sink, but pulled it out of the
river with a shout, our horses' flanks heaving.
Then recrossing the river, we lashed all the bedding
to four gentle saddle horses and led them over.
But to get our provisions across was no easy matter, for we were heavily loaded, having taken on
a supply at Doan's sufficient to last us until we
reached Dodge, a good month's journey.   Yet over
it must go, and we kept a string of horsemen crossing and recrossing for an hour, carrying everything
from pots and pans to axle grease, as well as the
staples of life.   When we had got the contents of
the wagon finally over and reloaded, there remained
nothing but crossing the saddle stock.

The wagon mules had been turned loose, harnessed, while we were crossing the wagon and other
effects; and when we drove the *remuda* into the
river, one of the wheel mules turned back, and in
spite of every man, reached the bank again.   Part
of the boys hurried the others across, but McCann
and I turned back after our wheeler.   We caught
him without any trouble, but our attempt to lead
him across failed.   In spite of all the profanity
addressed personally to him, he proved a credit to

his sire, and we lost ground in trying to force him into the river. The boys across the river watched a few minutes, when all recrossed to our assistance.

"Time's too valuable to monkey with a mule to-day," said Priest, as he rode up; "skin off that harness."

It was off at once, and we blindfolded and backed him up to the river bank; then taking a rope around his forelegs, we threw him, hog-tied him, and rolled him into the water. With a rope around his forelegs and through the ring in the bridle bit, we asked no further favors, but snaked him ignominiously over to the farther side and re-harnessed him into the team.

The afternoon was more than half spent when we reached the first bogged cattle, and by the time the wagon overtook us we had several tied up and ready for the mule team to give us a lift. The herd had been watered in the mean time and was grazing about in sight of the river, and as we occasionally drifted a freed animal out to the herd, we saw others being turned in down the river. About an hour before sunset, Flood rode up to us and reported having cleared the island ford, while a middle outfit under Forrest was working down towards it. During the twilight hours of evening, the wagon and saddle horses moved out to the herd and made ready to camp, but we remained until dark, and with but three horses released a number of light cows. We were the last outfit to reach the wagon, and as Honeyman had tied up our night horses, there was nothing for us to do but eat and go to bed, to which we required no coaxing, for we all knew that early morning would find us once more working with bogged cattle.

The night passed without incident, and the next morning in the division of the forces, Priest was again allowed the wagon to do the snaking out with, but only four men, counting McCann. The remainder of the outfit was divided into several gangs, working near enough each other to lend a hand in case an extra horse was needed on a pull. The third animal we struck in the river that morning was the black steer that had showed fight the day before. Knowing his temper would not be improved by soaking in the quicksand overnight, we changed our tactics. While we were tying up the steer's tail and legs, McCann secreted his team at a safe distance. Then he took a lariat, lashed the tongue of the wagon to a cottonwood tree, and jacking up a hind wheel, used it as a windlass. When all was ready, we tied the loose end of our cable rope to a spoke, and allowing the rope to coil on the hub, manned the windlass and drew him ashore. When the steer was freed, McCann, having no horse at hand, climbed into the wagon, while the rest of us sought safety in our saddles, and gave him a wide berth. When he came to his feet he was sullen with rage and refused to move out of his tracks. Priest rode out and baited him at a distance, and McCann, from his safe position, attempted to give him a scare, when he savagely charged the wagon. McCann reached down, and securing a handful of flour, dashed it into his eyes, which made him back away; and, kneeling, he fell to cutting the sand with his horns. Rising, he charged the wagon a second time, and catching the wagon sheet with his horns, tore two slits in it like slashes of a razor. By this time The Rebel ventured a little nearer, and attracted the steer's attention. He started for Priest, who gave the quirt to his horse, and for the first quarter mile had a close race. The steer, however, weakened by the severe treatment he had been subjected to, soon fell to the rear, and gave up the chase and continued on his way to the herd.

After this incident we worked down the river until the outfits met. We finished the work before noon, having lost three full days by the quicksands of the Canadian. As we pulled into the trail that afternoon near the first divide and looked back to take a parting glance at the river, we saw a dust cloud across the Canadian which we knew must be the Ellison herd under Nat Straw. Quince Forrest, noticing it at the same time as I did, rode forward and said to me, "Well, old Nat will get it in the neck this time, if that old girl dallies with him as she did with us. I don't wish him any bad luck, but I do hope he'll bog enough cattle to keep his hand in practice.   It will be just about his luck, though, to find it settled and solid enough to cross."

And the next morning we saw his signal in the sky about the same distance behind us, and knew he had forded without any serious trouble.

CHAPTER XII

THERE was never very much love lost between government soldiers and our tribe, so we swept past Camp Supply in contempt a few days later, and crossed the North Fork of the Canadian to camp for the night. Flood and McCann went into the post, as our supply of flour and navy beans was running rather low, and our foreman had hopes that he might be able to get enough of these staples from the sutler to last until we reached Dodge. He also hoped to receive some word from Lovell.

The rest of us had no lack of occupation, as a result of a chance find of mine that morning. Honeyman had stood my guard the night before, and in return, I had got up when he was called to help rustle the horses. We had every horse under hand before the sun peeped over the eastern horizon, and when returning to camp with the *remuda*, as I rode through a bunch of sumach bush, I found a wild turkey's nest with sixteen fresh eggs in it. Honeyman rode up, when I dismounted, and putting them in my hat, handed them up to Billy until I could mount, for they were beauties and as

precious to us as gold.   There was an egg for each
man in the outfit and one over, and McCann threw
a heap of swagger into the inquiry, "Gentlemen,
how will you have your eggs this morning?" just
as though it was an everyday affair.   They were
issued to us fried, and I naturally felt that the odd
egg, by rights, ought to fall to me, but the oppos-
ing majority was formidable, — fourteen to one,
— so I yielded.   A number of ways were suggested
to allot the odd egg, but the gambling fever in us
being rabid, raffling or playing cards for it seemed
to be the proper caper.   Raffling had few advo-
cates.

"It reflects on any man's raising," said Quince
Forrest, contemptuously, "to suggest the idea of
raffling, when we've got cards and all night to
play for that egg.   The very idea of raffling for it!
I'd like to see myself pulling straws or drawing
numbers from a hat, like some giggling girl at a
church fair.   Poker is a science; the highest court
in Texas has said so, and I want some little show
for my interest in that speckled egg.   What have I
spent twenty years learning the game for, will some
of you tell me?   Why, it lets me out if you raffle
it."   The argument remained unanswered, and the
play for it gave interest to that night.

As soon as supper was over and the first guard
had taken the herd, the poker game opened, each
man being given ten beans for chips.   We had
only one deck of cards, so one game was all that

could be run at a time, but there were six players, and when one was frozen out another sat in and took his place. As wood was plentiful, we had a good fire, and this with the aid of the cook's lantern gave an abundance of light. We unrolled a bed to serve as a table, sat down on it Indian fashion, and as fast as one seat was vacated there was a man ready to fill it, for we were impatient for our turns in the game. The talk turned on an accident which had happened that afternoon. While we were crossing the North Fork of the Canadian, Bob Blades attempted to ride out of the river below the crossing, when his horse bogged down. He instantly dismounted, and his horse after floundering around scrambled out and up the bank, but with a broken leg. Our foreman had ridden up and ordered the horse unsaddled and shot, to put him out of his suffering.

While waiting our turns, the accident to the horse was referred to several times, and finally Blades, who was sitting in the game, turned to us who were lounging around the fire, and asked, "Did you all notice that look he gave me as I was uncinching the saddle? If he had been human, he might have told what that look meant. Good thing he was a horse and could n't realize."

From then on, the yarning and conversation was strictly *horse*.

"It was always a mystery to me," said Billy Honeyman, "how a Mexican or Indian knows so

much more about a horse than any of us. I have
seen them trail a horse across a country for miles,
riding in a long lope, with not a trace or sign visible to me. I was helping a horseman once to
drive a herd of horses to San Antonio from the
lower Rio Grande country. We were driving them
to market, and as there were no railroads south
then, we had to take along saddle horses to ride
home on after disposing of the herd. We always
took favorite horses which we did n't wish to sell,
generally two apiece for that purpose. This time,
when we were at least a hundred miles from the
ranch, a Mexican, who had brought along a pet
horse to ride home, thought he would n't hobble
this pet one night, fancying the animal would n't
leave the others. Well, next morning his pet was
missing. We scoured the country around and the
trail we had come over for ten miles, but no horse.
As the country was all open, we felt positive he
would go back to the ranch.

"Two days later and about forty miles higher
up the road, the Mexican was riding in the lead
of the herd, when suddenly he reined in his horse,
throwing him back on his haunches, and waved for
some of us to come to him, never taking his eyes
off what he saw in the road. The owner was riding on one point of the herd and I on the other.
We hurried around to him and both rode up at
the same time, when the vaquero blurted out,
' There 's my horse 's track.'

" ' What horse? ' asked the owner.

" ' My own; the horse we lost two days ago,' replied the Mexican.

"' How do you know it's your horse's track from the thousands of others that fill the road?' demanded his employer.

" ' Don Tomas,' said the Aztec, lifting his hat, ' how do I know your step or voice from a thousand others?'

"We laughed at him. He had been a peon, and that made him respect our opinions — at least he avoided differing with us. But as we drove on that afternoon, we could see him in the lead, watching for that horse's track. Several times he turned in his saddle and looked back, pointed to some track in the road, and lifted his hat to us. At camp that night we tried to draw him out, but he was silent.

"But when we were nearing San Antonio, we overtook a number of wagons loaded with wool, lying over, as it was Sunday, and there among their horses and mules was our Mexican's missing horse. The owner of the wagons explained how he came to have the horse. The animal had come to his camp one morning, back about twenty miles from where we had lost him, while he was feeding grain to his work stock, and being a pet insisted on being fed. Since then, I have always had a lot of respect for a Greaser's opinion regarding a horse."

"Turkey eggs is too rich for my blood," said

Bob Blades, rising from the game. "I don't care a continental who wins the egg now, for whenever I get three queens pat beat by a four card draw, I have misgivings about the deal. And old Quince thinks he can stack cards. He couldn't stack hay."

"Speaking about Mexicans and Indians," said Wyatt Roundtree, "I've got more use for a good horse than I have for either of those grades of humanity. I had a little experience over east here, on the cut off from the Chisholm trail, a few years ago, that gave me all the Injun I want for some time to come. A band of renegade Cheyennes had hung along the trail for several years, scaring or begging passing herds into giving them a beef. Of course all the cattle herds had more or less strays among them, so it was easier to cut out one of these than to argue the matter. There was plenty of herds on the trail then, so this band of Indians got bolder than bandits. In the year I'm speaking of, I went up with a herd of horses belonging to a Texas man, who was in charge with us. When we came along with our horses — only six men all told — the chief of the band, called Running Bull Sheep, got on the bluff bigger than a wolf and demanded six horses. Well, that Texan wasn't looking for any particular Injun that day to give six of his own dear horses to. So we just drove on, paying no attention to Mr. Bull Sheep. About half a mile farther up the trail, the chief overtook

us with all his bucks, and they were an ugly looking lot.   Well, this time he held up four fingers,
meaning that four horses would be acceptable.
But the Texan was n't recognizing the Indian levy
of taxation that year.   When he refused them, the
Indians never parleyed a moment, but set up a
' ki yi ' and began circling round the herd on their
ponies, Bull Sheep in the lead.

"As the chief passed the owner, his horse on a
run, he gave a special shrill ' ki yi,' whipped a short
carbine out of its scabbard, and shot twice into
the rear of the herd.   Never for a moment considering consequences, the Texan brought his six-
shooter into action.   It was a long, purty shot, and
Mr. Bull Sheep threw his hands in the air and
came off his horse backward, hard hit.   This shooting in the rear of the horses gave them such a
scare that we never checked them short of a mile.
While the other Indians were holding a little powwow over their chief, we were making good time
in the other direction, considering that we had over
eight hundred loose horses.   Fortunately our wagon
and saddle horses had gone ahead that morning,
but in the run we overtook them.   As soon as we
checked the herd from its scare, we turned them
up the trail, stretched ropes from the wheels of
the wagon, ran the saddle horses in, and changed
mounts just a little quicker than I ever saw it
done before or since.   The cook had a saddle in
the wagon, so we caught him up a horse, clapped

leather on him, and tied him behind the wagon in case of an emergency. And you can just bet we changed to our best horses. When we overtook the herd, we were at least a mile and a half from where the shooting occurred, and there was no Indian in sight, but we felt that they had n't given it up. We had n't long to wait, though we would have waited willingly, before we heard their yells and saw the dust rising in clouds behind us. We quit the herd and wagon right there and rode for a swell of ground ahead that would give us a rear view of the scenery. The first view we caught of them was not very encouraging. They were riding after us like fiends and kicking up a dust like a wind storm. We had nothing but six-shooters, no good for long range. The owner of the horses admitted that it was useless to try to save the herd now, and if our scalps were worth saving it was high time to make ourselves scarce.

"Cantonment was a government post about twenty-five miles away, so we rode for it. Our horses were good Spanish stock, and the Indians' little bench-legged ponies were no match for them. But not satisfied with the wagon and herd falling into their hands, they followed us until we were within sight of the post. As hard luck would have it, the cavalry stationed at this post were off on some escort duty, and the infantry were useless in this case. When the cavalry returned a few days later, they tried to round up those Indians, and the Indian agent used his influence, but the horses were so divided up and scattered that they were never recovered."

"And did the man lose his horses entirely?" asked Flood, who had anteed up his last bean and joined us.

"He did. There was, I remember, a tin horn lawyer up about Dodge who thought he could recover their value, as these were agency Indians and the government owed them money. But all I got for three months' wages due me was the horse I got away on."

McCann had been frozen out during Roundtree's yarn, and had joined the crowd of story-tellers on the other side of the fire. Forrest was feeling quite gala, and took a special delight in taunting the vanquished as they dropped out.

"Is McCann there?" inquired he, well knowing he was. "I just wanted to ask, would it be any trouble to poach that egg for my breakfast and serve it with a bit of toast; I'm feeling a little bit dainty. You 'll poach it for me, won't you, please?"

McCann never moved a muscle as he replied, "Will you please go to hell?"

The story-telling continued for some time, and while Fox Quarternight was regaling us with the history of a little black mare that a neighbor of theirs in Kentucky owned, a dispute arose in the card game regarding the rules of discard and draw.

"I'm too old a girl," said The Rebel, angrily, to Forrest, "to allow a pullet like you to teach me this game. When it's my deal, I'll discard just when I please, and it's none of your business so long as I keep within the rules of the game;" which sounded final, and the game continued.

Quarternight picked up the broken thread of his narrative, and the first warning we had of the lateness of the hour was Bull Durham calling to us from the game, "One of you fellows can have my place, just as soon as we play this jack pot. I've got to saddle my horse and get ready for our guard. Oh, I'm on velvet, anyhow, and before this game ends, I'll make old Quince curl his tail; I've got him going south now."

It took me only a few minutes to lose my chance at the turkey egg, and I sought my blankets. At one A. M., when our guard was called, the beans were almost equally divided among Priest, Stallings, and Durham; and in view of the fact that Forrest, whom we all wanted to see beaten, had met defeat, they agreed to cut the cards for the egg, Stallings winning. We mounted our horses and rode out into the night, and the second guard rode back to our camp-fire, singing:—

> "Two little niggers upstairs in bed,
>   One turned ober to de oder an' said,
> 'How 'bout dat shortnin' bread,
>   How 'bout dat shortnin' bread?'"

CHAPTER XIII

DODGE

AT Camp Supply, Flood received a letter from Lovell, requesting him to come on into Dodge ahead of the cattle. So after the first night's camp above the Cimarron, Flood caught up a favorite horse, informed the outfit that he was going to quit us for a few days, and designated Quince Forrest as the *segundo* during his absence.

"You have a wide, open country from here into Dodge," said he, when ready to start, "and I'll make inquiry for you daily from men coming in, or from the buckboard which carries the mail to Supply. I'll try to meet you at Mulberry Creek, which is about ten miles south of Dodge. I'll make that town to-night, and you ought to make the Mulberry in two days. You will see the smoke of passing trains to the north of the Arkansaw, from the first divide south of Mulberry. When you reach that creek, in case I don't meet you, hold the herd there and three or four of you can come on into town. But I'm almost certain to meet you," he called back as he rode away.

"Priest," said Quince, when our foreman had gone, "I reckon you did n't handle your herd to suit the old man when he left us that time at Buffalo Gap. But I think he used rare judgment this time in selecting a *segundo*. The only thing that frets me is, I'm afraid he'll meet us before we reach the Mulberry, and that won't give me any chance to go in ahead like a sure enough foreman. Fact is I have business there; I deposited a few months' wages at the Long Branch gambling house last year when I was in Dodge, and failed to take a receipt. I just want to drop in and make inquiry if they gave me credit, and if the account is drawing interest. I think it's all right, for the man I deposited it with was a clever fellow and asked me to have a drink with him just as I was leaving. Still, I'd like to step in and see him again."

Early in the afternoon of the second day after our foreman left us, we sighted the smoke of passing trains, though they were at least fifteen miles distant, and long before we reached the Mulberry, a livery rig came down the trail to meet us. To Forrest's chagrin, Flood, all dressed up and with a white collar on, was the driver, while on a back seat sat Don Lovell and another cowman by the name of McNulta. Every rascal of us gave old man Don the glad hand as they drove around the herd, while he, liberal and delighted as a bridegroom, passed out the cigars by the handful. The cattle were looking fine, which put the old man in high spirits, and he inquired of each of us if our

health was good and if Flood had fed us well.
They loitered around the herd the rest of the evening, until we threw off the trail to graze and camp
for the night, when Lovell declared his intention
of staying all night with the outfit.

While we were catching horses during the evening, Lovell came up to me where I was saddling
my night horse, and recognizing me gave me news
of my brother Bob. "I had a letter yesterday from
him," he said, "written from Red Fork, which is
just north of the Cimarron River over on the Chisholm route. He reports everything going along
nicely, and I'm expecting him to show up here
within a week. His herd are all beef steers, and
are contracted for delivery at the Crow Indian
Agency. He's not driving as fast as Flood, but
we've got to have our beef for that delivery in
better condition, as they have a new agent there
this year, and he may be one of these knowing
fellows. Sorry you couldn't see your brother, but
if you have any word to send him, I'll deliver
it."

I thanked him for the interest he had taken in me,
and assured him that I had no news for Robert;
but took advantage of the opportunity to inquire
if our middle brother, Zack Quirk, was on the trail
with any of his herds. Lovell knew him, but felt
positive he was not with any of his outfits.

We had an easy night with the cattle. Lovell insisted on standing a guard, so he took Rod Wheat's

horse and stood the first watch, and after returning
to the wagon, he and McNulta, to our great interest,
argued the merits of the different trails until near
midnight.   McNulta had two herds coming in on
the Chisholm trail, while Lovell had two herds on
the Western and only one on the Chisholm.

The next morning Forrest, who was again in
charge, received orders to cross the Arkansaw
River shortly after noon, and then let half the outfit come into town.   The old trail crossed the river
about a mile above the present town of Dodge City,
Kansas, so when we changed horses at noon, the
first and second guards caught up their top horses,
ransacked their war bags, and donned their best
toggery.   We crossed the river about one o'clock
in order to give the boys a good holiday, the stage
of water making the river easily fordable.   McCann,
after dinner was over, drove down on the south
side for the benefit of a bridge which spanned the
river opposite the town.   It was the first bridge
he had been able to take advantage of in over
a thousand miles of travel, and to-day he spurned
the cattle ford as though he had never crossed at
one.   Once safely over the river, and with the
understanding that the herd would camp for the
night about six miles north on Duck Creek, six
of our men quit us and rode for the town in a long
gallop.   Before the rig left us in the morning,
McNulta, who was thoroughly familiar with Dodge,
and an older man than Lovell, in a friendly and

fatherly spirit, seeing that many of us were youngsters, had given us an earnest talk and plenty of
good advice.

"I 've been in Dodge every summer since '77,"
said the old cowman, "and I can give you boys
some points. Dodge is one town where the average bad man of the West not only finds his equal,
but finds himself badly handicapped. The buffalo
hunters and range men have protested against the
iron rule of Dodge's peace officers, and nearly
every protest has cost human life. Don't ever get
the impression that you can ride your horses into
a saloon, or shoot out the lights in Dodge; it may
go somewhere else, but it don't go there. So I
want to warn you to behave yourselves. You can
wear your six-shooters into town, but you 'd better
leave them at the first place you stop, hotel, livery,
or business house. And when you leave town, call
for your pistols, but don't ride out shooting; omit
that. Most cowboys think it 's an infringement on
their rights to give up shooting in town, and if it
is, it stands, for your six-shooters are no match
for Winchesters and buckshot; and Dodge's officers are as game a set of men as ever faced
danger."

Nearly a generation has passed since McNulta,
the Texan cattle drover, gave our outfit this advice
one June morning on the Mulberry, and in setting down this record, I have only to scan the
roster of the peace officials of Dodge City to admit

its correctness. Among the names that graced the official roster, during the brief span of the trail days, were the brothers Ed, Jim, and "Bat" Masterson, Wyatt Earp, Jack Bridges, "Doc" Holliday, Charles Bassett, William Tillman, "Shotgun" Collins, Joshua Webb, Mayor A. B. Webster, and "Mysterious" Dave Mather. The puppets of no romance ever written can compare with these officers in fearlessness. And let it be understood, there were plenty to protest against their rule; almost daily during the range season some equally fearless individual defied them.

"Throw up your hands and surrender," said an officer to a Texas cowboy, who had spurred an excitable horse until it was rearing and plunging in the street, leveling meanwhile a double-barreled shotgun at the horseman.

"Not to you, you white-livered s— of a b—," was the instant reply, accompanied by a shot.

The officer staggered back mortally wounded, but recovered himself, and the next instant the cowboy reeled from his saddle, a load of buckshot through his breast.

After the boys left us for town, the remainder of us, belonging to the third and fourth guard, grazed the cattle forward leisurely during the afternoon. Through cattle herds were in sight both up and down the river on either side, and on crossing the Mulberry the day before, we learned that several herds were holding out as far south as that

stream, while McNulta had reported over forty
herds as having already passed northward on the
trail.   Dodge was the meeting point for buyers
from every quarter.   Often herds would sell at
Dodge whose destination for delivery was beyond
the Yellowstone in Montana.   Herds frequently
changed owners when the buyer never saw the cattle.   A yearling was a yearling and a two year old
was a two year old, and the seller's word, that
they were " as good or better than the string I sold
you last year," was sufficient.   Cattle were classified as northern, central, and southern animals,
and, except in case of severe drouth in the preceding years, were pretty nearly uniform in size
throughout each section.   The prairie section of
the State left its indelible imprint on the cattle
bred in the open country, while the coast, as well
as the piney woods and black-jack sections, did the
same, thus making classification easy.

McCann overtook us early in the evening, and,
being an obliging fellow, was induced by Forrest
to stand the first guard with Honeyman so as to
make up the proper number of watches, though
with only two men on guard at a time, for it was
hardly possible that any of the others would return
before daybreak.   There was much to be seen in
Dodge, and as losing a night's sleep on duty was
considered nothing, in hilarious recreation sleep
would be entirely forgotten.   McCann had not
forgotten us, but had smuggled out a quart bottle

to cut the alkali in our drinking water. But a quart amongst eight of us was not dangerous, so the night passed without incident, though we felt a growing impatience to get into town. As we expected, about sunrise the next morning our men off on holiday rode into camp, having never closed an eye during the entire night. They brought word from Flood that the herd would only graze over to Saw Log Creek that day, so as to let the remainder of us have a day and night in town. Lovell would only advance half a month's wages — twenty-five dollars — to the man. It was ample for any personal needs, though we had nearly three months' wages due, and no one protested, for the old man was generally right in his decisions. According to their report the boys had had a hog-killing time, old man Don having been out with them all night. It seems that McNulta stood in well with a class of practical jokers which included the officials of the town, and whenever there was anything on the tapis, he always got the word for himself and friends. During breakfast Fox Quarternight told this incident of the evening.

"Some professor, a professor in the occult sciences I think he called himself, had written to the mayor to know what kind of a point Dodge would be for a lecture. The lecture was to be free, but he also intimated that he had a card or two on the side up his sleeve, by which he expected to graft onto some of the coin of the realm from the wayfaring man as well as the citizen. The mayor turned the letter over to Bat Masterson, the city marshal, who answered it, and invited the professor to come on, assuring him that he was deeply interested in the occult sciences, personally, and would take pleasure in securing him a hall and a date, besides announcing his coming through the papers.

"Well, he was billed to deliver his lecture last night. Those old long horns, McNulta and Lovell, got us in with the crowd, and while they did n't know exactly what was coming, they assured us that we could n't afford to miss it. Well, at the appointed hour in the evening, the hall was packed, not over half being able to find seats. It is safe to say there were over five hundred men present, as it was announced for 'men only.' Every gambler in town was there, with a fair sprinkling of cowmen and our tribe. At the appointed hour, Masterson, as chairman, rapped for order, and in a neat little speech announced the object of the meeting. Bat mentioned the lack of interest in the West in the higher arts and sciences, and bespoke our careful attention to the subject under consideration for the evening. He said he felt it hardly necessary to urge the importance of good order, but if any one had come out of idle curiosity or bent on mischief, as chairman of the meeting and a peace officer of the city, he would certainly brook no interruption. After a few other appropriate remarks, he introduced the speaker as Dr. J. Graves-Brown, the noted scientist.

"The professor was an oily-tongued fellow, and led off on the prelude to his lecture, while the audience was as quiet as mice and as grave as owls. After he had spoken about five minutes and was getting warmed up to his subject, he made an assertion which sounded a little fishy, and some one back in the audience blurted out, ' That 's a damned lie.' The speaker halted in his discourse and looked at Masterson, who arose, and, drawing two six-shooters, looked the audience over as if trying to locate the offender. Laying the guns down on the table, he informed the meeting that another interruption would cost the offender his life, if he had to follow him to the Rio Grande or the British possessions. He then asked the professor, as there would be no further interruptions, to proceed with his lecture. The professor hesitated about going on, when Masterson assured him that it was evident that his audience, with the exception of one skulking coyote, was deeply interested in the subject, but that no one man could interfere with the freedom of speech in Dodge as long as it was a free country and he was city marshal. After this little talk, the speaker braced up and launched out again on his lecture. When he was once more under good headway, he had occasion to relate an exhibition which he had witnessed while studying his profession in India. The incident related was a trifle rank for any one to swallow raw, when the same party who had interrupted before sang out, ' That 's another damn lie.'

"Masterson came to his feet like a flash, a gun in each hand, saying, 'Stand up, you measly skunk, so I can see you.' Half a dozen men rose in different parts of the house and cut loose at him, and as they did so the lights went out and the room filled with smoke. Masterson was blazing away with two guns, which so lighted up the rostrum that we could see the professor crouching under the table. Of course they were using blank cartridges, but the audience raised the long yell and poured out through the windows and doors, and the lecture was over. A couple of police came in later, so McNulta said, escorted the professor to his room in the hotel, and quietly advised him that Dodge was hardly capable of appreciating anything so advanced as a lecture on the occult sciences."

Breakfast over, Honeyman ran in the *remuda*, and we caught the best horses in our mounts, on which to pay our respects to Dodge. Forrest detailed Rod Wheat to wrangle the horses, for we intended to take Honeyman with us. As it was only about six miles over to the Saw Log, Quince advised that they graze along Duck Creek until after dinner, and then graze over to the former stream during the afternoon. Before leaving, we rode over and looked out the trail after it left Duck, for it was quite possible that we might re-

turn during the night; and we requested McCann
to hang out the lantern, elevated on the end of
the wagon tongue, as a beacon. After taking our
bearings, we reined southward over the divide to
Dodge.

"The very first thing I do," said Quince Forrest, as we rode leisurely along, "after I get a
shave and hair-cut and buy what few tricks I need,
is to hunt up that gambler in the Long Branch,
and ask him to take a drink with me — I took the
parting one on him. Then I'll simply set in and
win back every dollar I lost there last year.
There's something in this northern air that I
breathe in this morning that tells me that this is
my lucky day. You other kids had better let the
games alone and save your money to buy red silk
handkerchiefs and soda water and such harmless
jimcracks." The fact that The Rebel was ten
years his senior never entered his mind as he gave
us this fatherly advice, though to be sure the majority of us were his juniors in years.

On reaching Dodge, we rode up to the Wright
House, where Flood met us and directed our cavalcade across the railroad to a livery stable, the proprietor of which was a friend of Lovell's. We
unsaddled and turned our horses into a large corral, and while we were in the office of the livery,
surrendering our artillery, Flood came in and
handed each of us twenty-five dollars in gold, warning us that when that was gone no more would be

advanced.   On receipt of the money, we scattered
like partridges before a gunner.   Within an hour
or two, we began to return to the stable by ones
and twos, and were stowing into our saddle pockets
our purchases, which ran from needles and thread
to .45 cartridges, every mother's son reflecting the
art of the barber, while John Officer had his blond
mustaches blackened, waxed, and curled like a
French dancing master.   "If some of you boys
will hold him," said Moss Strayhorn, commenting
on Officer's appearance, "I'd like to take a good
smell of him, just to see if he took oil up there
where the end of his neck's haired over."   As
Officer already had several drinks comfortably
stowed away under his belt, and stood up strong
six feet two, none of us volunteered.

After packing away our plunder, we sauntered
around town, drinking moderately, and visiting
the various saloons and gambling houses.   I clung
to my bunkie, The Rebel, during the rounds, for
I had.learned to like him, and had confidence he
would lead me into no indiscretions.   At the
Long Branch, we found Quince Forrest and Wyatt
Roundtree playing the faro bank, the former keeping cases.   They never recognized us, but were
answering a great many questions, asked by the
dealer and lookout, regarding the possible volume
of the cattle drive that year.   Down at another
gambling house, The Rebel met Ben Thompson,
a faro dealer not on duty and an old cavalry com-

rade, and the two cronied around for over an hour like long lost brothers, pledging anew their friendship over several social glasses, in which I was always included. There was no telling how long this reunion would have lasted, but happily for my sake, Lovell — who had been asleep all the morning — started out to round us up for dinner with him at the Wright House, which was at that day a famous hostelry, patronized almost exclusively by the Texas cowmen and cattle buyers.

We made the rounds of the gambling houses, looking for our crowd. We ran across three of the boys piking at a monte game, who came with us reluctantly; then, guided by Lovell, we started for the Long Branch, where we felt certain we would find Forrest and Roundtree, if they had any money left. Forrest was broke, which made him ready to come, and Roundtree, though quite a winner, out of deference to our employer's wishes, cashed in and joined us. Old man Don could hardly do enough for us; and before we could reach the Wright House, had lined us up against three different bars; and while I had confidence in my navigable capacity, I found they were coming just a little too fast and free, seeing I had scarcely drunk anything in three months but branch water. As we lined up at the Wright House bar for the final before dinner, The Rebel, who was standing next to me, entered a waiver and took a cigar, which I understood to be a hint, and I did likewise.

We had a splendid dinner. Our outfit, with
McNulta, occupied a ten-chair table, while on the
opposite side of the room was another large table,
occupied principally by drovers who were waiting
for their herds to arrive. Among those at the
latter table, whom I now remember, was "Uncle"
Henry Stevens, Jesse Ellison, "Lum" Slaughter,
John Blocker, Ike Pryor, "Dun" Houston, and last
but not least, Colonel "Shanghai" Pierce. The
latter was possibly the most widely known cowman
between the Rio Grande and the British possessions. He stood six feet four in his stockings, was
gaunt and raw-boned, and the possessor of a voice
which, even in ordinary conversation, could be distinctly heard across the street.

"No, I'll not ship any more cattle to your
town," said Pierce to a cattle solicitor during the
dinner, his voice in righteous indignation resound-
ing like a foghorn through the dining-room, "until you adjust your yardage charges. Listen! I
can go right up into the heart of your city and get
a room for myself, with a nice clean bed in it,
plenty of soap, water, and towels, and I can occupy
that room for twenty-four hours for two bits.
And your stockyards, away out in the suburbs,
want to charge me twenty cents a head and let
my steer stand out in the weather."

After dinner, all the boys, with the exception
of Priest and myself, returned to the gambling
houses as though anxious to work overtime. Be-

fore leaving the hotel, Forrest effected the loan of
ten from Roundtree, and the two returned to the
Long Branch, while the others as eagerly sought
out a monte game.   But I was fascinated with the
conversation of these old cowmen, and sat around
for several hours listening to their yarns and cattle
talk.

"I was selling a thousand beef steers one time
to some Yankee army contractors," Pierce was
narrating to a circle of listeners, "and I got the
idea that they were not up to snuff in receiving
cattle out on the prairie.   I was holding a herd of
about three thousand, and they had agreed to take
a running cut, which showed that they had the
receiving agent fixed.   Well, my foreman and I
were counting the cattle as they came between us.
But the steers were wild, long-legged coasters, and
came through between us like scared wolves.   I
had lost the count several times, but guessed at
them and started over, the cattle still coming like
a whirlwind; and when I thought about nine
hundred had passed us, I cut them off and sang
out, ' Here they come and there they go; just an
even thousand, by gatlins!   What do you make
it, Bill?'

"' Just an even thousand, Colonel,' replied my
foreman.   Of course the contractors were counting
at the same time, and I suppose did n't like to
admit they could n't count a thousand cattle where
anybody else could, and never asked for a recount,

but accepted and paid for them. They had hired
an outfit, and held the cattle outside that night,
but the next day, when they cut them into car lots
and shipped them, they were a hundred and eighteen short. They wanted to come back on me to
make them good, but, shucks! I wasn't responsible
if their Jim Crow outfit lost the cattle."

Along early in the evening, Flood advised us
boys to return to the herd with him, but all the
crowd wanted to stay in town and see the sights.
Lovell interceded in our behalf, and promised to
see that we left town in good time to be in camp
before the herd was ready to move the next morning. On this assurance, Flood saddled up and
started for the Saw Log, having ample time to
make the ride before dark. By this time most of
the boys had worn off the wire edge for gambling
and were comparing notes. Three of them were
broke, but Quince Forrest had turned the tables
and was over a clean hundred winner for the day.
Those who had no money fortunately had good
credit with those of us who had, for there was yet
much to be seen, and in Dodge in '82 it took
money to see the elephant. There were several
variety theatres, a number of dance halls, and
other resorts which, like the wicked, flourish best
under darkness. After supper, just about dusk,
we went over to the stable, caught our horses,
saddled them, and tied them up for the night. We
fully expected to leave town by ten o'clock, for it

was a good twelve mile ride to the Saw Log. In
making the rounds of the variety theatres and
dance halls, we hung together. Lovell excused
himself early in the evening, and at parting we
assured him that the outfit would leave for camp
before midnight. We were enjoying ourselves
immensely over at the Lone Star dance hall, when
an incident occurred in which we entirely neglected
the good advice of McNulta, and had the sensation
of hearing lead whistle and cry around our ears
before we got away from town.

Quince Forrest was spending his winnings as
well as drinking freely, and at the end of a quad-
rille gave vent to his hilarity in an old-fashioned
Comanche yell. The bouncer of the dance hall of
course had his eye on our crowd, and at the end of
a change, took Quince to task. He was a surly
brute, and instead of couching his request in appropriate language, threatened to throw him out of
the house. Forrest stood like one absent-minded
and took the abuse, for physically he was no match
for the bouncer, who was armed, moreover, and
wore an officer's star. I was dancing in the same
set with a red-headed, freckled-faced girl, who
clutched my arm and wished to know if my friend
was armed. I assured her that he was not, or we
would have had notice of it before the bouncer's
invective was ended. At the conclusion of the
dance, Quince and The Rebel passed out, giving
the rest of us the word to remain as though no-

thing was wrong. In the course of half an hour, Priest returned and asked us to take our leave one at a time without attracting any attention, and meet at the stable. I remained until the last, and noticed The Rebel and the bouncer taking a drink together at the bar, — the former apparently in a most amiable mood. We passed out together shortly afterward, and found the other boys mounted and awaiting our return, it being now about midnight. It took but a moment to secure our guns, and once in the saddle, we rode through the town in the direction of the herd. On the outskirts of the town, we halted. "I'm going back to that dance hall," said Forrest, "and have one round at least with that whore-herder. No man who walks this old earth can insult me, as he did, not if he has a hundred stars on him. If any of you don't want to go along, ride right on to camp, but I'd like to have you all go. And when I take his measure, it will be the signal to the rest of you to put out the lights. All that's going, come on."

There were no dissenters to the programme. I saw at a glance that my bunkie was heart and soul in the play, and took my cue and kept my mouth shut. We circled round the town to a vacant lot within a block of the rear of the dance hall. Honeyman was left to hold the horses; then, taking off our belts and hanging them on the pommels of our saddles, we secreted our six-shooters inside the waistbands of our trousers. The hall was still crowded with the revelers when we entered, a few at a time, Forrest and Priest being the last to arrive. Forrest had changed hats with The Rebel, who always wore a black one, and as the bouncer circulated around, Quince stepped squarely in front of him. There was no waste of words, but a gun-barrel flashed in the lamplight, and the bouncer, struck with the six-shooter, fell like a beef. Before the bewildered spectators could raise a hand, five six-shooters were turned into the ceiling. The lights went out at the first fire, and amidst the rush of men and the screaming of women, we reached the outside, and within a minute were in our saddles. All would have gone well had we returned by the same route and avoided the town; but after crossing the railroad track, anger and pride having not been properly satisfied, we must ride through the town.

On entering the main street, leading north and opposite the bridge on the river, somebody of our party in the rear turned his gun loose into the air. The Rebel and I were riding in the lead, and at the clattering of hoofs and shooting behind us, our horses started on the run, the shooting by this time having become general. At the second street crossing, I noticed a rope of fire belching from a Winchester in the doorway of a store building. There was no doubt in my mind but we were the object of the manipulator of that carbine, and as we reached the next cross street, a man kneeling

CELEBRATING IN DODGE

in the shadow of a building opened fire on us with a six-shooter. Priest reined in his horse, and not having wasted cartridges in the open-air shooting, returned the compliment until he emptied his gun. By this time every officer in the town was throwing lead after us, some of which cried a little too close for comfort. When there was no longer any shooting on our flanks, we turned into a cross street and soon left the lead behind us. At the outskirts of the town we slowed up our horses and took it leisurely for a mile or so, when Quince Forrest halted us and said, "I'm going to drop out here and see if any one follows us. I want to be alone, so that if any officers try to follow us up, I can have it out with them."

As there was no time to lose in parleying, and as he had a good horse, we rode away and left him. On reaching camp, we secured a few hours' sleep, but the next morning, to our surprise, Forrest failed to appear. We explained the situation to Flood, who said if he did not show up by noon, he would go back and look for him. We all felt positive that he would not dare to go back to town; and if he was lost, as soon as the sun arose he would be able to get his bearings. While we were nooning about seven miles north of the Saw Log, some one noticed a buggy coming up the trail. As it came nearer we saw that there were two other occupants of the rig besides the driver. When it drew up old Quince, still wearing The Rebel's hat, stepped out of the rig, dragged out his saddle from under the seat, and invited his companions to dinner. They both declined, when Forrest, taking out his purse, handed a twenty-dollar gold piece to the driver with an oath. He then asked the other man what he owed him, but the latter very haughtily declined any recompense, and the conveyance drove away.

"I suppose you fellows don't know what all this means," said Quince, as he filled a plate and sat down in the shade of the wagon. "Well, that horse of mine got a bullet plugged into him last night as we were leaving town, and before I could get him to Duck Creek, he died on me. I carried my saddle and blankets until daylight, when I hid in a draw and waited for something to turn up. I thought some of you would come back and look for me sometime, for I knew you wouldn't understand it, when all of a sudden here comes this livery rig along with that drummer — going out to Jetmore, I believe he said. I explained what I wanted, but he decided that his business was more important than mine, and refused me. I referred the matter to Judge Colt, and the judge decided that it was more important that I overtake this herd. I'd have made him take pay, too, only he acted so mean about it."

After dinner, fearing arrest, Forrest took a horse and rode on ahead to the Solomon River. We were a glum outfit that afternoon, but after a

good night's rest were again as fresh as daisies.
When McCann started to get breakfast, he hung
his coat on the end of the wagon rod, while he
went for a bucket of water.   During his absence,
John Officer was noticed slipping something into
Barney's coat pocket, and after breakfast when our
cook went to his coat for his tobacco, he unearthed
a lady's cambric handkerchief, nicely embroidered,
and a silver mounted garter.   He looked at the
articles a moment, and, grasping the situation at
a glance, ran his eye over the outfit for the cul-
prit.   But there was not a word or a smile.   He
walked over and threw the articles into the fire,
remarking, "Good whiskey and bad women will
be the ruin of you varmints yet."

CHAPTER XIV

SLAUGHTER'S BRIDGE

HERDS bound for points beyond the Yellowstone, in Montana, always considered Dodge as the half-way landmark on the trail, though we had hardly covered half the distance to the destination of our Circle Dots. But with Dodge in our rear, all felt that the backbone of the drive was broken, and it was only the middle of June. In order to divide the night work more equitably, for the remainder of the trip the first and fourth guards changed, the second and third remaining as they were. We had begun to feel the scarcity of wood for cooking purposes some time past, and while crossing the plains of western Kansas, we were frequently forced to resort to the old bed grounds of a year or two previous for cattle chips. These chips were a poor substitute, and we swung a cowskin under the reach of the wagon, so that when we encountered wood on creeks and rivers we could lay in a supply. Whenever our wagon was in the rear, the riders on either side of the herd were always on the skirmish for fuel, which they left alongside the wagon track, and our cook was sure to stow it away underneath on the cowskin.

In spite of any effort on our part, the length of the days made long drives the rule. The cattle could be depended on to leave the bed ground at dawn, and before the outfit could breakfast, secure mounts, and overtake the herd, they would often have grazed forward two or three miles. Often we never threw them on the trail at all, yet when it came time to bed them at night, we had covered twenty miles. They were long, monotonous days; for we were always sixteen to eighteen hours in the saddle, while in emergencies we got the benefit of the limit. We frequently saw mirages, though we were never led astray by shady groves of timber or tempting lakes of water, but always kept within a mile or two of the trail. The evening of the third day after Forrest left us, he returned as we were bedding down the cattle at dusk, and on being assured that no officers had followed us, resumed his place with the herd. He had not even reached the Solomon River, but had stopped with a herd of Millet's on Big Boggy. This creek he reported as bottomless, and the Millet herd as having lost between forty and fifty head of cattle in attempting to force it at the regular crossing the day before his arrival. They had scouted the creek both up and down since without finding a safe crossing. It seemed that there had been unusually heavy June rains through that section, which accounted for Boggy being in its dangerous condition. Millet's foreman had not considered it

necessary to test such an insignificant stream until
he got a couple of hundred head of cattle floundering in the mire. They had saved the greater
portion of the mired cattle, but quite a number
were trampled to death by the others, and now
the regular crossing was not approachable for the
stench of dead cattle. Flood knew the stream, and
so did a number of our outfit, but none of them
had any idea that it could get into such an impassable condition as Forrest reported.

The next morning Flood started to the east and
Priest to the west to look out a crossing, for we
were then within half a day's drive of the creek.
Big Boggy paralleled the Solomon River in our
front, the two not being more than five miles
apart. The confluence was far below in some set-
tlements, and we must keep to the westward of all
immigration, on account of the growing crops in the
fertile valley of the Solomon. On the westward,
had a favorable crossing been found, we would
almost have had to turn our herd backward, for
we were already within the half circle which this
creek described in our front. So after the two
men left us, we allowed the herd to graze forward,
keeping several miles to the westward of the trail
in order to get the benefit of the best grazing.
Our herd, when left to itself, would graze from
a mile to a mile and a half an hour, and by the
middle of the forenoon the timber on Big Boggy
and the Solomon beyond was sighted. On reach-

ing this last divide, some one sighted a herd about
five or six miles to the eastward and nearly parallel
with us. As they were three or four miles beyond
the trail, we could easily see that they were grazing along like ourselves, and Forrest was appealed
to to know if it was the Millet herd. He said not,
and pointed out to the northeast about the location
of the Millet cattle, probably five miles in advance
of the stranger on our right. When we overtook
our wagon at noon, McCann, who had never left
the trail, reported having seen the herd. They
looked to him like heavy beef cattle, and had two
yoke of oxen to their chuck wagon, which served
further to proclaim them as strangers.

Neither Priest nor Flood returned during the
noon hour, and when the herd refused to lie down
and rest longer, we grazed them forward till the
fringe of timber which grew along the stream
loomed up not a mile distant in our front. From
the course we were traveling, we would strike the
creek several miles above the regular crossing, and
as Forrest reported that Millet was holding below
the old crossing on a small rivulet, all we could do
was to hold our wagon in the rear, and await the
return of our men out on scout for a ford. Priest
was the first to return, with word that he had ridden the creek out for twenty-five miles and had
found no crossing that would be safe for a mud
turtle. On hearing this, we left two men with the
herd, and the rest of the outfit took the wagon,

went on to Boggy, and made camp. It was a deceptive-looking stream, not over fifty or sixty feet wide. In places the current barely moved, shallowing and deepening, from a few inches in places to several feet in others, with an occasional pool that would swim a horse. We probed it with poles until we were satisfied that we were up against a proposition different from anything we had yet encountered. While we were discussing the situation, a stranger rode up on a fine roan horse, and inquired for our foreman. Forrest informed him that our boss was away looking for a crossing, but we were expecting his return at any time; and invited the stranger to dismount. He did so, and threw himself down in the shade of our wagon. He was a small, boyish-looking fellow, of sandy complexion, not much, if any, over twenty years old, and smiled continuously.

"My name is Pete Slaughter," said he, by way of introduction, "and I 've got a herd of twenty-eight hundred beef steers, beyond the trail and a few miles back. I 've been riding since daybreak down the creek, and I 'm prepared to state that the chance of crossing is as good right here as anywhere. I wanted to see your foreman, and if he 'll help, we 'll bridge her. I 've been down to see this other outfit, but they ridicule the idea, though I think they 'll come around all right. I borrowed their axe, and to-morrow morning you 'll see me with my outfit cutting timber to bridge Big Boggy.

That's right, boys; it's the only thing to do. The trouble is I've only got eight men all told. I don't aim to travel over eight or ten miles a day, so I don't need a big outfit. You say your foreman's name is Flood? Well, if he don't return before I go, some of you tell him that he's wasting good time looking for a ford, for there ain't none."

In the conversation which followed, we learned that Slaughter was driving for his brother Lum, a widely known cowman and drover, whom we had seen in Dodge. He had started with the grass from north Texas, and by the time he reached the Platte, many of his herd would be fit to ship to market, and what were not would be in good demand as feeders in the corn belt of eastern Nebraska. He asked if we had seen his herd during the morning, and on hearing we had, got up and asked McCann to let him see our axe. This he gave a critical examination, before he mounted his horse to go, and on leaving said, —

"If your foreman don't want to help build a bridge, I want to borrow that axe of yours. But you fellows talk to him. If any of you boys has ever been over on the Chisholm trail, you will remember the bridge on Rush Creek, south of the Washita River. I built that bridge in a day with an outfit of ten men. Why, shucks! if these outfits would pull together, we could cross to-morrow evening. Lots of these old foremen don't like to

listen to a cub like me, but, holy snakes! I've
been over the trail oftener than any of them.
Why, when I wasn't big enough to make a hand
with the herd, — only ten years old, — in the days
when we drove to Abilene, they used to send me
in the lead with an old cylinder gun to shoot at
the buffalo and scare them off the trail. And I've
made the trip every year since. So you tell Flood
when he comes in, that Pete Slaughter was here,
and that he's going to build a bridge, and would
like to have him and his outfit help."

Had it not been for his youth and perpetual
smile, we might have taken young Slaughter more
seriously, for both Quince Forrest and The Rebel
remembered the bridge on Rush Creek over on
the Chisholm. Still there was an air of confident
assurance in the young fellow; and the fact that
he was the trusted foreman of Lum Slaughter, in
charge of a valuable herd of cattle, carried weight
with those who knew that drover. The most un-
welcome thought in the project was that it required
the swinging of an axe to fell trees and to cut them
into the necessary lengths, and, as I have said before, the Texan never took kindly to manual labor.
But Priest looked favorably on the suggestion, and
so enlisted my support, and even pointed out a
spot where timber was most abundant as a suitable place to build the bridge.

"Hell's fire," said Joe Stallings, with infinite
contempt, "there's thousands of places to build a

bridge, and the timber's there, but the idea is to cut it." And his sentiments found a hearty approval in the majority of the outfit.

Flood returned late that evening, having ridden as far down the creek as the first settlement. The Rebel, somewhat antagonized by the attitude of the majority, reported the visit and message left for him by young Slaughter. Our foreman knew him by general reputation amongst trail bosses, and when Priest vouched for him as the builder of the Rush Creek bridge on the Chisholm trail, Flood said, "Why, I crossed my herd four years ago on that Rush Creek bridge within a week after it was built, and wondered who it could be that had the nerve to undertake that task. Rush isn't over half as wide a bayou as Boggy, but she's a true little sister to this miry slough. So he's going to build a bridge anyhow, is he?"

The next morning young Slaughter was at our camp before sunrise, and never once mentioning his business or waiting for the formality of an invitation, proceeded to pour out a tin cup of coffee and otherwise provide himself with a substantial breakfast. There was something amusing in the audacity of the fellow which all of us liked, though he was fifteen years the junior of our foreman. McCann pointed out Flood to him, and taking his well-loaded plate, he went over and sat down by our foreman, and while he ate talked rapidly, to enlist our outfit in the building of the bridge.

During breakfast, the outfit listened to the two
bosses as they discussed the feasibility of the
project, — Slaughter enthusiastic, Flood reserved,
and asking all sorts of questions as to the mode
of procedure. Young Pete met every question
with promptness, and assured our foreman that
the building of bridges was his long suit. After
breakfast, the two foremen rode off down the creek
together, and within half an hour Slaughter's
wagon and *remuda* pulled up within sight of the
regular crossing, and shortly afterwards our foreman returned, and ordered our wagon to pull down
to a clump of cottonwoods which grew about half
a mile below our camp. Two men were detailed
to look after our herd during the day, and the
remainder of us returned with our foreman to the
site selected for the bridge. On our arrival three
axes were swinging against as many cottonwoods,
and there was no doubt in any one's mind that we
were going to be under a new foreman for that
day at least. Slaughter had a big negro cook who
swung an axe in a manner which bespoke him a job
for the day, and McCann was instructed to provide
dinner for the extra outfit.

The site chosen for the bridge was a miry bottom over which oozed three or four inches of water,
where the width of the stream was about sixty feet,
with solid banks on either side. To get a good
foundation was the most important matter, but the
brush from the trees would supply the material for

that; and within an hour, brush began to arrive, dragged from the pommels of saddles, and was piled into the stream. About this time a call went out for a volunteer who could drive oxen, for the darky was too good an axeman to be recalled. As I had driven oxen as a boy, I was going to offer my services, when Joe Stallings eagerly volunteered in order to avoid using an axe. Slaughter had some extra chain, and our four mules were pressed into service as an extra team in snaking logs. As McCann was to provide for the inner man, the mule team fell to me; and putting my saddle on the nigh wheeler, I rode jauntily past Mr. Stallings as he trudged alongside his two yoke of oxen.

About ten o'clock in the morning, George Jacklin, the foreman of the Millet herd, rode up with several of his men, and seeing the bridge taking shape, turned in and assisted in dragging brush for the foundation. By the time all hands knocked off for dinner, we had a foundation of brush twenty feet wide and four feet high, to say nothing about what had sunk in the mire. The logs were cut about fourteen feet long, and old Joe and I had snaked them up as fast as the axemen could get them ready. Jacklin returned to his wagon for dinner and a change of horses, though Slaughter, with plenty of assurance, had invited him to eat with us, and when he declined had remarked, with no less confidence, "Well, then, you'll be back right after dinner. And say, bring all the men you can spare; and if you 've got any gunny sacks or old tarpaulins, bring them; and by all means don't forget your spade."

Pete Slaughter was a harsh master, considering he was working volunteer labor; but then we all felt a common interest in the bridge, for if Slaughter's beeves could cross, ours could, and so could Millet's. All the men dragging brush changed horses during dinner, for there was to be no pause in piling in a good foundation as long as the material was at hand. Jacklin and his outfit returned, ten strong, and with thirty men at work, the bridge grew. They began laying the logs on the brush after dinner, and the work of sodding the bridge went forward at the same time. The bridge stood about two feet above the water in the creek, but when near the middle of the stream was reached, the foundation gave way, and for an hour ten horses were kept busy dragging brush to fill that sink hole until it would bear the weight of the logs. We had used all the acceptable timber on our side of the stream for half a mile either way, and yet there were not enough logs to complete the bridge. When we lacked only some ten or twelve logs, Slaughter had the boys sod a narrow strip across the remaining brush, and the horsemen led their mounts across to the farther side. Then the axemen crossed, felled the nearest trees, and the last logs were dragged up from the pommels of our saddles.

It now only remained to sod over and dirt the bridge thoroughly. With only three spades the work was slow, but we cut sod with axes, and after several hours' work had it finished. The two yoke of oxen were driven across and back for a test, and the bridge stood it nobly. Slaughter then brought up his *remuda*, and while the work of dirting the bridge was still going on, crossed and recrossed his band of saddle horses twenty times. When the bridge looked completed to every one else, young Pete advised laying stringers across on either side; so a number of small trees were felled and guard rails strung across the ends of the logs and staked. Then more dirt was carried in on tarpaulins and in gunny sacks, and every chink and crevice filled with sod and dirt. It was now getting rather late in the afternoon, but during the finishing touches, young Slaughter had dispatched his outfit to bring up his herd; and at the same time Flood had sent a number of our outfit to bring up our cattle. Now Slaughter and the rest of us took the oxen, which we had unyoked, and went out about a quarter of a mile to meet his herd coming up. Turning the oxen in the lead, young Pete took one point and Flood the other, and pointed in the lead cattle for the bridge. On reaching it the cattle hesitated for a moment, and it looked as though they were going to balk, but finally one of the oxen took the lead, and they began to cross in almost Indian file. They were big four and five year old beeves, and too many of them on the bridge at one time might have sunk it, but Slaughter rode back down the line of cattle and called to the men to hold them back.

"Don't crowd the cattle," he shouted. "Give them all the time they want. We're in no hurry now; there's lots of time."

They were a full half hour in crossing, the chain of cattle taking the bridge never for a moment being broken. Once all were over, his men rode to the lead and turned the herd up Boggy, in order to have it well out of the way of ours, which were then looming up in sight. Slaughter asked Flood if he wanted the oxen; and as our cattle had never seen a bridge in their lives, the foreman decided to use them; so we brought them back and met the herd, now strung out nearly a mile. Our cattle were naturally wild, but we turned the oxen in the lead, and the two bosses again taking the points, moved the herd up to the bridge. The oxen were again slow to lead out in crossing, and several hundred head of cattle had congested in front of the new bridge, making us all rather nervous, when a big white ox led off, his mate following, and the herd began timidly to follow. Our cattle required careful handling, and not a word was spoken as we nursed them forward, or rode through them to scatter large bunches. A number of times we cut the train of cattle off entirely, as they were congesting at the bridge entrance, and, in crossing, shied and crowded so that several were forced off the bridge into the mire. Our herd crossed in considerably less time than did Slaughter's beeves, but we had five head to pull out; this, however, was considered nothing, as they were light, and the mire was as thin as soup. Our wagon and saddle horses crossed while we were pulling out the bogged cattle, and about half the outfit, taking the herd, drifted them forward towards the Solomon. Since Millet intended crossing that evening, herds were likely to be too thick for safety at night. The sun was hardly an hour high when the last herd came up to cross. The oxen were put in the lead, as with ours, and all four of the oxen took the bridge, but when the cattle reached the bridge, they made a decided balk and refused to follow the oxen. Not a hoof of the herd would even set foot on the bridge. The oxen were brought back several times, but in spite of all coaxing and nursing, and our best endeavors and devices, they would not risk it. We worked with them until dusk, when all three of the foremen decided it was useless to try longer, but both Slaughter and Flood promised to bring back part of their outfits in the morning and make another effort.

McCann's camp-fire piloted us to our wagon, at least three miles from the bridge, for he had laid in a good supply of wood during the day; and on our arrival our night horses were tied up, and everything made ready for the night. The next morning we started the herd, but Flood took four of us with him and went back to Big Boggy. The Millet herd was nearly two miles back from the bridge, where we found Slaughter at Jacklin's wagon; and several more of his men were, we learned, coming over with the oxen at about ten o'clock. That hour was considered soon enough by the bosses, as the heat of the day would be on the herd by that time, which would make them lazy. When the oxen arrived at the bridge, we rode out twenty strong and lined the cattle up for another trial. They had grazed until they were full and sleepy, but the memory of some of them was too vivid of the hours they had spent in the slimy ooze of Big Boggy once on a time, and they began milling on sight of the stream. We took them back and brought them up a second time with the same results. We then brought them around in a circle a mile in diameter, and as the rear end of the herd was passing, we turned the last hundred, and throwing the oxen into their lead, started them for the bridge; but they too sulked and would have none of it. It was now high noon, so we turned the herd and allowed them to graze back while we went to dinner. Millet's foreman was rather discouraged with the outlook, but Slaughter said they must be crossed if he had to lay over a week and help. After dinner, Jacklin asked us if we wanted a change of horses, and as we could see a twenty mile ride ahead of us in overtaking our herd, Flood accepted.

When all was ready to start, Slaughter made a suggestion. "Let's go out," he said, "and bring them up slowly in a solid body, and when we get them opposite the bridge, round them in gradually as if we were going to bed them down. I'll take a long lariat to my white wheeler, and when they have quieted down perfectly, I'll lead old Blanco through them and across the bridge, and possibly they'll follow. There's no use crowding them, for that only excites them, and if you ever start them milling, the jig's up. They're nice, gentle cattle, but they've been balked once and they haven't forgotten it."

What we needed right then was a leader, for we were all ready to catch at a straw, and Slaughter's suggestion was welcome, for he had established himself in our good graces until we preferred him to either of the other foremen as a leader. Riding out to the herd, which were lying down, we roused and started them back towards Boggy. While drifting them back, we covered a front a quarter of a mile in width, and as we neared the bridge we gave them perfect freedom. Slaughter had caught out his white ox, and we gradually worked them into a body, covering perhaps ten acres, in front of the bridge. Several small bunches attempted to mill, but some of us rode in and split them up, and after about half an hour's wait, they quieted down. Then Slaughter rode in whistling and leading his white ox at the end of a thirty-five foot lariat, and as he rode through them they were so logy that he had to quirt them out of the way. When he came to the bridge, he stopped the white wheeler until everything had quieted down; then he led old Blanco on again, but giving him all the time he needed and stopping every few feet. We held our breath, as one or two of the herd started to follow him, but they shied and turned back, and our hopes of the moment were crushed. Slaughter detained the ox on the bridge for several minutes, but seeing it was useless, he dismounted and drove him back into the herd. Again and again he tried the same ruse, but it was of no avail. Then we threw the herd back about half a mile, and on Flood's suggestion cut off possibly two hundred head, a bunch which with our numbers we ought to handle readily in spite of their will, and by putting their *remuda* of over a hundred saddle horses in the immediate lead, made the experiment of forcing them. We took the saddle horses down and crossed and recrossed the bridge several times with them, and as the cattle came up turned the horses into the lead and headed for the bridge. With a cordon of twenty riders around them, no animal could turn back, and the horses crossed the bridge on a trot, but the cattle turned tail and positively refused to have anything to do with it. We held them like a block in a vise, so compactly that they could not even mill, but they would not cross the bridge.

When it became evident that it was a fruitless effort, Jacklin, usually a very quiet man, gave vent
to a fit of profanity which would have put the
army in Flanders to shame.   Slaughter, somewhat
to our amusement, reproved him: "Don't fret,
man; this is nothing, — I balked a herd once in
crossing a railroad track, and after trying for two
days to cross them, had to drive ten miles and
put them under a culvert.   You want to cultivate
patience, young fellow, when you 're handling
dumb brutes."

If Slaughter's darky cook had been thereabouts
then, and suggested a means of getting that herd
to take the bridge, his suggestion would have been
welcomed, for the bosses were at their wits' ends.
Jacklin swore that he would bed that herd at the
entrance, and hold them there until they starved
to death or crossed, before he would let an animal
turn back.   But cooler heads were present, and
The Rebel mentioned a certain adage, to the effect
that when a bird or a girl, he did n't know which,
could sing and would n't, she or it ought to be
made to sing.   He suggested that we hold the four
oxen on the bridge, cut off fifteen head of cattle,
and give them such a running start, they would n't
know which end their heads were on when they
reached the bridge.   Millet's foreman approved of
the idea, for he was nursing his wrath.   The four
oxen were accordingly cut out, and Slaughter and
one of his men, taking them, started for the bridge

with instructions to hold them on the middle. The
rest of us took about a dozen head of light cattle,
brought them within a hundred yards of the bridge,
then with a yell started them on a run from which
they could not turn back. They struck the entrance squarely, and we had our first cattle on the
bridge. Two men held the entrance, and we
brought up another bunch in the same manner,
which filled the bridge. Now, we thought, if the
herd could be brought up slowly, and this bridge-
ful let off in their lead, they might follow. To
june a herd of cattle across in this manner would
have been shameful, and the foreman of the herd
knew it as well as any one present; but no one
protested, so we left men to hold the entrance securely and went back after the herd. When we
got them within a quarter of a mile of the creek,
we cut off about two hundred head of the leaders
and brought them around to the rear, for amongst
these leaders were certain to be the ones which had
been bogged, and we wanted to have new leaders
in this trial. Slaughter was on the farther end of
the bridge, and could be depended on to let the
oxen lead off at the opportune moment. We
brought them up cautiously, and when the herd
came within a few rods of the creek the cattle on
the bridge lowed to their mates in the herd, and
Slaughter, considering the time favorable, opened
out and allowed them to leave the bridge on the
farther side. As soon as the cattle started leaving

on the farther side, we dropped back, and the leaders of the herd to the number of a dozen, after smelling the fresh dirt and seeing the others crossing, walked cautiously up on the bridge. It was a moment of extreme anxiety. None of us spoke a word, but the cattle crowding off the bridge at the farther end set it vibrating. That was enough: they turned as if panic-stricken and rushed back to the body of the herd. I was almost afraid to look at Jacklin. He could scarcely speak, but he rode over to me, ashen with rage, and kept repeating, "Well, would n't that beat hell!"

Slaughter rode back across the bridge, and the men came up and gathered around Jacklin. We seemed to have run the full length of our rope. No one even had a suggestion to offer, and if any one had had, it needed to be a plausible one to find approval, for hope seemed to have vanished. While discussing the situation, a one-eyed, pox-marked fellow belonging to Slaughter's outfit, galloped up from the rear, and said almost breathlessly, "Say, fellows, I see a cow and calf in the herd. Let 's rope the calf, and the cow is sure to follow. Get the rope around the calf's neck, and when it chokes him, he 's liable to bellow, and that will call the steers. And if you never let up on the choking till you get on the other side of the bridge, I think it 'll work. Let 's try it, anyhow."

We all approved, for we knew that next to the smell of blood, nothing will stir range cattle like the bellowing of a calf. At the mere suggestion, Jacklin's men scattered into the herd, and within a few minutes we had a rope round the neck of the calf. As the roper came through the herd leading the calf, the frantic mother followed, with a train of excited steers at her heels. And as the calf was dragged bellowing across the bridge, it was followed by excited, struggling steers who never knew whether they were walking on a bridge or on *terra firma*. The excitement spread through the herd, and they thickened around the entrance until it was necessary to hold them back, and only let enough pass to keep the chain unbroken.

They were nearly a half hour in crossing, for it was fully as large a herd as ours; and when the last animal had crossed, Pete Slaughter stood up in his stirrups and led the long yell. The sun went down that day on nobody's wrath, for Jacklin was so tickled that he offered to kill the fattest beef in his herd if we would stay overnight with him. All three of the herds were now over, but had not this herd balked on us the evening before, over nine thousand cattle would have crossed Slaughter's bridge the day it was built.

It was now late in the evening, and as we had to wait some little time to get our own horses, we stayed for supper. It was dark before we set out to overtake the herd, but the trail was plain, and letting our horses take their own time, we jollied along until after midnight. We might have missed the camp, but, by the merest chance, Priest sighted our camp-fire a mile off the trail, though it had burned to embers. On reaching camp, we changed saddles to our night horses, and, calling Officer, were ready for our watch. We were expecting the men on guard to call us any minute, and while Priest was explaining to Officer the trouble we had had in crossing the Millet herd, I dozed off to sleep there as I sat by the rekindled embers. In that minute's sleep my mind wandered in a dream to my home on the San Antonio River, but the next moment I was aroused to the demands of the hour by The Rebel shaking me and saying, —

"Wake up, Tom, and take a new hold. They 're calling us on guard. If you expect to follow the trail, son, you must learn to do your sleeping in the winter."

CHAPTER XV

AFTER leaving the country tributary to the Solomon River, we crossed a wide tableland for nearly a hundred miles, and with the exception of the Kansas Pacific Railroad, without a landmark worthy of a name. Western Kansas was then classified, worthily too, as belonging to the Great American Desert, and most of the country for the last five hundred miles of our course was entitled to a similar description. Once the freshness of spring had passed, the plain took on her natural sunburnt color, and day after day, as far as the eye could reach, the monotony was unbroken, save by the variations of the mirages on every hand. Except at morning and evening, we were never out of sight of these optical illusions, sometimes miles away, and then again close up, when an antelope standing half a mile distant looked as tall as a giraffe. Frequently the lead of the herd would be in eclipse from these illusions, when to the men in the rear the horsemen and cattle in the lead would appear like giants in an old fairy story. If the monotony of the sea can be charged with dulling men's sensibilities until they become pirates, surely this desolate, arid plain might be equally charged with the wrongdoing of not a few of our craft.

On crossing the railroad at Grinnell, our foreman received a letter from Lovell, directing him to go to Culbertson, Nebraska, and there meet a man who was buying horses for a Montana ranch. Our employer had his business eye open for a possible purchaser for our *remuda*, and if the horses could be sold for delivery after the herd had reached its destination, the opportunity was not to be overlooked. Accordingly, on reaching Beaver Creek, where we encamped, Flood left us to ride through to the Republican River during the night. The trail crossed this river about twenty miles west of Culbertson, and if the Montana horse buyer were yet there, it would be no trouble to come up to the trail crossing and look at our horses.

So after supper, and while we were catching up our night horses, Flood said to us, "Now, boys, I'm going to leave the outfit and herd under Joe Stallings as *segundo*. It's hardly necessary to leave you under any one as foreman, for you all know your places. But some one must be made responsible, and one bad boss will do less harm than half a dozen that might n't agree. So you can put Honeyman on guard in your place at night, Joe, if you don't want to stand your own watch. Now behave yourselves, and when I meet you on the Republican, I'll bring out a box of cigars and have it charged up as axle grease when we get supplies at Ogalalla. And don't sit up all night telling fool stories."

"Now, that's what I call a good cow boss," said Joe Stallings, as our foreman rode away in the twilight; "besides, he used passable good judgment in selecting a *segundo*. Now, Honeyman, you heard what he said. Billy dear, I won't rob you of this chance to stand a guard. McCann, have you got on your next list of supplies any jam and jelly for Sundays? You have? That's right, son — that saves you from standing a guard to-night. Officer, when you come off guard at 3.30 in the morning, build the cook up a good fire. Let me see; yes, and I'll detail young Tom Quirk and The Rebel to grease the wagon and harness your mules before starting in the morning. I want to impress it on your mind, McCann, that I can appreciate a thoughtful cook. What's that, Honeyman? No, indeed, you can't ride my night horse. Love me, love my dog; my horse shares this snap. Now, I don't want to be under the necessity of speaking to any of you first guard, but flop into your saddles ready to take the herd. My turnip says it's eight o'clock now."

"Why, you've missed your calling — you'd make a fine second mate on a river steamboat, driving niggers," called back Quince Forrest, as the first guard rode away.

When our guard returned, Officer intentionally

walked across Stallings's bed, and catching his spur
in the tarpaulin, fell heavily across our *segundo*.

"Excuse me," said John, rising, "but I was just
nosing around looking for the foreman. Oh, it's
you, is it? I just wanted to ask if 4.30 would n't
be plenty early to build up the fire. Wood's a
little scarce, but I'll burn the prairies if you say
so. That's all I wanted to know; you may lay
down now and go to sleep."

Our camp-fire that night was a good one, and
in the absence of Flood, no one felt like going to
bed until drowsiness compelled us. So we lounged
around the fire smoking the hours away, and in
spite of the admonition of our foreman, told stories
far into the night. During the early portion of
the evening, dog stories occupied the boards. As
the evening wore on, the subject of revisiting the
old States came up for discussion.

"You all talk about going back to the old
States," said Joe Stallings, "but I don't take very
friendly to the idea. I felt that way once and
went home to Tennessee; but I want to tell you
that after you live a few years in the sunny Southwest and get onto her ways, you can't stand it
back there like you think you can. Now, when I
went back, and I reckon my relations will average
up pretty well, — fought in the Confederate army,
vote the Democratic ticket, and belong to the
Methodist church, — they all seemed to be rapidly
getting locoed. Why, my uncles, when they think

of planting the old buck field or the widow's acre
into any crop, they first go projecting around in
the soil, and, as they say, analyze it, to see what
kind of a fertilizer it will require to produce the
best results. Back there if one man raises ten
acres of corn and his neighbor raises twelve, the
one raising twelve is sure to look upon the other
as though he lacked enterprise or had modest am-
bitions. Now, up around that old cow town, Abilene, Kansas, it's a common sight to see the corn-
fields stretch out like an ocean.

"And then their stock — they are all locoed
about that. Why, I know people who will pay
a hundred dollars for siring a colt, and if there's
one drop of mongrel blood in that sire's veins for
ten generations back on either side of his ancestral
tree, it condemns him, though he may be a good
horse otherwise. They are strong on standard
bred horses; but as for me, my mount is all right.
I wouldn't trade with any man in this outfit, without it would be Flood, and there's none of them
standard bred either. Why, shucks! if you had
the pick of all the standard bred horses in Tennessee, you couldn't handle a herd of cattle like ours
with them, without carrying a commissary with
you to feed them. No; they would never fit here
— it takes a range-raised horse to run cattle; one
that can rustle and live on grass.

"Another thing about those people back in those
old States: Not one in ten, I'll gamble, knows the

STORY TELLING

teacher he sends his children to school to. But
when he has a promising colt to be shod, the owner
goes to the blacksmith shop himself, and he and
the smith will sit on the back sill of the shop, and
they will discuss how to shoe that filly so as to
give her certain knee action which she seems to
need. Probably, says one, a little weight on her
toe would give her reach. And there they will sit
and powwow and make medicine for an hour or
two. And while the blacksmith is shoeing her,
the owner will tell him in confidence what a won-
derful burst of speed she developed yesterday,
while he was speeding her on the back stretch.
And then just as he turned her into the home
stretch, she threw a shoe and he had to check her
in; but if there 'd been any one to catch her time,
he was certain it was better than a two-ten clip.
And that same colt, you couldn't cut a lame cow
out of the shade of a tree on her. A man back
there — he 's rich, too, though his father made it
— gave a thousand dollars for a pair of dogs before
they were born. The terms were one half cash and
the balance when they were old enough to ship to
him. And for fear they were not the proper mus-
tard, he had that dog man sue him in court for
the balance, so as to make him prove the pedigree.
Now Bob, there, thinks that old hound of his is
the real stuff, but he wouldn't do now; almost
every year the style changes in dogs back in the
old States. One year maybe it 's a little white dog

with red eyes, and the very next it's a long bench-
legged, black dog with a Dutch name that right
now I disremember. Common old pot hounds and
everyday yellow dogs have gone out of style entirely. No, you can all go back that want to, but
as long as I can hold a job with Lovell and Flood,
I 'll try and worry along in my own way."

On finishing his little yarn, Stallings arose, saying, "I must take a listen to my men on herd. It
always frets me for fear my men will ride too near
the cattle."

A minute later he called us, and when several of
us walked out to where he was listening, we recognized Roundtree's voice, singing: —

> " Little black bull came down the hillside,
>   Down the hillside, down the hillside,
> Little black bull came down the hillside,
>   Long time ago."

"Whenever my men sing that song on guard, it
tells me that everything is amply serene," remarked
our *segundo*, with the air of a field-marshal, as we
walked back to the fire.

The evening had passed so rapidly it was now
almost time for the second guard to be called, and
when the lateness of the hour was announced, we
skurried to our blankets like rabbits to their war-
rens. The second guard usually got an hour or
two of sleep before being called, but in the absence of our regular foreman, the mice would play.
When our guard was called at one o'clock, as

usual, Officer delayed us several minutes looking for his spurs, and I took the chance to ask The Rebel why it was that he never wore spurs.

"It's because I'm superstitious, son," he answered. "I own a fine pair of silver-plated spurs that have a history, and if you're ever at Lovell's ranch I'll show them to you. They were given to me by a mortally wounded Federal officer the day the battle of Lookout Mountain was fought. I was an orderly, carrying dispatches, and in passing through a wood from which the Union army had been recently driven, this officer was sitting at the root of a tree, fatally wounded. He motioned me to him, and when I dismounted, he said, 'Johnny Reb, please give a dying man a drink.' I gave him my canteen, and after drinking from it he continued, 'I want you to have my spurs. Take them off. Listen to their history: as you have taken them off me to-day, so I took them off a Mexican general the day the American army entered the capital of Mexico.'"

CHAPTER XVI

THE outfit were awakened out of sleep the next morning by shouts of " Whoa, *mula !* Whoa, you mongrel outcasts ! Catch them blankety blank mules !" accompanied by a rattle of chain harness, and Quince Forrest dashed across our *segundo's* bed, shaking a harness in each hand. We kicked the blankets off, and came to our feet in time to see the offender disappear behind the wagon, while Stallings sat up and yawningly inquired "what other locoed fool had got funny." But the camp was awake, for the cattle were leisurely leaving the bed ground, while Honeyman, who had been excused from the herd with the first sign of dawn, was rustling up the horses in the valley of the Beaver below camp. With the understanding that the Republican River was a short three days' drive from our present camp, the herd trailed out the first day with not an incident to break the monotony of eating and sleeping, grazing and guarding. But near noon of the second day, we were overtaken by an old, long-whiskered man and a boy of possibly fifteen. They were riding in a light, rickety vehicle, drawn by a small Spanish mule and a rough but

clean-limbed bay mare. The strangers appealed to
our sympathy, for they were guileless in appearance,
and asked so many questions, indicating that ours
might have been the first herd of trail cattle they
had ever seen. The old man was a free talker, and
innocently allowed us to inveigle it out of him that
he had been down on the North Beaver, looking up
land to homestead, and was then on his way up to
take a look at the lands along the Republican. We
invited him and the boy to remain for dinner, for in
that monotonous waste, we would have been only
too glad to entertain a bandit, or an angel for
that matter, provided he would talk about something else than cattle. In our guest, however, we
found a good conversationalist, meaty with stories
not eligible to the retired list; and in return, the
hospitality of our wagon was his and welcome. The
travel-stained old rascal proved to be a good mixer,
and before dinner was over he had won us to a man,
though Stallings, in the capacity of foreman, felt it
incumbent on him to act the host in behalf of the
outfit. In the course of conversation, the old man
managed to unearth the fact that our acting foreman was a native of Tennessee, and when he had
got it down to town and county, claimed acquaint-
anceship with a family of men in that locality who
were famed as breeders of racehorses. Our guest
admitted that he himself was a native of that State,
and in his younger days had been a devotee of the
racecourse, with the name of every horseman in

that commonwealth as well as the bluegrass regions of Kentucky on his tongue's end. But adversity had come upon him, and now he was looking out a new country in which to begin life over again.

After dinner, when our *remuda* was corralled to catch fresh mounts, our guest bubbled over with admiration of our horses, and pointed out several as promising speed and action. We took his praise of our horseflesh as quite a compliment, never suspecting flattery at the hands of this nomadic patriarch. He innocently inquired which was considered the fastest horse in the *remuda*, when Stallings pointed out a brown, belonging to Flood's mount, as the best quarter horse in the band. He gave him a critical examination, and confessed he would never have picked him for a horse possessing speed, though he admitted that he was unfamiliar with range-raised horses, this being his first visit in the West. Stallings offered to loan him a horse out of his mount, and as the old man had no saddle, our *segundo* prevailed on McCann to loan his for the afternoon. I am inclined to think there was a little jealousy amongst us that afternoon, as to who was best entitled to entertain our company; and while he showed no partiality, Stallings seemed to monopolize his countryman to our disadvantage. The two jollied along from point to rear and back again, and as they passed us riders in the swing, Stallings ignored us entirely, though the old man always had a pleasant word as he rode by.

"If we don't do something to wean our *segundo*
from that old man," said Fox Quarternight, as he
rode up and overtook me, " he 's liable to quit the
herd and follow that old fossil back to Tennessee
or some other port. Just look at the two now, will
you? Old Joe 's putting on as much dog as though
he was asking the Colonel for his daughter. Between me and you and the gatepost, Quirk, I 'm a
little dubious about the old varmint — he talks too
much."

But I had warmed up to our guest, and gave
Fox's criticism very little weight, well knowing if
any one of us had been left in charge, he would
have shown the old man similar courtesies. In this
view I was correct, for when Stallings had ridden
on ahead to look up water that afternoon, the very
man that entirely monopolized our guest for an
hour was Mr. John Fox Quarternight. Nor did
he jar loose until we reached water, when Stallings
cut him off by sending all the men on the right of
the herd to hold the cattle from grazing away until
every hoof had had ample time to drink. During
this rest, the old man circulated around, asking
questions as usual, and when I informed him that,
with a half mile of water front, it would take a
full hour to water the herd properly, he expressed
an innocent amazement which seemed as simple as
sincere. When the wagon and *remuda* came up,
I noticed the boy had tied his team behind our
wagon, and was riding one of Honeyman's horses

bareback, assisting the wrangler in driving the saddle stock. After the wagon had crossed the creek, and the kegs had been filled and the teams watered, Stallings took the old man with him and the two rode away in the lead of the wagon and *remuda* to select a camp and a bed ground for the night. The rest of us grazed the cattle, now thoroughly watered, forward until the wagon was sighted, when, leaving two men as usual to nurse them up to bed, the remainder of us struck out for camp. As I rode in, I sought out my bunkie to get his opinion regarding our guest. But The Rebel was reticent, as usual, of his opinions of people, so my inquiries remained unanswered, which only served to increase my confidence in the old man.

On arriving at camp we found Stallings and Honeyman entertaining our visitor in a little game of freeze-out for a dollar a corner, while McCann looked wistfully on, as if regretting that his culinary duties prevented his joining in. Our arrival should have been the signal to our wrangler for rounding in the *remuda* for night horses, but Stallings was too absorbed in the game even to notice the lateness of the hour and order in the saddle stock. Quarternight, however, had a few dollars burning holes in his pocket, and he called our horse rustler's attention to the approaching twilight; not that he was in any hurry, but if Honeyman vacated, he saw an opportunity to get into the game. The foreman gave the necessary order, and

Quarternight at once bargained for the wrangler's remaining beans, and sat into the game. While we were catching up our night horses, Honeyman told us that the old man had been joking Stallings about the speed of Flood's brown, even going so far as to intimate that he did n't believe that the gelding could outrun that old bay harness mare which he was driving. He had confessed that he was too hard up to wager much on it, but he would risk a few dollars on his judgment on a running horse any day. He also said that Stallings had come back at him, more in earnest than in jest, that if he really thought his harness mare could outrun the brown, he could win every dollar the outfit had. They had codded one another until Joe had shown some spirit, when the old man suggested they play a little game of cards for fun, but Stallings had insisted on stakes to make it interesting, and on the old homesteader pleading poverty, they had agreed to make it for a dollar on the corner. After supper our *segundo* wanted to renew the game; the old man protested that he was too unlucky and could not afford to lose, but was finally persuaded to play one more game, " just to pass away the evening." Well, the evening passed, and within the short space of two hours, there also passed to the supposed lean purse of our guest some twenty dollars from the feverish pockets of the outfit. Then the old man felt too sleepy to play any longer, but loitered around some time, and casually inquired of his boy if he had picketed their mare where she would get a good bait of grass. This naturally brought up the proposed race for discussion.

" If you really think that that old bay palfrey of yours can outrun any horse in our *remuda*," said Stallings, tauntingly, " you 're missing the chance of your life not to pick up a few honest dollars as you journey along. You stay with us to-morrow, and when we meet our foreman at the Republican, if he 'll loan me the horse, I 'll give you a race for any sum you name, just to show you that I 've got a few drops of sporting blood in me. And if your mare can outrun a cow, you stand an easy chance to win some money."

Our visitor met Joe's bantering in a timid manner. Before turning in, however, he informed us that he appreciated our hospitality, but that he expected to make an early drive in the morning to the Republican, where he might camp several days. With this the old man and the boy unrolled their blankets, and both were soon sound asleep. Then our *segundo* quietly took Fox Quarternight off to one side, and I heard the latter agree to call him when the third guard was aroused. Having notified Honeyman that he would stand his own watch that night, Stallings, with the rest of the outfit, soon joined the old man in the land of dreams. Instead of the rough shaking which was customary on arousing a guard, when we of the third watch were called, we were awakened in a manner so cautious as to betoken something unusual in the air. The atmosphere of mystery soon cleared after reaching the herd, when Bob Blades informed us that it was the intention of Stallings and Quarternight to steal the old man's harness mare off the picket rope, and run her against their night horses in a trial race. Like love and war, everything is fair in horse racing, but the audacity of this proposition almost passed belief. Both Blades and Durham remained on guard with us, and before we had circled the herd half a dozen times, the two conspirators came riding up to the bed ground, leading the bay mare. There was a good moon that night; Quarternight exchanged mounts with John Officer, as the latter had a splendid night horse that had outstripped the outfit in every stampede so far, and our *segundo* and the second guard rode out of hearing of both herd and camp to try out the horses.

After an hour, the quartette returned, and under solemn pledges of secrecy Stallings said, " Why, that old bay harness mare can't run fast enough to keep up with a funeral. I rode her myself, and if she's got any run in her, rowel and quirt won't bring it out. That chestnut of John's ran away from her as if she was hobbled and side-lined, while this coyote of mine threw dust in her face every jump in the road from the word ' go.' If the old man is n't bluffing and will back his mare, we 'll get back our freeze-out money with good interest. Mind you, now, we must keep it a dead secret from Flood — that we've tried the mare; he might get funny and tip the old man."

We all swore great oaths that Flood should never hear a breath of it. The conspirators and their accomplices rode into camp, and we resumed our sentinel rounds. I had some money, and figured that betting in a cinch like this would be like finding money in the road.

But The Rebel, when we were returning from guard, said, " Tom, you keep out of this race the boys are trying to jump up. I 've met a good many innocent men in my life, and there 's something about this old man that reminds me of people who have an axe to grind. Let the other fellows run on the rope if they want to, but you keep your money in your pocket. Take an older man's advice this once. And I 'm going to round up John in the morning, and try and beat a little sense into his head, for he thinks it 's a dead immortal cinch."

I had made it a rule, during our brief acquaintance, never to argue matters with my bunkie, well knowing that his years and experience in the ways of the world entitled his advice to my earnest consideration. So I kept silent, though secretly wishing he had not taken the trouble to throw cold water on my hopes, for I had built several air castles with the money which seemed within my grasp. We had been out then over four months, and I, like many of the other boys, was getting ragged, and with Ogalalla within a week's drive, a town which it took money to see properly, I thought it a burning shame to let this opportunity pass. When I awoke the next morning the camp was astir, and my first look was in the direction of the harness mare, grazing peacefully on the picket rope where she had been tethered the night before.

Breakfast over, our venerable visitor harnessed in his team, preparatory to starting. Stallings had made it a point to return to the herd for a parting word.

"Well, if you must go on ahead," said Joe to the old man, as the latter was ready to depart, "remember that you can get action on your money, if you still think that your bay mare can outrun that brown cow horse which I pointed out to you yesterday. You need n't let your poverty interfere, for we 'll run you to suit your purse, light or heavy. The herd will reach the river by the middle of the afternoon, or a little later, and you be sure and stay overnight there, — stay with us if you want to, — and we 'll make up a little race for any sum you say, from marbles and chalk to a hundred dollars. I may be as badly deceived in your mare as I think you are in my horse; but if you 're a Tennesseean, here 's your chance."

But beyond giving Stallings his word that he would see him again during the afternoon or evening, the old man would make no definite proposition, and drove away. There was a difference of opinion amongst the outfit, some asserting that we would never see him again, while the larger portion of us were at least hopeful that we would. After our guest was well out of sight, and before the wagon started, Stallings corralled the *remuda* a second time, and taking out Flood's brown and Officer's chestnut, tried the two horses for a short dash of about a hundred yards. The trial confirmed the general opinion of the outfit, for the brown outran the chestnut over four lengths, starting half a neck in the rear. A general canvass of the outfit was taken, and to my surprise there was over three hundred dollars amongst us. I had over forty dollars, but I only promised to loan mine if it was needed, while Priest refused flat-footed either to lend or bet his. I wanted to bet, and it would grieve me to the quick if there was any chance and I did n't take it — but I was young then.

Flood met us at noon about seven miles out from the Republican with the superintendent of a cattle company in Montana, and, before we started the herd after dinner, had sold our *remuda*, wagon, and mules for delivery at the nearest railroad point to the Blackfoot Agency sometime during September. This cattle company, so we afterwards learned from Flood, had headquarters at Helena, while their ranges were somewhere on the headwaters of the Missouri. But the sale of the horses seemed to us an insignificant matter, compared with the race

which was on the tapis; and when Stallings had
made the ablest talk of his life for the loan of the
brown, Flood asked the new owner, a Texan himself, if he had any objections.

"Certainly not," said he; "let the boys have a
little fun. I 'm glad to know that the *remuda* has
fast horses in it. Why did n't you tell me, Flood?
— I might have paid you extra if I had known I
was buying racehorses. Be sure and have the
race come off this evening, for I want to see it."

And he was not only good enough to give his
consent, but added a word of advice. "There 's
a deadfall down here on the river," said he, "that
robs a man going and coming. They 've got booze
to sell you that would make a pet rabbit fight a
wolf. And if you can't stand the whiskey, why,
they have skin games running to fleece you as fast
as you can get your money to the centre. Be sure,
lads, and let both their whiskey and cards alone."

While changing mounts after dinner, Stallings
caught out the brown horse and tied him behind
the wagon, while Flood and the horse buyer returned to the river in the conveyance, our foreman
having left his horse at the ford. When we reached
the Republican with the herd about two hours before
sundown, and while we were crossing and watering,
who should ride up on the Spanish mule but our
Tennessee friend. If anything, he was a trifle more
talkative and boastful than before, which was easily
accounted for, as it was evident that he was drink-

ing; and producing a large bottle which had but a
few drinks left in it, insisted on every one taking
a drink with him. He said he was encamped half a
mile down the river, and that he would race his
mare against our horse for fifty dollars; that if we
were in earnest, and would go back with him and
post our money at the tent, he would cover it. Then
Stallings in turn became crafty and diplomatic, and
after asking a number of unimportant questions
regarding conditions, returned to the joint with the
old man, taking Fox Quarternight. To the rest of
us it looked as though there was going to be no
chance to bet a dollar even. But after the herd
had been watered and we had grazed out some distance from the river, the two worthies returned.
They had posted their money, and all the conditions were agreed upon; the race was to take place
at sundown over at the saloon and gambling joint.
In reply to an earnest inquiry by Bob Blades,
the outfit were informed that we might get some
side bets with the gamblers, but the money already
posted was theirs, win or lose. This selfishness was
not looked upon very favorably, and some harsh
comments were made, but Stallings and Quarternight were immovable.

We had an early supper, and pressing in Mc-
Cann to assist The Rebel in grazing the herd until
our return, the cavalcade set out, Flood and the
horse buyer with us. My bunkie urged me to let
him keep my money, but under the pretense of

some of the outfit wanting to borrow. it, I took it with me. The race was to be catch weights, and as Rod Wheat was the lightest in our outfit, the riding fell to him. On the way over I worked Bull Durham out to one side, and after explaining the jacketing I had got from Priest, and the partial promise I had made not to bet, gave him my forty dollars to wager for me if he got a chance. Bull and I were good friends, and on the understanding that it was to be a secret, I intimated that some of the velvet would line his purse. On reaching the tent, we found about half a dozen men loitering around, among them the old man, who promptly invited us all to have a drink with him. A number of us accepted and took a chance against the vintage of this canvas roadhouse, though the warnings of the Montana horse buyer were fully justified by the quality of the goods dispensed. While taking the drink, the old man was lamenting his poverty, which kept him from betting more money, and after we had gone outside, the saloonkeeper came and said to him, in a burst of generous feeling, —

" Old sport, you 're a stranger to me, but I can see at a glance that you 're a dead game man. Now, if you need any more money, just give me a bill of sale of your mare and mule, and I 'll advance you a hundred. Of course I know nothing about the merits of the two horses, but I noticed your team as you drove up to-day, and if you can use any more money, just ask for it."

The old man jumped at the proposition in delighted surprise; the two reëntered the tent, and after killing considerable time in writing out a bill of sale, the old graybeard came out shaking a roll of bills at us. He was promptly accommodated, Bull Durham making the first bet of fifty; and as I caught his eye, I walked away, shaking hands with myself over my crafty scheme. When the old man's money was all taken, the hangers-on of the place became enthusiastic over the betting, and took every bet while there was a dollar in sight amongst our crowd, the horse buyer even making a wager. When we were out of money they offered to bet against our saddles, six-shooters, and watches. Flood warned us not to bet our saddles, but Quarternight and Stallings had already wagered theirs, and were stripping them from their horses to turn them over to the saloonkeeper as stakeholder. I managed to get a ten-dollar bet on my six-shooter, though it was worth double the money, and a similar amount on my watch. When the betting ended, every watch and six-shooter in the outfit was in the hands of the stakeholder, and had it not been for Flood our saddles would have been in the same hands.

It was to be a three hundred yard race, with an ask and answer start between the riders. Stallings and the old man stepped off the course parallel with the river, and laid a rope on the ground to mark the start and the finish. The sun had already set

and twilight was deepening when the old man signaled to his boy in the distance to bring up the
mare. Wheat was slowly walking the brown horse
over the course, when the boy came up, canter-
ing the mare, blanketed with an old government
blanket, over the imaginary track also. These preliminaries thrilled us like the tuning of a fiddle for
a dance. Stallings and the old homesteader went
out to the starting point to give the riders the
terms of the race, while the remainder of us congregated at the finish. It was getting dusk when
the blanket was stripped from the mare and the
riders began jockeying for a start. In that twilight stillness we could hear the question, " Are
you ready ? " and the answer " No," as the two
jockeys came up to the starting rope. But finally
there was an affirmative answer, and the two horses
were coming through like arrows in their flight.
My heart stood still for the time being, and when
the bay mare crossed the rope at the outcome an
easy winner, I was speechless. Such a crestfallen-
looking lot of men as we were would be hard to
conceive. We had been beaten, and not only felt
it but looked it. Flood brought us to our senses
by calling our attention to the approaching darkness, and setting off in a gallop toward the herd.
The rest of us trailed along silently after him in
threes and fours. After the herd had been bedded
and we had gone in to the wagon my spirits were
slightly lightened at the sight of the two arch con-

spirators, Stallings and Quarternight, meekly riding in bareback. I enjoyed the laughter of The Rebel and McCann at their plight; but when my bunkie noticed my six-shooter missing, and I admitted having bet it, he turned the laugh on me.

"That's right, son," he said; "don't you take anybody's advice. You're young yet, but you'll learn. And when you learn it for yourself, you'll remember it that much better."

That night when we were on guard together, I eased my conscience by making a clean breast of the whole affair to my bunkie, which resulted in his loaning me ten dollars with which to redeem my six-shooter in the morning. But the other boys, with the exception of Officer, had no banker to call on as we had, and when Quarternight and Stallings asked the foreman what they were to do for saddles, the latter suggested that one of them could use the cook's, while the other could take it bareback or ride in the wagon. But the Montana man interceded in their behalf, and Flood finally gave in and advanced them enough to redeem their saddles. Our foreman had no great amount of money with him, but McCann and the horse buyer came to the rescue for what they had, and the guns were redeemed; not that they were needed, but we would have been so lonesome without them. I had worn one so long I didn't trim well without it, but toppled forward and couldn't maintain my balance. But the most cruel exposure of the whole affair occurred

when Nat Straw, riding in ahead of his herd, overtook us one day out from Ogalalla.

" I met old 'Says I' Littlefield," said Nat, " back
at the ford of the Republican, and he tells me that
they won over five hundred dollars off this Circle
Dot outfit on a horse race. He showed me a whole
basketful of your watches. I used to meet old
'Says I' over on the Chisholm trail, and he's a
foxy old innocent. He told me that he put tar on
his harness mare's back to see if you fellows had
stolen the nag off the picket rope at night, and when
he found you had, he robbed you to a finish. He
knew you fool Texans would bet your last dollar
on such a cinch. That's one of his tricks. You
see the mare you tried wasn't the one you ran the
race against. I've seen them both, and they look
as much alike as two pint bottles. My, but you
fellows are easy fish ! "

And then Jim Flood lay down on the grass and
laughed until the tears came into his eyes, and we
understood that there were tricks in other trades
than ours.

CHAPTER XVII

FROM the head of Stinking Water to the South Platte was a waterless stretch of forty miles. But by watering the herd about the middle of one forenoon, after grazing, we could get to water again the following evening. With the exception of the meeting with Nat Straw, the drive was featureless, but the night that Nat stayed with us, he regaled us with his experiences, in which he was as lucky as ever. Where we had lost three days on the Canadian with bogged cattle, he had crossed it within fifteen minutes after reaching it. His herd was sold before reaching Dodge, so that he lost no time there, and on reaching Slaughter's bridge, he was only two days behind our herd. His cattle were then en route for delivery on the Crazy Woman in Wyoming, and, as he put it, " any herd was liable to travel faster when it had a new owner."

Flood had heard from our employer at Culbertson, learning that he would not meet us at Ogalalla, as his last herd was due in Dodge about that time. My brother Bob's herd had crossed the Arkansaw a week behind us, and was then possibly a hundred and fifty miles in our rear.

We all regretted not being able to see old man Don, for he believed that nothing was too good for his men, and we all remembered the good time he had shown us in Dodge. The smoke of passing trains hung for hours in signal clouds in our front, during the afternoon of the second day's dry drive, but we finally scaled the last divide, and there, below us in the valley of the South Platte, nestled Ogalalla, the Gomorrah of the cattle trail. From amongst its half hundred buildings, no church spire pointed upward, but instead three fourths of its business houses were dance halls, gambling houses, and saloons. We all knew the town by reputation, while the larger part of our outfit had been in it before. It was there that Joel Collins and his outfit rendezvoused when they robbed the Union Pacific train in October, '77. Collins had driven a herd of cattle for his father and brother, and after selling them in the Black Hills, gambled away the proceeds. Some five or six of his outfit returned to Ogalalla with him, and being moneyless, concluded to recoup their losses at the expense of the railway company. Going eighteen miles up the river to Big Springs, seven of them robbed the express and passengers, the former yielding sixty thousand dollars in gold. The next morning they were in Ogalalla, paying debts, and getting their horses shod. In Collins's outfit was Sam Bass, and under his leadership, until he met his death the following spring at the hands of Texas Rangers, the course of the outfit southward was marked by a series of daring bank and train robberies.

We reached the river late that evening, and after watering, grazed until dark and camped for the night. But it was not to be a night of rest and sleep, for the lights were twinkling across the river in town; and cook, horse wrangler, and all, with the exception of the first guard, rode across the river after the herd had been bedded. Flood had quit us while we were watering the herd and gone in ahead to get a draft cashed, for he was as moneyless as the rest of us. But his letter of credit was good anywhere on the trail where money was to be had, and on reaching town, he took us into a general outfitting store and paid us twenty-five dollars apiece. After warning us to be on hand at the wagon to stand our watches, he left us, and we scattered like lost sheep. Officer and I paid our loans to The Rebel, and the three of us wandered around for several hours in company with Nat Straw. When we were in Dodge, my bunkie had shown no inclination to gamble, but now he was the first one to suggest that we make up a " cow," and let him try his luck at monte. Straw and Officer were both willing, and though in rags, I willingly consented and contributed my five to the general fund.

Every gambling house ran from two to three monte layouts, as it was a favorite game of cowmen, especially when they were from the far southern country. Priest soon found a game to his liking, and after watching his play through several deals, Officer and I left him with the understanding that he would start for camp promptly at midnight. There was much to be seen, though it was a small place, for the ends of the earth's iniquity had gathered in Ogalalla. We wandered through the various gambling houses, drinking moderately, meeting an occasional acquaintance from Texas, and in the course of our rounds landed in the Dew-Drop-In dance hall. Here might be seen the frailty of women in every grade and condition. From girls in their teens, launching out on a life of shame, to the adventuress who had once had youth and beauty in her favor, but was now discarded and ready for the final dose of opium and the coroner's verdict, — all were there in tinsel and paint, practicing a careless exposure of their charms. In a town which has no night, the hours pass rapidly; and before we were aware, midnight was upon us. Returning to the gambling house where we had left Priest, we found him over a hundred dollars winner, and, calling his attention to the hour, persuaded him to cash in and join us. We felt positively rich, as he counted out to each partner his share of the winnings! Straw was missing to receive his, but we knew he could be found on the morrow, and after a round of drinks, we forded the river. As we rode along, my bunkie said, —

"I'm superstitious, and I can't help it. But

I 've felt for a day or so that I was in luck, and I
wanted you lads in with me if my warning was
true. I never was afraid to go into battle but
once, and just as we were ordered into action, a
shell killed my horse under me and I was left behind. I 've had lots of such warnings, good and
bad, and I'm influenced by them. If we get off
to-morrow, and I'm in the mood, I'll go back
there and make some monte bank look sick."

We reached the wagon in good time to be called
on our guard, and after it was over secured a few
hours' sleep before the foreman aroused us in the
morning. With herds above and below us, we
would either have to graze contrary to our course
or cross the river. The South Platte was a wide,
sandy river with numerous channels, and as easily
crossed as an alkali flat of equal width, so far as
water was concerned. The sun was not an hour
high when we crossed, passing within two hundred
yards of the business section of the town, which
lay under a hill. The valley on the north side of
the river, and beyond the railroad, was not over
half a mile wide, and as we angled across it, the
town seemed as dead as those that slept in the
graveyard on the first hill beside the trail.

Finding good grass about a mile farther on, we
threw the herd off the trail, and leaving orders to
graze until noon, the foreman with the first and
second guard returned to town. It was only about
ten miles over to the North Platte, where water

was certain; and in the hope that we would be permitted to revisit the village during the afternoon, we who were on guard threw riders in the lead of the grazing cattle, in order not to be too far away should permission be granted us. That was a long morning for us of the third and fourth guards, with nothing to do but let the cattle feed, while easy money itched in our pockets. Behind us lay Ogalalla — and our craft did dearly love to break the monotony of our work by getting into town. But by the middle of the forenoon, the wagon and saddle horses overtook us, and ordering McCann into camp a scant mile in our lead, we allowed the cattle to lie down, they having grazed to contentment. Leaving two men on guard, the remainder of us rode in to the wagon, and lightened with an hour's sleep in its shade the time which hung heavy on our hands. We were aroused by our horse wrangler, who had sighted a cavalcade down the trail, which, from the color of their horses, he knew to be our outfit returning. As they came nearer and their numbers could be made out, it was evident that our foreman was not with them, and our hopes rose. On coming up, they informed us that we were to have a half holiday, while they would take the herd over to the North River during the afternoon. Then emergency orders rang out to Honeyman and McCann, and as soon as a change of mounts could be secured, our dinners bolted, and the herders relieved, we were ready to go. Two of the six who returned had shed their rags and swaggered about in new, cheap suits; the rest, although they had money, simply had not had the time to buy clothes in a place with so many attractions.

When the herders came in deft hands transferred their saddles to waiting mounts while they swallowed a hasty dinner, and we set out for Ogalalla, happy as city urchins in an orchard. We were less than five miles from the burg, and struck a free gait in riding in, where we found several hundred of our craft holding high jinks. A number of herds had paid off their outfits and were sending them home, while from the herds for sale, holding along the river, every man not on day herd was paying his respects to the town. We had not been there five minutes when a horse race was run through the main street, Nat Straw and Jim Flood acting as judges on the outcome. The officers of Ogalalla were a different crowd from what we had encountered at Dodge, and everything went. The place suited us. Straw had entirely forgotten our "cow" of the night before, and when The Rebel handed him his share of the winnings, he tucked it away in the watch pocket of his trousers without counting. But he had arranged a fiddling match between a darky cook of one of the returning outfits and a locoed white man, a mendicant of the place, and invited us to be present. Straw knew the foreman of the outfit to which the darky belonged, and the two had fixed it up to pit the two in

a contest, under the pretense that a large wager had
been made on which was the better fiddler. The
contest was to take place at once in the corral of
the Lone Star livery stable, and promised to be
humorous if nothing more. So after the race was
over, the next number on the programme was the
fiddling match, and we followed the crowd. The
Rebel had given us the slip during the race, though
none of us cared, as we knew he was hungering for
a monte game. It was a motley crowd which had
gathered in the corral, and all seemed to know of
the farce to be enacted, though the Texas outfit to
which the darky belonged were flashing their money
on their dusky cook, " as the best fiddler that ever
crossed Red River with a cow herd."

"Oh, I don't know that your man is such an
Ole Bull as all that," said Nat Straw. "I just got
a hundred posted which says he can't even play a
decent second to my man. And if we can get a
competent set of judges to decide the contest, I'll
wager a little more on the white against the black,
though I know your man is a cracker-jack."

A canvass of the crowd was made for judges, but
as nearly every one claimed to be interested in the
result, having made wagers, or was incompetent to
sit in judgment on a musical contest, there was
some little delay. Finally, Joe Stallings went to
Nat Straw and told him that I was a fiddler, whereupon he instantly appointed me as judge, and the
other side selected a redheaded fellow belonging to

one of Dillard Fant's herds.   Between the two of
us we selected as the third judge a bartender whom
I had met the night before.   The conditions gov-
erning the contest were given us, and two chuck
wagons were drawn up alongside each other, in one
of which were seated the contestants and in the
other the judges.   The gravity of the crowd was
only broken as some enthusiast cheered his favorite or defiantly offered to wager on the man of his
choice.   Numerous sham bets were being made,
when the redheaded judge arose and announced
the conditions, and urged the crowd to remain quiet,
that the contestants might have equal justice.   Each
fiddler selected his own piece.   The first number
was a waltz, on the conclusion of which partisan-
ship ran high, each faction cheering its favorite
to the echo.   The second number was a jig, and as
the darky drew his bow several times across the
strings tentatively, his foreman, who stood six
inches taller than any man in a crowd of tall men,
tapped himself on the breast with one forefinger,
and with the other pointed at his dusky champion,
saying, "Keep your eye on me, Price.   We're
going home together, remember.   You black rascal,
you can make a mocking bird ashamed of itself if
you try.   You know I've swore by you through
thick and thin ; now win this money.   Pay no attention to any one else.   Keep your eye on me."

Straw, not to be outdone in encouragement,
cheered his man with promises of reward, and his

faction of supporters raised such a din that Fant's man arose, and demanded quiet so the contest could proceed. Though boisterous, the crowd was good-tempered, and after the second number was disposed of, the final test was announced, which was to be in sacred music. On this announcement, the tall foreman waded through the crowd, and drawing the darky to him, whispered something in his ear, and then fell back to his former position. The dusky artist's countenance brightened, and with a few preliminaries he struck into "The Arkansaw Traveler," throwing so many contortions into its execution that it seemed as if life and liberty depended on his exertions. The usual applause greeted him on its conclusion, when Nat Straw climbed up on the wagon wheel, and likewise whispered something to his champion. The little, old, weazened mendicant took his cue, and cut into "The Irish Washerwoman" with a great flourish, and in the refrain chanted an unintelligible gibberish like the yelping of a coyote, which the audience so cheered that he repeated it several times. The crowd now gathered around the wagons and clamored for the decision, and after consulting among ourselves some little time, and knowing that a neutral or indefinite verdict was desired, we delegated the bartender to announce our conclusions. Taking off his hat, he arose, and after requesting quietness, pretended to read our decision.

"Gentlemen," he began, "your judges feel a

delicacy in passing on the merits of such distinguished artists, but in the first number the decision is unanimously in favor of the darky, while the second is clearly in favor of the white contestant. In regard to the last test, your judges cannot reach any decision, as the selections rendered fail to qualify under the head of " —

But two shots rang out in rapid succession across the street, and the crowd, including the judges and fiddlers, rushed away to witness the new excitement. The shooting had occurred in a restaurant, and quite a mob gathered around the door, when the sheriff emerged from the building.

" It 's nothing," said he ; " just a couple of punchers, who had been drinking a little, were eating a snack, and one of them asked for a second dish of prunes, when the waiter got gay and told him that he could n't have them, — 'that he was full of prunes now.' So the lad took a couple of shots at him, just to learn him to be more courteous to strangers. There was no harm done, as the puncher was too unsteady."

As the crowd dispersed from the restaurant, I returned to the livery stable, where Straw and several of our outfit were explaining to the old mendicant that he had simply outplayed his opponent, and it was too bad that they were not better posted in sacred music. Under Straw's leadership, a purse was being made up amongst them, and the old man's eyes brightened as he received several crisp bills and a handful of silver. Straw was urging the old fiddler to post himself in regard to sacred music, and he would get up another match for the next day, when Rod Wheat came up and breathlessly informed Officer and myself that The Rebel wanted us over at the Black Elephant gambling hall. As we turned to accompany him, we eagerly inquired if there were any trouble. Wheat informed us there was not, but that Priest was playing in one of the biggest streaks of luck that ever happened. " Why, the old man is just wallowing in velvet," said Rod, as we hurried along, " and the dealer has lowered the limit from a hundred to fifty, for old Paul is playing them as high as a cat's back. He is n't drinking a drop, and is as cool as a cucumber. I don't know what he wants with you fellows, but he begged me to hunt you up and send you to him."

The Black Elephant was about a block from the livery, and as we entered, a large crowd of bystanders were watching the playing around one of the three monte games which were running. Elbowing our way through the crowd, we reached my bunkie, whom Officer slapped on the back and inquired what he wanted.

" Why, I want you and Quirk to bet a little money for me," he replied. " My luck is with me to-day, and when I try to crowd it, this layout gets foxy and pinches the limit down to fifty. Here, take this money and cover both those other games.

Call out as they fall the layouts, and I 'll pick the card to bet the money on. And bet her carelessly, boys, for she 's velvet."

As he spoke he gave Officer and myself each a handful of uncounted money, and we proceeded to carry out his instructions. I knew the game perfectly, having spent several years' earnings on my tuition, and was past master in the technical Spanish terms of the game, while Officer was equally informed. John took the table to the right, while I took the one on the left, and waiting for a new deal, called the cards as they fell. I inquired the limit of the dealer, and was politely informed that it was fifty to-day. At first our director ordered a number of small bets made, as though feeling his way, for cards will turn; but as he found the old luck was still with him, he gradually increased them to the limit. After the first few deals, I caught on to his favorite cards, which were the queen and seven, and on these we bet the limit. Alces and a "face against an ace" were also favorite bets of The Rebel's, but for a smaller sum. During the first hour of my playing — to show the luck of cards — the queen won five consecutive times, once against a favorite at the conclusion of a deal. My judgment was to take up this bet, but Priest ordered otherwise, for it was one of his principles never to doubt a card as long as it won for you.

The play had run along some time, and as I was absorbed with watching, some one behind me laid a friendly hand on my shoulder. Having every card in the layout covered with a bet at the time, and supposing it to be some of our outfit, I never looked around, when there came a slap on my back which nearly loosened my teeth. Turning to see who was making so free with me when I was absorbed, my eye fell on my brother Zack, but I had not time even to shake hands with him, for two cards won in succession and the dealer was paying me, while the queen and seven were covered to the limit and were yet to be drawn for. When the deal ended and while the dealer was shuffling, I managed to get a few words with my brother, and learned that he had come through with a herd belonging to one-armed Jim Reed, and that they were holding about ten miles up the river. He had met Flood, who told him that I was in town; but as he was working on first guard with their herd, it was high time he was riding. The dealer was waiting for me to cut the cards, and stopping only to wring Zack's hand in farewell, I turned again to the monte layout.

Officer was not so fortunate as I was, partly by reason of delays, the dealer in his game changing decks on almost every deal, and under Priest's orders, we counted the cards with every change of the deck. A gambler would rather burn money than lose to a citizen, and every hoodoo which the superstition of the craft could invoke to turn the run of the cards was used to check us. Several hours passed and the lamps were lighted, but we constantly added to the good — to the discomfiture of the owners of the games. Dealers changed, but our vigilance never relaxed for a moment. Suddenly an altercation sprang up between Officer and the dealer of his game. The seven had proved the most lucky card to John, which fact was as plain to dealer as to player, but the dealer, by slipping one seven out of the pack after it had been counted, which was possible in the hands of an adept in spite of all vigilance, threw the percentage against the favorite card and in favor of the bank. Officer had suspected something wrong, for the seven had been loser during several deals, when with a seven-king layout, and two cards of each class yet in the pack, the dealer drew down until there were less than a dozen cards left, when the king came, which lost a fifty dollar bet on the seven. Officer laid his hand on the money, and, as was his privilege, said to the dealer, " Let me look over the remainder of those cards. If there's two sevens there, you have won. If there isn't, don't offer to touch this bet."

But the gambler declined the request, and Officer repeated his demand, laying a blue-barreled six-shooter across the bet with the remark, " Well, if you expect to rake in this bet you have my terms."

Evidently the demand would not have stood the test, for the dealer bunched the deck among the passed cards, and Officer quietly raked in the money. " When I want a skin game," said John, as he arose, " I 'll come back and see you. You saw me take this money, did you? Well, if you 've got anything to say, now 's your time to spit it out."

But his calling had made the gambler discreet, and he deigned no reply to the lank Texan, who, chafing under the attempt to cheat him, slowly returned his six-shooter to its holster. Although holding my own in my game, I was anxious to have it come to a close, but neither of us cared to suggest it to The Rebel; it was his money. But Officer passed outside the house shortly afterward, and soon returned with Jim Flood and Nat Straw.

As our foreman approached the table at which Priest was playing, he laid his hand on The Rebel's shoulder and said, " Come on, Paul, we 're all ready to go to camp. Where 's Quirk?"

Priest looked up in innocent amazement, — as though he had been awakened out of a deep sleep, for, in the absorption of the game, he had taken no note of the passing hours and did not know that the lamps were burning. My bunkie obeyed as promptly as though the orders had been given by Don Lovell in person, and, delighted with the turn of affairs, I withdrew with him. Once in the street, Nat Straw threw an arm around The Rebel's neck and said to him, " My dear sir, the secret of successful gambling is to quit when you 're winner, and before luck turns. You may think this is a low down trick, but we 're your friends, and when we heard that you were a big winner, we were deter-

mined to get you out of there if we had to rope
and drag you out. How much are you winner?"

Before the question could be correctly answered,
we sat down on the sidewalk and the three of us
disgorged our winnings, so that Flood and Straw
could count. Priest was the largest winner, Officer
the smallest, while I never will know the amount
of mine, as I had no idea what I started with. But
the tellers' report showed over fourteen hundred
dollars among the three of us. My bunkie consented to allow Flood to keep it for him, and the
latter attempted to hurrah us off to camp, but John
Officer protested.

"Hold on a minute, Jim," said Officer. "We're
in rags; we need some clothes. We've been in
town long enough, and we've got the price, but it's
been such a busy afternoon with us that we simply
have n't had the time."

Straw took our part, and Flood giving in, we
entered a general outfitting store, from which we
emerged within a quarter of an hour, wearing
cheap new suits, the color of which we never knew
until the next day. Then bidding Straw a hearty
farewell, we rode for the North Platte, on which
the herd would encamp. As we scaled the bluffs,
we halted for our last glimpse of the lights of
Ogalalla, and The Rebel remarked, "Boys, I've
traveled some in my life, but that little hole back
there could give Natchez-under-the-hill cards and
spades, and then outhold her as a tough town."

CHAPTER XVIII

It was now July. We had taken on new supplies at Ogalalla, and a week afterwards the herd was snailing along the North Platte on its way to the land of the Blackfeet. It was always hard to get a herd past a supply point. We had the same trouble when we passed Dodge. Our long hours in the saddle, coupled with the monotony of our work, made these supply points of such interest to us that they were like oases in desert lands to devotees on pilgrimage to some consecrated shrine. We could have spent a week in Ogalalla and enjoyed our visit every blessed moment of the time. But now, a week later, most of the headaches had disappeared and we had settled down to our daily work.

At Horse Creek, the last stream of water before entering Wyoming, a lad who cut the trail at that point for some cattle companies, after trimming us up, rode along for half a day through their range, and told us of an accident which happened about a week before. The horse of some peeler, working with one of Shanghai Pierce's herds, acted up one morning, and fell backward with him so that his gun was accidentally discharged.   The outfit lay over a day and gave him as decent a burial as they could. We would find the new-made grave ahead on Squaw Creek, beyond the crossing, to the right hand side in a clump of cottonwoods.   The next day, while watering the herd at this creek, we all rode over and looked at the grave.   The outfit had fixed things up quite nicely.   They had built a square pen of rough cottonwood logs around the grave, and had marked the head and foot with a big flat stone, edged up, heaping up quite a mound of stones to keep the animals away.   In a tree his name was cut — sounded natural, too, though none of us knew him, as Pierce always drove from the east coast country.   There was nothing different about this grave from the hundreds of others which made landmarks on the Old Western Trail, except it was the latest.

That night around the camp-fire some of the boys were moved to tell their experiences.   This accident might happen to any of us, and it seemed rather short notice to a man enjoying life, even though his calling was rough.

"As for myself," said Rod Wheat, " I 'm not going to fret.   You can't avoid it when it comes, and every now and then you miss it by a hair.   I had an uncle who served four years in the Confederate army, went through thirty engagements, was wounded half a dozen times, and came home well and sound.   Within a month after his return, a plough handle kicked him in the side and we buried him within a week."

" Oh, well," said Fox, commenting on the sudden call of the man whose grave we had seen, " it won't make much difference to this fellow back here when the horn toots and the graves give up their dead. He might just as well start from there as anywhere. I don't envy him none, though ; but if I had any pity to offer now, it would be for a mother or sister who might wish that he slept nearer home."

This last remark carried our minds far away from their present surroundings to other graves which were not on the trail. There was a long silence. We lay around the camp-fire and gazed into its depths, while its flickering light threw our shadows out beyond the circle. Our reverie was finally broken by Ash Borrowstone, who was by all odds the most impressionable and emotional one in the outfit, a man who always argued the moral side of every question, yet could not be credited with possessing an iota of moral stamina. Gloomy as we were, he added to our depression by relating a pathetic incident which occurred at a child's funeral, when Flood reproved him, saying, —

" Well, neither that one you mention, nor this one of Pierce's man is any of our funeral. We 're on the trail with Lovell's cattle. You should keep nearer the earth."

There was a long silence after this reproof of the foreman. It was evident there was a gloom settling

over the outfit. Our thoughts were ranging wide.
At last Rod Wheat spoke up and said that in order
to get the benefit of all the variations, the blues
were not a bad thing to have.

But the depression of our spirits was not so
easily dismissed. In order to avoid listening to the
gloomy tales that were being narrated around the
camp-fire, a number of us got up and went out as
if to look up the night horses on picket. The
Rebel and I pulled our picket pins and changed
our horses to fresh grazing, and after lying down
among the horses, out of hearing of the camp, for
over an hour, returned to the wagon expecting to
retire. A number of the boys were making down
their beds, as it was already late; but on our
arrival at the fire one of the boys had just concluded a story, as gloomy as the others which had
preceded it.

"These stories you are all telling to-night," said
Flood, "remind me of what Lige Link said to
the book agent when he was shearing sheep. 'I
reckon,' said Lige, 'that book of yours has a heap
sight more poetry in it than there is in shearing
sheep.' I wish I had gone on guard to-night, so I
could have missed these stories."

At this juncture the first guard rode in, having
been relieved, and John Officer, who had exchanged
places on guard that night with Moss Strayhorn,
remarked that the cattle were uneasy.

"This outfit," said he, "didn't half water the

herd to-day. One third of them has n't bedded down yet, and they don't act as if they aim to, either. There 's no excuse for it in a well-watered country like this. I 'll leave the saddle on my horse, anyhow."

"Now that 's the result," said our foreman, " of the hour we spent around that grave to-day, when we ought to have been tending to our job. This outfit," he continued, when Officer returned from picketing his horse, " have been trying to hold funeral services over that Pierce man's grave back there. You 'd think so, anyway, from the tales they 've been telling. I hope you won't get the sniffles and tell any."

" This letting yourself get gloomy," said Officer, " reminds me of a time we once had at the ' J. H.' camp in the Cherokee Strip. It was near Christmas, and the work was all done up. The boys had blowed in their summer's wages and were feeling glum all over. One or two of the boys were lamenting that they had n't gone home to see the old folks. This gloomy feeling kept spreading until they actually would n't speak to each other. One of them would go out and sit on the wood pile for hours, all by himself, and make a new set of good resolutions. Another would go out and sit on the ground, on the sunny side of the corrals, and dig holes in the frozen earth with his knife. They would n't come to meals when the cook called them.

" Now, Miller, the foreman, did n't have any

sympathy for them; in fact he delighted to see them in that condition. He had n't any use for a man who was n't dead tough under any condition. I 've known him to camp his outfit on alkali water, so the men would get out in the morning, and every rascal beg leave to ride on the outside circle on the morning roundup.

" Well, three days before Christmas, just when things were looking gloomiest, there drifted up from the Cheyenne country one of the old timers. None of them had seen him in four years, though he had worked on that range before, and with the exception of myself, they all knew him. He was riding the chuckline all right, but Miller gave him a welcome, as he was the real thing. He had been working out in the Pan-handle country, New Mexico, and the devil knows where, since he had left that range. He was meaty with news and scarey stories. The boys would sit around and listen to him yarn, and now and then a smile would come on their faces. Miller was delighted with his guest. He had shown no signs of letting up at eleven o'clock the first night, when he happened to mention where he was the Christmas before.

" ' There was a little woman at the ranch,' said he, ' wife of the owner, and I was helping her get up dinner, as we had quite a number of folks at the ranch. She asked me to make the bear sign — doughnuts, she called them — and I did, though she had to show me how some little. Well, fellows, you ought to have seen them — just sweet enough, browned to a turn, and enough to last a week. All the folks at dinner that day praised them. Since then, I've had a chance to try my hand several times, and you may not tumble to the diversity of all my accomplishments, but I'm an artist on bear sign.'

"Miller arose, took him by the hand, and said, 'That's straight, now, is it?'

"'That's straight. Making bear sign is my long suit.'

"'Mouse,' said Miller to one of the boys, 'go out and bring in his saddle from the stable and put it under my bed. Throw his horse in the big pasture in the morning. He stays here until spring; and the first spear of green grass I see, his name goes on the pay roll. This outfit is shy on men who can make bear sign. Now, I was thinking that you could spread down your blankets on the hearth, but you can sleep with me to-night. You go to work on this specialty of yours right after breakfast in the morning, and show us what you can do in that line.'

"They talked quite a while longer, and then turned in for the night. The next morning after breakfast was over, he got the needed articles together and went to work. But there was a surprise in store for him. There was nearly a dozen men lying around, all able eaters. By ten o'clock he began to turn them out as he said he could. When

the regular cook had to have the stove to get dinner, the taste which we had had made us ravenous
for more.   Dinner over, he went at them again in
earnest.   A boy riding towards the railroad with
an important letter dropped in, and as he claimed
he could only stop for a moment, we stood aside
until he had had a taste, though he filled himself
like a poisoned pup.   After eating a solid hour,
he filled his pockets and rode away.   One of our
regular men called after him, 'Don't tell anybody
what we got.'

"We did n't get any supper that night.   Not a
man could have eaten a bite.   Miller made him
knock off along in the shank of the evening, as he
had done enough for any one day.   The next morning after breakfast he fell to at the bear sign once
more.   Miller rolled a barrel of flour into the
kitchen from the storehouse, and told him to fly
at them.   'About how many do you think you 'll
want?' asked our bear sign man.

"'That big tub full won't be any too many,'
answered Miller.   'Some of these fellows have n't
had any of this kind of truck since they were little
boys.   If this gets out, I look for men from other
camps.'

"The fellow fell to his work like a thorough-
bred, which he surely was.   About ten o'clock two
men rode up from a camp to the north, which the
boy had passed the day before with the letter.
They never went near the dug-out, but straight

to the kitchen. That movement showed that they were on to the racket. An hour later old Tom Cave rode in, his horse all in a lather, all the way from Garretson's camp, twenty-five miles to the east. The old sinner said that he had been on the frontier some little time, and that there were the best bear sign he had tasted in forty years. He refused to take a stool and sit down like civilized folks, but stood up by the tub and picked out the ones which were a pale brown.

" After dinner our man threw off his overshirt, unbuttoned his red undershirt and turned it in until you could see the hair on his breast. Rolling up his sleeves, he flew at his job once more. He was getting his work reduced to a science by this time. He rolled his dough, cut his dough, and turned out the fine brown bear sign to the satisfaction of all.

" His capacity, however, was limited. About two o'clock Doc Langford and two of his peelers were seen riding up. When he came into the kitchen, Doc swore by all that was good and holy that he had n't heard that our artist had come back to that country. But any one that was noticing could see him edge around to the tub. It was easy to see that he was lying. This luck of ours was circulating faster than a secret amongst women. Our man, though, stood at his post like the boy on the burning deck. When night came on, he had n't covered the bottom of the tub. When he knocked

off, Doc Langford and his men gobbled up what
was left. We gave them a mean look as they rode
off, but they came back the next day, five strong.
Our regular men around camp did n't like it, the
way things were going. They tried to act polite
to " —

"Calling bear sign doughnuts," interrupted
Quince Forrest, "reminds me what" —

"Will you kindly hobble your lip," said Officer;
"I have the floor at present. As I was saying,
they tried to act polite to company that way, but
we had n't got a smell the second day. Our man
showed no signs of fatigue, and told several good
stories that night. He was tough. The next day
was Christmas, but he had no respect for a holiday, and made up a large batch of dough before
breakfast. It was a good thing he did, for early
that morning 'Original' John Smith and four of
his peelers rode in from the west, their horses all
covered with frost. They must have started at
daybreak — it was a good twenty-two mile ride.
They wanted us to believe that they had simply
come over to spend Christmas with us. Company
that way, you can't say anything. But the easy
manner in which they gravitated around that tub
— not even waiting to be invited — told a different
tale. They were not nearly satisfied by noon.

"Then who should come drifting in as we were
sitting down to dinner, but Billy Dunlap and Jim
Hale from Quinlin's camp, thirty miles south on

the Cimarron. Dunlap always holed up like a
bear in the winter, and several of the boys spilled
their coffee at sight of him. He put up a thin excuse just like the rest. Any one could see through
it. But there it was again — he was company.
Lots of us had eaten at his camp and complained
of his chuck; therefore, we were nice to him.
Miller called our man out behind the kitchen and
told him to knock off if he wanted to. But he
would n't do it. He was clean strain — I 'm not
talking. Dunlap ate hardly any dinner, we noticed,
and the very first batch of bear sign turned out, he
loads up a tin plate and goes out and sits behind
the storehouse in the sun, all alone in his glory.
He satisfied himself out of the tub after that.

"He and Hale stayed all night, and Dunlap
kept every one awake with the nightmare. Yes,
kept fighting the demons all night. The next
morning Miller told him that he was surprised
that an old gray-haired man like him did n't know
when he had enough, but must gorge himself like
some silly kid. Miller told him that he was welcome to stay a week if he wanted to, but he would
have to sleep in the stable. It was cruel to the
horses, but the men were entitled to a little sleep,
at least in the winter. Miller tempered his remarks with all kindness, and Dunlap acted as if he
was sorry, and as good as admitted that his years
were telling on him. That day our man filled his
tub. He was simply an artist on bear sign."

" Calling bear sign doughnuts," cut in Quince
Forrest again, as soon as he saw an opening, " reminds me what the little boy said who went " —

But there came a rumbling of many hoofs from
the bed ground. " There's hell for you," said half
a dozen men in a chorus, and every man in camp
ran for his horse but the cook, and he climbed into
the wagon. The roar of the running cattle was
like approaching thunder, but the flash from the
six-shooters of the men on guard indicated they
were quartering by camp, heading out towards the
hills. Horses became so excited they were difficult to bridle. There was plenty of earnest and
sincere swearing done that night. All the fine
sentiment and melancholy of the hour previous
vanished in a moment, as the men threw themselves into their saddles, riding deep, for it was
uncertain footing to horses.

Within two minutes from the time the herd left
the bed ground, fourteen of us rode on their left
point and across their front, firing our six-shooters
in their faces. By the time the herd had covered a
scant mile, we had thrown them into a mill. They
had run so compactly that there were no stragglers,
so we loosened out and gave them room; but it
was a long time before they relaxed any, but continued going round and round like a water wheel
or an endless chain. The foreman ordered three
men on the heaviest horses to split them. The men
rode out a short distance to get the required mo-

mentum, wheeled their horses, and, wedge-shaped,
struck this sea of cattle and entered, but it instantly closed in their wake as though it had been
water. For an hour they rode through the herd,
back and forth, now from this quarter, now from
that, and finally the mill was broken. After midnight, as luck would have it, heavy dark clouds
banked in the northwest, and lightning flashed,
and before a single animal had lain down, a driz-
zling rain set in. That settled it; it was an all-
night job now. We drifted about hither and yon.
Horses, men, and cattle turned their backs to the
wind and rain and waited for morning. We were
so familiar with the signs of coming day that we
turned them loose half an hour before dawn, leaving herders, and rode for camp.

As we groped our way in that dark hour before
dawn, hungry, drenched, and bedraggled, there
was nothing gleeful about us, while Bob Blades
expressed his disgust over our occupation. "If
ever I get home again," said he, and the tones of
his voice were an able second to his remarks, "you
all can go up the trail that want to, but here's one
chicken that won't. There isn't a cowman in
Texas who has money enough to hire me again."

"Ah, hell, now," said Bull, "you ought n't to let
a little rain ruffle your feathers that way. Cheer
up, sonny; you may be rich some day yet and walk
on brussels and velvet."

CHAPTER XIX

FORTY ISLANDS FORD

AFTER securing a count on the herd that morning and finding nothing short, we trailed out up the North Platte River. It was an easy country in which to handle a herd; the trail in places would run back from the river as far as ten miles, and again follow close in near the river bottoms. There was an abundance of small creeks putting into this fork of the Platte from the south, which afforded water for the herd and good camp grounds at night. Only twice after leaving Ogalalla had we been compelled to go to the river for water for the herd, and with the exception of thunderstorms and occasional summer rains, the weather had been all one could wish. For the past week as we trailed up the North Platte, some one of us visited the river daily to note its stage of water, for we were due to cross at Forty Islands, about twelve miles south of old Fort Laramie. The North Platte was very similar to the South Canadian, — a wide sandy stream without banks; and our experience with the latter was fresh in our memories. The stage of water had not been favorable, for this river also had its source in the mountains, and as now mid-

summer was upon us, the season of heavy rainfall
in the mountains, augmented by the melting snows,
the prospect of finding a fordable stage of water at
Forty Islands was not very encouraging.

We reached this well-known crossing late in the
afternoon the third day after leaving the Wyoming
line, and found one of the Prairie Cattle Company's herds waterbound. This herd had been
wintered on one of that company's ranges on the
Arkansaw River in southern Colorado, and their
destination was in the Bad Lands near the mouth
of the Yellowstone, where the same company had
a northern range. Flood knew the foreman, Wade
Scholar, who reported having been waterbound
over a week already with no prospect of crossing
without swimming. Scholar knew the country
thoroughly, and had decided to lie over until the
river was fordable at Forty Islands, as it was much
the easiest crossing on the North Platte, though
there was a wagon ferry at Fort Laramie. He
returned with Flood to our camp, and the two
talked over the prospect of swimming it on the
morrow.

"Let's send the wagons up to the ferry in the
morning," said Flood, "and swim the herds. If
you wait until this river falls, you are liable to
have an experience like we had on the South Canadian, — lost three days and bogged over a hundred
cattle. When one of these sandy rivers has had
a big freshet, look out for quicksands; but you

know that as well as I do. Why, we've swum over half a dozen rivers already, and I'd much rather swim this one than attempt to ford it just after it has fallen. We can double our outfits and be safely across before noon. I've got nearly a thousand miles yet to make, and have just *got* to get over. Think it over to-night, and have your wagon ready to start with ours."

Scholar rode away without giving our foreman any definite answer as to what he would do, though earlier in the evening he had offered to throw his herd well out of the way at the ford, and lend us any assistance at his command. But when it came to the question of crossing his own herd, he seemed to dread the idea of swimming the river, and could not be induced to say what he would do, but said that we were welcome to the lead. The next morning Flood and I accompanied our wagon up to his camp, when it was plainly evident that he did not intend to send his wagon with ours, and McCann started on alone, though our foreman renewed his efforts to convince Scholar of the feasibility of swimming the herds. Their cattle were thrown well away from the ford, and Scholar assured us that his outfit would be on hand whenever we were ready to cross, and even invited all hands of us to come to his wagon for dinner. When returning to our herd, Flood told me that Scholar was considered one of the best foremen on the trail, and why he should refuse to swim his cattle was unexplainable. He must have time to burn, but that did n't seem reasonable, for the earlier through cattle were turned loose on their winter range the better. We were in no hurry to cross, as our wagon would be gone all day, and it was nearly high noon when we trailed up to the ford.

With the addition to our force of Scholar and nine or ten of his men, we had an abundance of help, and put the cattle into the water opposite two islands, our saddle horses in the lead as usual. There was no swimming water between the south shore and the first island, though it wet our saddle skirts for some considerable distance, this channel being nearly two hundred yards wide. Most of our outfit took the water, while Scholar's men fed our herd in from the south bank, a number of their men coming over as far as the first island. The second island lay down the stream some little distance; and as we pushed the cattle off the first one we were in swimming water in no time, but the saddle horses were already landing on the second island, and our lead cattle struck out, and, breasting the water, swam as proudly as swans. The middle channel was nearly a hundred yards wide, the greater portion of which was swimming, though the last channel was much wider. But our saddle horses had already taken it, and when within fifty yards of the farther shore, struck solid footing. With our own outfit we crowded the leaders to keep the chain of cattle unbroken, and before

Honeyman could hustle his horses out of the river,
our lead cattle had caught a foothold, were heading
up stream and edging out for the farther shore.

I had one of the best swimming horses in our
outfit, and Flood put me in the lead on the point.
As my horse came out on the farther bank, I am
certain I never have seen a herd of cattle, before
or since, which presented a prettier sight when
swimming than ours did that day.   There was fully
four hundred yards of water on the angle by which
we crossed, nearly half of which was swimming, but
with the two islands which gave them a breath-
ing spell, our Circle Dots were taking the water
as steadily as a herd leaving their bed ground.
Scholar and his men were feeding them in, while
half a dozen of our men on each island were keeping them moving.   Honeyman and I pointed them
out of the river; and as they grazed away from
the shore, they spread out fan-like, many of them
kicking up their heels after they left the water
in healthy enjoyment of their bath.   Long before
they were half over, the usual shouting had ceased,
and we simply sat in our saddles and waited for
the long train of cattle to come up and cross.
Within less than half an hour from the time our
saddle horses entered the North Platte, the tail
end of our herd had landed safely on the farther
bank.

As Honeyman and I were the only ones of our
outfit on the north side of the river during the pas-

SWIMMING THE PLATTE

sage, Flood called to us from across the last channel to graze the herd until relieved, when the remainder of the outfit returned to the south side to
recover their discarded effects and to get dinner
with Scholar's wagon. I had imitated Honeyman,
and tied my boots to my cantle strings, so that
my effects were on the right side of the river; and
as far as dinner was concerned, — well, I 'd much
rather miss it than swim the Platte twice in its
then stage of water.   There is a difference in
daring in one's duty and in daring out of pure
venturesomeness, and if we missed our dinners it
would not be the first time, so we were quite willing to make the sacrifice. If the Quirk family
never achieve fame for daring by field and flood,
until this one of the old man's boys brings the
family name into prominence, it will be hopelessly
lost to posterity.

We allowed the cattle to graze of their own free
will, and merely turned in the sides and rear, but
on reaching the second bottom of the river, where
they caught a good breeze, they lay down for their
noonday siesta, which relieved us of all work but
keeping watch over them.   The saddle horses were
grazing about in plain view on the first bottom, so
Honeyman and I dismounted on a little elevation
overlooking our charges.   We were expecting the
outfit to return promptly after dinner was over,
for it was early enough in the day to have trailed
eight or ten miles farther.   It would have been no

trouble to send some one up the river to meet our
wagon and pilot McCann to the herd, for the trail
left on a line due north from the river. We had
been lounging about for an hour while the cattle
were resting, when our attention was attracted by
our saddle horses in the bottom. They were looking at the ford, to which we supposed their attention had been attracted by the swimming of the
outfit, but instead only two of the boys showed up,
and on sighting us nearly a mile away, they rode
forward very leisurely. Before their arrival we
recognized them by their horses as Ash Borrowstone and Rod Wheat, and on their riding up the
latter said as he dismounted, —

"Well, they 're going to cross the other herd,
and they want you to come back and point the
cattle with that famous swimming horse of yours.
You 'll learn after a while not to blow so much
about your mount, and your cutting horses, and
your night horses, and your swimming horses. I
wish every horse of mine had a nigger brand on
him, and I had to ride in the wagon, when it comes
to swimming these rivers. And I 'm not the only
one that has a distaste for a wet proposition, for
I would n't have to guess twice as to what 's the
matter with Scholar. But Flood has pounded him
on the back ever since he met him yesterday evening to swim his cattle, until it 's either swim or
say he 's afraid to, — it 's ' Shoot, Luke, or give up
the gun ' with him. Scholar 's a nice fellow, but

I 'll bet my interest in goose heaven that I know
what 's the matter with him. And I 'm not blam-
ing him, either; but I can't understand why our
boss should take such an interest in having him
swim. It 's none of his business if he swims now,
or fords a month hence, or waits until the river
freezes over in the winter and crosses on the ice.
But let the big augers wrangle it out; you noticed,
Ash, that not one of Scholar's outfit ever said a
word one way or the other, but Flood poured it
into him until he consented to swim. So fork that
swimming horse of yours and wet your big toe
again in the North Platte."

As the orders had come from the foreman, there
was nothing to do but obey. Honeyman rode as
far as the river with me, where after shedding my
boots and surplus clothing and secreting them, I
rode up above the island and plunged in. I was
riding the gray which I had tried in the Rio
Grande the day we received the herd, and now
that I understood handling him better, I preferred
him to Nigger Boy, my night horse. We took the
first and second islands with but a blowing spell
between, and when I reached the farther shore, I
turned in my saddle and saw Honeyman wave his
hat to me in congratulation. On reaching their
wagon, I found the herd was swinging around
about a mile out from the river, in order to get a
straight shoot for the entrance at the ford. I hur-
riedly swallowed my dinner, and as we rode out to

meet the herd, asked Flood if Scholar were not going to send his wagon up to the ferry to cross, for there was as yet no indication of it. Flood replied that Scholar expected to go with the wagon, as he needed some supplies which he thought he could get from the sutler at Fort Laramie.

Flood ordered me to take the lower point again, and I rode across the trail and took my place when the herd came within a quarter of a mile of the river, while the remainder of the outfit took positions near the lead on the lower side. It was a slightly larger herd than ours, — all steers, three-year-olds that reflected in their glossy coats the benefits of a northern winter. As we came up to the water's edge, it required two of their men to force their *remuda* into the water, though it was much smaller than ours, — six horses to the man, but better ones than ours, being northern wintered. The cattle were well trail-broken, and followed the leadership of the saddle horses nicely to the first island, but they would have balked at this second channel, had it not been for the amount of help at hand. We lined them out, however, and they breasted the current, and landed on the second island. The saddle horses gave some little trouble on leaving for the farther shore, and before they were got off, several hundred head of cattle had landed on the island. But they handled obediently and were soon trailing out upon terra firma, the herd following across without a broken link in the

chain. There was nothing now to do but keep the
train moving into the water on the south bank, see
that they did not congest on the islands, and that
they left the river on reaching the farther shore.
When the saddle horses reached the farther bank,
they were thrown up the river and turned loose, so
that the two men would be available to hold the
herd after it left the water. I had crossed with
the first lead cattle to the farther shore, and was
turning them up the river as fast as they struck
solid footing on that side. But several times I was
compelled to swim back to the nearest island, and
return with large bunches which had hesitated to
take the last channel.

The two outfits were working promiscuously together, and I never knew who was the directing
spirit in the work; but when the last two or three
hundred of the tail-enders were leaving the first
island for the second, and the men working in the
rear started to swim the channel, amid the general
hilarity I recognized a shout that was born of fear
and terror. A hushed silence fell over the riotous
riders in the river, and I saw those on the sand bar
nearest my side rush down the narrow island and
plunge back into the middle channel. Then it
dawned on my mind in a flash that some one had
lost his seat, and that terrified cry was for help.
I plunged my gray into the river and swam to
the first bar, and from thence to the scene of the
trouble. Horses and men were drifting with the

current down the channel, and as I appealed to the men I could get no answer but their blanched faces, though it was plain in every countenance that one of our number was under water if not drowned.   There were not less than twenty horsemen drifting in the middle channel in the hope that whoever it was would come to the surface, and a hand could be stretched out in succor.

About two hundred yards down the river was an island near the middle of the stream.   The current carried us near it, and, on landing, I learned that the unfortunate man was none other than Wade Scholar, the foreman of the herd.   We scattered up and down this middle island and watched every ripple and floating bit of flotsam in the hope that he would come to the surface, but nothing but his hat was seen.   In the disorder into which the outfits were thrown by this accident, Flood first regained his thinking faculties, and ordered a few of us to cross to either bank, and ride down the river and take up positions on the other islands, from which that part of the river took its name.   A hundred conjectures were offered as to how it occurred; but no one saw either horse or rider after sinking.   A free horse would be hard to drown, and on the nonappearance of Scholar's mount it was concluded that he must have become entangled in the reins or that Scholar had clutched them in his death grip, and horse and man thus met death together.   It was believed by

his own outfit that Scholar had no intention until
the last moment to risk swimming the river, but
when he saw all the others plunge into the channel, his better judgment was overcome, and rather
than remain behind and cause comment, he had
followed and lost his life.

We patrolled the river until darkness without
result, the two herds in the mean time having been
so neglected that they had mixed. Our wagon
returned along the north bank early in the evening, and Flood ordered Priest to go in and make
up a guard from the two outfits and hold the herd
for the night. Some one of Scholar's outfit went
back and moved their wagon up to the crossing,
within hailing distance of ours. It was a night
of muffled conversation, and every voice of the
night or cry of waterfowl in the river sent creepy
sensations over us. The long night passed, however, and the sun rose in Sabbath benediction, for
it was Sunday, and found groups of men huddled
around two wagons in silent contemplation of what
the day before had brought. A more broken and
disconsolate set of men than Scholar's would be
hard to imagine.

Flood inquired of their outfit if there was any
sub-foreman, or *segundo* as they were generally
called. It seemed there was not, but their outfit
was unanimous that the leadership should fall to a
boyhood acquaintance of Scholar's by the name of
Campbell, who was generally addressed as "Black "

Jim. Flood at once advised Campbell to send their wagon up to Laramie and cross it, promising that we would lie over that day and make an effort to recover the body of the drowned foreman. Campbell accordingly started his wagon up to the ferry, and all the remainder of the outfits, with the exception of a few men on herd, started out in search of the drowned man. Within a mile and a half below the ford, there were located over thirty of the forty islands, and at the lower end of this chain of sand bars we began and searched both shores, while three or four men swam to each island and made a vigorous search.

The water in the river was not very clear, which called for a close inspection; but with a force of twenty-five men in the hunt, we covered island and shore rapidly in our search. It was about eight in the morning, and we had already searched half of the islands, when Joe Stallings and two of Scholar's men swam to an island in the river which had a growth of small cottonwoods covering it, while on the upper end was a heavy lodgment of driftwood. John Officer, The Rebel, and I had taken the next island above, and as we were riding the shallows surrounding it we heard a shot in our rear that told us the body had been found. As we turned in the direction of the signal, Stallings was standing on a large driftwood log, and signaling. We started back to him, partly wading and partly swimming, while from both sides of the river men were swimming their horses for the brushy island. Our squad, on nearing the lower bar, was compelled to swim around the driftwood, and some twelve or fifteen men from either shore reached the scene before us. The body was lying face upward, in about eighteen inches of eddy water. Flood and Campbell waded out, and taking a lariat, fastened it around his chest under the arms. Then Flood, noticing I was riding my black, asked me to tow the body ashore. Forcing a passage through the driftwood, I took the loose end of the lariat and started for the north bank, the double outfit following. On reaching the shore, the body was carried out of the water by willing hands, and one of our outfit was sent to the wagon for a tarpaulin to be used as a stretcher.

Meanwhile, Campbell took possession of the drowned foreman's watch, six-shooter, purse, and papers. The watch was as good as ruined, but the leather holster had shrunk and securely held the gun from being lost in the river. On the arrival of the tarpaulin, the body was laid upon it, and four mounted men, taking the four corners of the sheet, wrapped them on the pommels of their saddles and started for our wagon. When the corpse had been lowered to the ground at our camp, a look of inquiry passed from face to face which seemed to ask, "What next?" But the inquiry was answered a moment later by Black Jim Campbell, the friend of the dead man. Memory may have dimmed the lesser details of that Sunday morning on the North Platte, for over two decades have since gone, but his words and manliness have lived, not only in my mind, but in the memory of every other survivor of those present. "This accident," said he in perfect composure, as he gazed into the calm, still face of his dead friend, "will impose on me a very sad duty. I expect to meet his mother some day. She will want to know everything. I must tell her the truth, and I'd hate to tell her we buried him like a dog, for she's a Christian woman. And what makes it all the harder, I know that this is the third boy she has lost by drowning. Some of you may not have understood him, but among those papers which you saw me take from his pockets was a letter from his mother, in which she warned him to guard against just what has happened. Situated as we are, I'm going to ask you all to help me give him the best burial we can. No doubt it will be crude, but it will be some solace to her to know we did the best we could."

Every one of us was eager to lend his assistance. Within five minutes Priest was galloping up the north bank of the river to intercept the wagon at the ferry, a well-filled purse in his pocket with which to secure a coffin at Fort Laramie. Flood and Campbell selected a burial place, and with our wagon spade a grave was being dug on a near-by grassy mound, where there were two other graves.

There was not a man among us who was hypocrite enough to attempt to conduct a Christian burial service, but when the subject came up, McCann said as he came down the river the evening before he noticed an emigrant train of about thirty wagons going into camp at a grove about five miles up the river. In a conversation which he had had with one of the party, he learned that they expected to rest over Sunday. Their respect for the Sabbath day caused Campbell to suggest that there might be some one in the emigrant camp who could conduct a Christian burial, and he at once mounted his horse and rode away to learn.

In preparing the body for its last resting-place we were badly handicapped, but by tearing a new wagon sheet into strips about a foot in width and wrapping the body, we gave it a humble bier in the shade of our wagon, pending the arrival of the coffin. The features were so ashened by having been submerged in the river for over eighteen hours, that we wrapped the face also, as we preferred to remember him as we had seen him the day before, strong, healthy, and buoyant. During the interim, awaiting the return of Campbell from the emigrant camp and of the wagon, we sat around in groups and discussed the incident. There was a sense of guilt expressed by a number of our outfit over their hasty decision regarding the courage of the dead man. When we understood that two of his brothers had met a similar fate in Red River within the past five years, every guilty thought or hasty word spoken came back to us with tenfold weight. Priest and Campbell returned together; the former reported having secured a coffin which would arrive within an hour, while the latter had met in the emigrant camp a superannuated minister who gladly volunteered his services. He had given the old minister such data as he had, and two of the minister's granddaughters had expressed a willingness to assist by singing at the burial services. Campbell had set the hour for four, and several conveyances would be down from the emigrant camp. The wagon arriving shortly afterward, we had barely time to lay the corpse in the coffin before the emigrants drove up. The minister was a tall, homely man, with a flowing beard, which the frosts of many a winter had whitened, and as he mingled amongst us in the final preparations, he had a kind word for every one. There were ten in his party; and when the coffin had been carried out to the grave, the two granddaughters of the old man opened the simple service by singing very impressively the first three verses of the Portuguese Hymn. I had heard the old hymn sung often before, but the impression of the last verse rang in my ears for days afterward.

> " When through the deep waters I call thee to go,
> The rivers of sorrow shall not overflow;
> For I will be with thee thy troubles to bless,
> And sanctify to thee thy deepest distress."

As the notes of the hymn died away, there was
for a few moments profound stillness, and not a
move was made by any one.   The touching words
of the old hymn expressed quite vividly the disaster of the previous day, and awakened in us
many memories of home.   For a time we were
silent, while eyes unused to weeping filled with
tears.   I do not know how long we remained so.
It may have been only for a moment, it probably
was; but I do know the silence was not broken
till the aged minister, who stood at the head of
the coffin, began his discourse.   We stood with
uncovered heads during the service, and when the
old minister addressed us he spoke as though he
might have been holding family worship and we
had been his children.   He invoked Heaven to
comfort and sustain the mother when the news of
her son's death reached her, as she would need
more than human aid in that hour; he prayed that
her faith might not falter and that she might again
meet and be with her loved ones forever in the
great beyond.   He then took up the subject of
life, — spoke of its brevity, its many hopes that
are never realized, and the disappointments from
which no prudence or foresight can shield us.   He
dwelt at some length on the strange mingling of
sunshine and shadow that seemed to belong to every
life; on the mystery everywhere, and nowhere more
impressively than in ourselves.   With his long
bony finger he pointed to the cold, mute form that

lay in the coffin before us, and said, "But this, my friends, is the mystery of all mysteries." The fact that life terminated in death, he said, only emphasized its reality; that the death of our companion was not an accident, though it was sudden and unexpected; that the difficulties of life are such that it would be worse than folly in us to try to meet them in our own strength. Death, he said, might change, but it did not destroy; that the soul still lived and would live forever; that death was simply the gateway out of time into eternity; and if we were to realize the high aim of our being, we could do so by casting our burdens on Him who was able and willing to carry them for us. He spoke feelingly of the Great Teacher, the lowly Nazarene, who also suffered and died, and he concluded with an eloquent description of the blessed life, the immortality of the soul, and the resurrection of the body. After the discourse was ended and a brief and earnest prayer was offered, the two young girls sang the hymn, "Shall we meet beyond the river?" The services being at an end, the coffin was lowered into the grave.

Campbell thanked the old minister and his two granddaughters on their taking leave, for their presence and assistance; and a number of us boys also shook hands with the old man at parting.

CHAPTER XX

THE two herds were held together a second night, but after they had grazed a few hours the next morning, the cattle were thrown together, and the work of cutting out ours commenced. With a double outfit of men available, about twenty men were turned into the herd to do the cutting, the remainder holding the main herd and looking after the cut. The morning was cool, every one worked with a vim, and in about two hours the herds were again separated and ready for the final trimming. Campbell did not expect to move out until he could communicate with the head office of the company, and would go up to Fort Laramie for that purpose during the day, hoping to be able to get a message over the military wire. When his outfit had finished retrimming our herd, and we had looked over his cattle for the last time, the two outfits bade each other farewell, and our herd started on its journey.

The unfortunate accident at the ford had depressed our feelings to such an extent that there was an entire absence of hilarity by the way. This morning the farewell songs generally used in parting with a river which had defied us were omitted. The herd trailed out like an immense serpent, and was guided and controlled by our men as if by mutes. Long before the noon hour, we passed out of sight of Forty Islands, and in the next few days, with the change of scene, the gloom gradually lifted. We were bearing almost due north, and passing through a delightful country. To our left ran a range of mountains, while on the other hand sloped off the apparently limitless plain. The scarcity of water was beginning to be felt, for the streams which had not a source in the mountains on our left had dried up weeks before our arrival. There was a gradual change of air noticeable too, for we were rapidly gaining altitude, the heat of summer being now confined to a few hours at noonday, while the nights were almost too cool for our comfort.

When about three days out from the North Platte, the mountains disappeared on our left, while on the other hand appeared a rugged-looking country, which we knew must be the approaches of the Black Hills. Another day's drive brought us into the main stage road connecting the railroad on the south with the mining camps which nestled somewhere in those rocky hills to our right. The stage road followed the trail some ten or fifteen miles before we parted company with it on a dry fork of the Big Cheyenne River. There was a road house and stage stand where these two thor-

oughfares separated, the one to the mining camp
of Deadwood, while ours of the Montana cattle
trail bore off for the Powder River to the northwest. At this stage stand we learned that some
twenty herds had already passed by to the northern ranges, and that after passing the next fork
of the Big Cheyenne we should find no water until
we struck the Powder River, — a stretch of eighty
miles. The keeper of the road house, a genial
host, informed us that this drouthy stretch in our
front was something unusual, this being one of the
dryest summers that he had experienced since the
discovery of gold in the Black Hills.

Here was a new situation to be met, an eighty-
mile dry drive; and with our experience of a few
months before at Indian Lakes fresh in our memories, we set our house in order for the under-
taking before us. It was yet fifteen miles to the
next and last water from the stage stand. There
were several dry forks of the Cheyenne beyond,
but as they had their source in the tablelands of
Wyoming, we could not hope for water in their
dry bottoms. The situation was serious, with only
this encouragement: other herds had crossed this
arid belt since the streams had dried up, and our
Circle Dots could walk with any herd that ever
left Texas. The wisdom of mounting us well for
just such an emergency reflected the good cow
sense of our employer; and we felt easy in regard
to our mounts, though there was not a horse or

a man too many. In summing up the situation, Flood said, "We 've got this advantage over the Indian Lake drive: there is a good moon, and the days are cool. We 'll make twenty-five miles a day covering this stretch, as this herd has never been put to a test yet to see how far they could walk in a day. They 'll have to do their sleeping at noon; at least cut it into two shifts, and if we get any sleep we 'll have to do the same. Let her come as she will; every day's drive is a day nearer the Blackfoot agency."

We made a dry camp that night on the divide between the road house and the last water, and the next forenoon reached the South Fork of the Big Cheyenne. The water was not even running in it, but there were several long pools, and we held the cattle around them for over an hour, until every hoof had been thoroughly watered. McCann had filled every keg and canteen in advance of the arrival of the herd, and Flood had exercised sufficient caution, in view of what lay before us, to buy an extra keg and a bull's-eye lantern at the road house. After watering, we trailed out some four or five miles and camped for noon, but the herd were allowed to graze forward until they lay down for their noonday rest. As the herd passed opposite the wagon, we cut a fat two-year-old stray heifer and killed her for beef, for the inner man must be fortified for the journey before us. After a two hours' siesta, we threw the herd on the trail

and started on our way. The wagon and saddle
horses were held in our immediate rear, for there
was no telling when or where we would make our
next halt of any consequence. We trailed and
grazed the herd alternately until near evening,
when the wagon was sent on ahead about three
miles to get supper, while half the outfit went
along to change mounts and catch up horses for
those remaining behind with the herd. A half
hour before the usual bedding time, the relieved
men returned and took the grazing herd, and the
others rode in to the wagon for supper and a
change of mounts. While we shifted our saddles,
we smelled the savory odor of fresh beef frying.

"Listen to that good old beef talking, will
you?" said Joe Stallings, as he was bridling his
horse. "McCann, I'll take my *carne fresco* a trifle rare to-night, garnished with a sprig of parsley
and a wee bit of lemon."

Before we had finished supper, Honeyman had
rehooked the mules to the wagon, while the *remuda*
was at hand to follow. Before we left the wagon,
a full moon was rising on the eastern horizon, and
as we were starting out Flood gave us these general directions: "I'm going to take the lead with
the cook's lantern, and one of you rear men take
the new bull's-eye. We'll throw the herd on the
trail; and between the lead and rear light, you
swing men want to ride well outside, and you
point men want to hold the lead cattle so the rear

will never be more than a half a mile behind.
I 'll admit that this is somewhat of an experiment
with me, but I don't see any good reason why she
won't work.   After the moon gets another hour
high we can see a quarter of a mile, and the cattle are so well trail broke they 'll never try to scatter.   If it works all right, we 'll never bed them
short of midnight, and that will put us ten miles
farther.   Let 's ride, lads.''

By the time the herd was eased back on the
trail, our evening camp-fire had been passed, while
the cattle led out as if walking on a wager.   After
the first mile on the trail, the men on the point
were compelled to ride in the lead if we were to
hold them within the desired half mile.   The men
on the other side, or the swing, were gradually
widening, until the herd must have reached fully
a mile in length; yet we swing riders were never
out of sight of each other, and it would have been
impossible for any cattle to leave the herd unno-
ticed.   In that moonlight the trail was as plain
as day, and after an hour, Flood turned his lantern
over to one of the point men, and rode back around
the herd to the rear.   From my position that first
night near the middle of the swing, the lanterns
both rear and forward being always in sight, I
was as much at sea as any one as to the length of
the herd, knowing the deceitfulness of distance of
campfires and other lights by night.   The foreman
appealed to me as he rode down the column, to

know the length of the herd, but I could give him
no more than a simple guess. I could assure him,
however, that the cattle had made no effort to drop
out and leave the trail. But a short time after he
passed me I noticed a horseman galloping up the
column on the opposite side of the herd, and knew
it must be the foreman. Within a short time,
some one in the lead wig-wagged his lantern; it
was answered by the light in the rear, and the
next minute the old rear song, —

> " Ip-e-la-ago, go 'long little doggie,
> You 'll make a beef-steer by-and-by," —

reached us riders in the swing, and we knew the rear
guard of cattle was being pushed forward. The
distance between the swing men gradually narrowed
in our lead, from which we could tell the leaders
were being held in, until several times cattle grazed
out from the herd, due to the checking in front.
At this juncture Flood galloped around the herd a
second time, and as he passed us riding along our
side, I appealed to him to let them go in front, as
it now required constant riding to keep the cattle
from leaving the trail to graze. When he passed
up the opposite side, I could distinctly hear the men
on that flank making a similar appeal, and shortly
afterwards the herd loosened out and we struck
our old gait for several hours.

Trailing by moonlight was a novelty to all of us,
and in the stillness of those splendid July nights
we could hear the point men chatting across the

lead in front, while well in the rear, the rattling
of our heavily loaded wagon and the whistling of
the horse wrangler to his charges reached our ears.
The swing men were scattered so far apart there
was no chance for conversation amongst us, but
every once in a while a song would be started, and
as it surged up and down the line, every voice,
good, bad, and indifferent, joined in.   Singing is
supposed to have a soothing effect on cattle, though
I will vouch for the fact that none of our Circle
Dots stopped that night to listen to our vocal efforts.   The herd was traveling so nicely that our
foreman hardly noticed the passing hours, but
along about midnight the singing ceased, and we
were nodding in our saddles and wondering if they
in. the lead were never going to throw off the trail,
when a great wig-wagging occurred in front, and
presently we overtook The Rebel, holding the lantern and turning the herd out of the trail.   It was
then after midnight, and within another half hour
we had the cattle bedded down within a few hundred yards of the trail.   One-hour guards was the
order of the night, and as soon as our wagon and
saddle horses came up, we stretched ropes and
caught out our night horses.   These we either tied
to the wagon wheels or picketed near at hand, and
then we sought our blankets for a few hours' sleep.
It was half past three in the morning when our
guard was called, and before the hour passed, the
first signs of day were visible in the east.   But

even before our watch had ended, Flood and the last guard came to our relief, and we pushed the sleeping cattle off the bed ground and started them grazing forward.

Cattle will not graze freely in a heavy dew or too early in the morning, and before the sun was high enough to dry the grass, we had put several miles behind us. When the sun was about an hour high, the remainder of the outfit overtook us, and shortly afterward the wagon and saddle horses passed on up the trail, from which it was evident that "breakfast would be served in the dining car ahead," as the traveled Priest aptly put it. After the sun was well up, the cattle grazed freely for several hours; but when we sighted the *remuda* and our commissary some two miles in our lead, Flood ordered the herd lined up for a count. The Rebel was always a reliable counter, and he and the foreman now rode forward and selected the crossing of a dry wash for the counting. On receiving their signal to come on, we allowed the herd to graze slowly forward, but gradually pointed them into an immense "V," and as the point of the herd crossed the dry arroyo, we compelled them to pass in a narrow file between the two counters, when they again spread out fan-like and continued their feeding.

The count confirmed the success of our driving by night, and on its completion all but two men rode to the wagon for breakfast. By the time the

morning meal was disposed of, the herd had come
up parallel with the wagon but a mile to the westward, and as fast as fresh mounts could be saddled,
we rode away in small squads to relieve the herders
and to turn the cattle into the trail.   It was but a
little after eight o'clock in the morning when the
herd was again trailing out on the Powder River
trail, and we had already put over thirty miles of
the dry drive behind us, while so far neither horses
nor cattle had been put to any extra exertion.   The
wagon followed as usual, and for over three hours
we held the trail without a break, when sighting
a divide in our front, the foreman went back and
sent the wagon around the herd with instructions
to make the noon camp well up on the divide.
We threw the herd off the trail, within a mile of
this stopping place, and allowed them to graze,
while two thirds of the outfit galloped away to
the wagon.

We allowed the cattle to lie down and rest to
their complete satisfaction until the middle of the
afternoon; meanwhile all hands, with the exception of two men on herd, also lay down and slept
in the shade of the wagon.   When the cattle had
had several hours' sleep, the want of water made
them restless, and they began to rise and graze
away.   Then all hands were aroused and we threw
them upon the trail.   The heat of the day was already over, and until the twilight of the evening, we
trailed a three-mile clip, and again threw the herd

off to graze. By our traveling and grazing gaits, we could form an approximate idea as to the distance we had covered, and the consensus of opinion of all was that we had already killed over half the distance. The herd was beginning to show the want of water by evening, but amongst our saddle horses the lack of water was more noticeable, as a horse subsisting on grass alone weakens easily; and riding them made them all the more gaunt. When we caught up our mounts that evening, we had used eight horses to the man since we had left the South Fork, and another one would be required at midnight, or whenever we halted.

We made our drive the second night with more confidence than the one before, but there were times when the train of cattle must have been nearly two miles in length, yet there was never a halt as long as the man with the lead light could see the one in the rear. We bedded the herd about midnight; and at the first break of day, the fourth guard with the foreman joined us on our watch and we started the cattle again. There was a light dew the second night, and the cattle, hungered by their night walk, went to grazing at once on the damp grass, which would allay their thirst slightly. We allowed them to scatter over several thousand acres, for we were anxious to graze them well before the sun absorbed the moisture, but at the same time every step they took was one less to the coveted Powder River.

When we had grazed the herd forward several miles, and the sun was nearly an hour high, the wagon failed to come up, which caused our foreman some slight uneasiness. Nearly another hour passed, and still the wagon did not come up nor did the outfit put in an appearance. Soon afterwards, however, Moss Strayhorn overtook us, and reported that over forty of our saddle horses were missing, while the work mules had been overtaken nearly five miles back on the trail. On account of my ability as a trailer, Flood at once dispatched me to assist Honeyman in recovering the missing horses, instructing some one else to take the *remuda*, and the wagon and horses to follow up the herd. By the time I arrived, most of the boys at camp had secured a change of horses, and I caught up my *grulla*, that I was saving for the last hard ride, for the horse hunt which confronted us. McCann, having no fire built, gave Honeyman and myself an impromptu breakfast and two canteens of water; but before we let the wagon get away, we rustled a couple of cans of tomatoes and buried them in a cache near the camp-ground, where we would have no trouble in finding them on our return. As the wagon pulled out, we mounted our horses and rode back down the trail.

Billy Honeyman understood horses, and at once volunteered the belief that we would have a long ride overtaking the missing saddle stock. The absent horses, he said, were principally the ones which had been under saddle the day before, and as we both knew, a tired, thirsty horse will go miles for water. He recalled, also, that while we were asleep at noon the day before, twenty miles back on the trail, the horses had found quite a patch of wild sorrel plant, and were foolish over leaving it. Both of us being satisfied that this would hold them for several hours at least, we struck a free gait for it. After we passed the point where the mules had been overtaken, the trail of the horses was distinct enough for us to follow in an easy canter. We saw frequent signs that they left the trail, no doubt to graze, but only for short distances, when they would enter it again, and keep it for miles. Shortly before noon, as we gained the divide above our noon camp of the day before, there about two miles distant we saw our missing horses, feeding over an alkali flat on which grew wild sorrel and other species of sour plants. We rounded them up, and finding none missing, we first secured a change of mounts. The only two horses of my mount in this portion of the *remuda* had both been under saddle the afternoon and night before, and were as gaunt as rails, and Honeyman had one unused horse of his mount in the band. So when, taking down our ropes, we halted the horses and began riding slowly around them, forcing them into a compact body, I had my eye on a brown horse of Flood's that had not had a saddle on in a week, and told Billy to fasten

to him if he got a chance. This was in violation
of all custom, but if the foreman kicked, I had a
good excuse to offer.

Honeyman was left-handed and threw a rope
splendidly; and as we circled around the horses on
opposite sides, on a signal from him we whirled
our lariats and made casts simultaneously. The
wrangler fastened to the brown I wanted, and
my loop settled around the neck of his unridden
horse. As the band broke away from our swinging ropes, a number of them ran afoul of my rope;
but I gave the rowel to my *grulla*, and we shook
them off. When I returned to Honeyman, and we
had exchanged horses and were shifting our saddles, I complimented him on the long throw he
had made in catching the brown, and incidentally
mentioned that I had read of vaqueros in California who used a sixty-five foot lariat. "Hell," said
Billy, in ridicule of the idea, "there wasn't a man
ever born who could throw a sixty-five foot rope its
full length — without he threw it down a well."

The sun was straight overhead when we started
back to overtake the herd. We struck into a little
better than a five-mile gait on the return trip, and
about two o'clock sighted a band of saddle horses
and a wagon camped perhaps a mile forward and
to the side of the trail. On coming near enough,
we saw at a glance it was a cow outfit, and after
driving our loose horses a good push beyond their
camp, turned and rode back to their wagon.

"We'll give them a chance to ask us to eat," said Billy to me, "and if they don't, why, they'll miss a hell of a good chance to entertain hungry men."

But the foreman with the stranger wagon proved to be a Bee County Texan, and our doubts did him an injustice, for, although dinner was over, he invited us to dismount and ordered his cook to set out something to eat. They had met our wagon, and McCann had insisted on their taking a quarter of our beef, so we fared well. The outfit was from a ranch near Miles City, Montana, and were going down to receive a herd of cattle at Cheyenne, Wyoming. The cattle had been bought at Ogalalla for delivery at the former point, and this wagon was going down with their ranch outfit to take the herd on its arrival. They had brought along about seventy-five saddle horses from the ranch, though in buying the herd they had taken its *remuda* of over a hundred saddle horses. The foreman informed us that they had met our cattle about the middle of the forenoon, nearly twenty-five miles out from Powder River. After we had satisfied the inner man, we lost no time getting off, as we could see a long ride ahead of us; but we had occasion as we rode away to go through their *remuda* to cut out a few of our horses which had mixed, and I found I knew over a dozen of their horses by the ranch brands, while Honeyman also recognized quite a few. Though we felt a pride in our mounts, we had to admit that theirs were better; for the effect of climate had transformed horses that we had once ridden on ranches in southern Texas. It does seem incredible, but it is a fact nevertheless, that a horse, having reached the years of maturity in a southern climate, will grow half a hand taller and carry two hundred pounds more flesh, when he has undergone the rigors of several northern winters.

We halted at our night camp to change horses and to unearth our cached tomatoes, and again set out. By then it was so late in the day that the sun had lost its force, and on this last leg in overtaking the herd we increased our gait steadily until the sun was scarcely an hour high, and yet we never sighted a dust-cloud in our front. About sundown we called a few minutes' halt, and after eating our tomatoes and drinking the last of our water, again pushed on. Twilight had faded into dusk before we reached a divide which we had had in sight for several hours, and which we had hoped to gain in time to sight the timber on Powder River before dark. But as we put mile after mile behind us, that divide seemed to move away like a mirage, and the evening star had been shining for an hour before we finally reached it, and sighted, instead of Powder's timber, the campfire of our outfit about five miles ahead. We fired several shots on seeing the light, in the hope that they might hear us in camp and wait; otherwise we knew they would start the herd with the rising of the moon.

When we finally reached camp, about nine o'clock at night, everything was in readiness to start, the moon having risen sufficiently. Our shooting, however, had been heard, and horses for a change were tied to the wagon wheels, while the remainder of the *remuda* was under herd in charge of Rod Wheat. The runaways were thrown into the horse herd while we bolted our suppers. Meantime McCann informed us that Flood had ridden that afternoon to the Powder River, in order to get the lay of the land. He had found it to be ten or twelve miles distant from the present camp, and the water in the river barely knee deep to a saddle horse. Beyond it was a fine valley. Before we started, Flood rode in from the herd, and said to Honeyman, "I'm going to send the horses and wagon ahead to-night, and you and McCann want to camp on this side of the river, under the hill and just a few hundred yards below the ford. Throw your saddle horses across the river, and build a fire before you go to sleep, so we will have a beacon light to pilot us in, in case the cattle break into a run on scenting the water. The herd will get in a little after midnight, and after crossing, we'll turn her loose just for luck."

It did me good to hear the foreman say the herd was to be turned loose, for I had been in the saddle since three that morning, had ridden over eighty miles, and had now ten more in sight, while Honeyman would complete the day with over a hundred to his credit. We let the *remuda* take the lead in pulling out, so that the wagon mules could be spurred to their utmost in keeping up with the loose horses. Once they were clear of the herd, we let the cattle into the trail. They had refused to bed down, for they were uneasy with thirst, but the cool weather had saved them any serious suffering. We all felt gala as the herd strung out on the trail. Before we halted again there would be water for our dumb brutes and rest for ourselves. There was lots of singing that night. "There's One more River to cross," and "Roll, Powder, roll," were wafted out on the night air to the coyotes that howled on our flanks, or to the prairie dogs as they peeped from their burrows at this weird caravan of the night, and the lights which flickered in our front and rear must have been real Jack-o'-lanterns or Will-o'-the-wisps to these occupants of the plain. Before we had covered half the distance, the herd was strung out over two miles, and as Flood rode back to the rear every half hour or so, he showed no inclination to check the lead and give the sore-footed rear guard a chance to close up the column; but about an hour before midnight we saw a light low down in our front, which gradually increased until the treetops were distinctly visible, and we knew that our wagon had reached the river. On sighting this beacon, the long yell went up and down the column, and the herd walked as only long-legged, thirsty Texas cattle can walk when they scent water. Flood called all the swing men to the rear, and we threw out a half-circle skirmish line covering a mile in width, so far back that only an occasional glimmer of the lead light could be seen. The trail struck the Powder on an angle, and when within a mile of the river, the swing cattle left the deep-trodden paths and started for the nearest water.

The left flank of our skirmish line encountered the cattle as they reached the river, and prevented them from drifting up the stream. The point men abandoned the leaders when within a few hundred yards of the river. Then the rear guard of cripples and sore-footed cattle came up, and the two flanks of horsemen pushed them all across the river until they met, when we turned and galloped into camp, making the night hideous with our yelling. The longest dry drive of the trip had been successfully made, and we all felt jubilant. We stripped bridles and saddles from our tired horses, and unrolling our beds, were soon lost in well-earned sleep.

The stars may have twinkled overhead, and sundry voices of the night may have whispered to us as we lay down to sleep, but we were too tired for poetry or sentiment that night.

CHAPTER XXI

THE tramping of our *remuda* as they came trotting up to the wagon the next morning, and Honeyman's calling, "Horses, horses," brought us to the realization that another day had dawned with its duty. McCann had stretched the ropes of our corral, for Flood was as dead to the world as any of us were, but the tramping of over a hundred and forty horses and mules, as they crowded inside the ropes, brought him into action as well as the rest of us. We had had a good five hours' sleep, while our mounts had been transformed from gaunt animals to round-barreled saddle horses, — that fought and struggled amongst themselves or artfully dodged the lariat loops which were being cast after them. Honeyman reported the herd quietly grazing across the river, and after securing our mounts for the morning, we breakfasted before looking after the cattle. It took us less than an hour to round up and count the cattle, and turn them loose again under herd to graze. Those of us not on herd returned to the wagon, and our foreman instructed McCann to make a two hours' drive down the river and camp for noon, as he pro-

posed only to graze the herd that morning. After
seeing the wagon safely beyond the rocky crossing,
we hunted up a good bathing pool and disported
ourselves for half an hour, taking a much needed
bath. There were trails on either side of the
Powder, and as our course was henceforth to the
northwest, we remained on the west side and grazed
or trailed down it. It was a beautiful stream of
water, having its source in the Big Horn Mountains, frequently visible on our left. For the next
four or five days we had easy work. There were
range cattle through that section, but fearful of
Texas fever, their owners gave the Powder River
a wide berth. With the exception of holding the
herd at night, our duties were light. We caught
fish and killed grouse; and the respite seemed like
a holiday after our experience of the past few days.
During the evening of the second day after reaching the Powder, we crossed the Crazy Woman, a
clear mountainous fork of the former river, and
nearly as large as the parent stream. Once or
twice we encountered range riders, and learned
that the Crazy Woman was a stock country, a number of beef ranches being located on it, stocked with
Texas cattle.

Somewhere near or about the Montana line, we
took a left-hand trail. Flood had ridden it out
until he had satisfied himself that it led over to
the Tongue River and the country beyond. While
large trails followed on down the Powder, their

direction was wrong for us, as they led towards the
Bad Lands and the lower Yellowstone country.
On the second day out, after taking the left-hand
trail, we encountered some rough country in passing across a saddle in a range of hills forming the
divide between the Powder and Tongue rivers.
We were nearly a whole day crossing it, but had
a well-used trail to follow, and down in the foot-
hills made camp that night on a creek which emptied into the Tongue. The roughness of the trail
was well compensated for, however, as it was a par-
adise of grass and water. We reached the Tongue
River the next afternoon, and found it a similar
stream to the Powder, — clear as crystal, swift, and
with a rocky bottom. As these were but minor
rivers, we encountered no trouble in crossing them,
the greatest danger being to our wagon. On the
Tongue we met range riders again, and from them
we learned that this trail, which crossed the Yellowstone at Frenchman's Ford, was the one in use
by herds bound for the Musselshell and remoter
points on the upper Missouri. From one rider we
learned that the first herd of the present season
which went through on this route were cattle wintered on the Niobrara in western Nebraska, whose
destination was Alberta in the British possessions.
This herd outclassed us in penetrating northward,
though in distance they had not traveled half as
far as our Circle Dots.

After following the Tongue River several days

and coming out on that immense plain tributary to the Yellowstone, the trail turned to the northwest, gave us a short day's drive to the Rosebud River, and after following it a few miles, bore off again on the same quarter. In our rear hung the mountains with their sentinel peaks, while in our front stretched the valley tributary to the Yellowstone, in extent, itself, an inland empire. The month was August, and, with the exception of cool nights, no complaint could be made, for that rarefied atmosphere was a tonic to man and beast, and there was pleasure in the primitive freshness of the country which rolled away on every hand. On leaving the Rosebud, two days' travel brought us to the east fork of Sweet Grass, an insignificant stream, with a swift current and rocky crossings. In the first two hours after reaching it, we must have crossed it half a dozen times, following the grassy bottoms, which shifted from one bank to the other. When we were full forty miles distant from Frenchman's Ford on the Yellowstone, the wagon, in crossing Sweet Grass, went down a sidling bank into the bottom of the creek, the left hind wheel collided with a boulder in the water, dishing it, and every spoke in the wheel snapped off at the shoulder in the felloe. McCann never noticed it, but poured the whip into the mules, and when he pulled out on the opposite bank left the felloe of his wheel in the creek behind. The herd was in the lead at the time, and when Honey-

man overtook us and reported the accident, we
threw the herd off to graze, and over half the outfit returned to the wagon.

When we reached the scene, McCann had recovered the felloe, but every spoke in the hub was
hopelessly ruined. Flood took in the situation at
a glance. He ordered the wagon unloaded and
the reach lengthened, took the axe, and, with The
Rebel, went back about a mile to a thicket of lodge
poles which we had passed higher up the creek.
While the rest of us unloaded the wagon, McCann,
who was swearing by both note and rhyme, unearthed his saddle from amongst the other plunder and cinched it on his nigh wheeler. We had
the wagon unloaded and had reloaded some of the
heaviest of the plunder in the front end of the
wagon box, by the time our foreman and Priest
returned, dragging from their pommels a thirty-
foot pole as perfect as the mast of a yacht. We
knocked off all the spokes not already broken at
the hub of the ruined wheel, and after jacking up
the hind axle, attached the "crutch." By cutting
a half notch in the larger end of the pole, so that it
fitted over the front axle, lashing it there securely,
and allowing the other end to trail behind on the
ground, we devised a support on which the hub
of the broken wheel rested, almost at its normal
height. There was sufficient spring to the pole to
obviate any jolt or jar, while the rearrangement we
had effected in distributing the load would relieve

it of any serious burden. We took a rope from
the coupling pole of the wagon and loosely noosed
it over the crutch, which allowed leeway in turning,
but prevented the hub from slipping off the support on a short turn to the left. Then we lashed
the tire and felloe to the front end of the wagon,
and with the loss of but a couple of hours our
commissary was again on the move.

The trail followed the Sweet Grass down to the
Yellowstone; and until we reached it, whenever
there were creeks to ford or extra pulls on hills,
half a dozen of us would drop back and lend a
hand from our saddle pommels. The gradual de-
cline of the country to the river was in our favor
at present, and we should reach the ford in two
days at the farthest, where we hoped to find a
wheelwright. In case we did not, our foreman
thought he could effect a trade for a serviceable
wagon, as ours was a new one and the best make
in the market. The next day Flood rode on ahead
to Frenchman's Ford, and late in the day returned
with the information that the Ford was quite a
pretentious frontier village of the squatter type.
There was a blacksmith and a wheelwright shop
in the town, but the prospect of an exchange
was discouraging, as the wagons there were of the
heavy freighting type, while ours was a wide tread
— a serious objection, as wagons manufactured for
southern trade were eight inches wider than those
in use in the north, and therefore would not track

on the same road. The wheelwright had assured
Flood that the wheel could be filled in a day, with
the exception of painting, and as paint was not
important, he had decided to move up within three
or four miles of the Ford and lie over a day for
repairing the wagon, and at the same time have
our mules reshod. Accordingly we moved up the
next morning, and after unloading the wagon, both
box and contents, over half the outfit — the first
and second guards — accompanied the wagon into
the Ford. They were to return by noon, when the
remainder of us were to have our turn in seeing
the sights of Frenchman's Ford. The horse wrangler remained behind with us, to accompany the
other half of the outfit in the afternoon. The herd
was no trouble to hold, and after watering about
the middle of the forenoon, three of us went into
camp and got dinner. As this was the first time
since starting that our cook was absent, we rather
enjoyed the opportunity to practice our culinary
skill. Pride in our ability to cook was a weakness
in our craft. The work was divided up between
Joe Stallings, John Officer, and myself, Honeyman
being excused on agreeing to rustle the wood and
water. Stallings prided himself on being an artist
in making coffee, and while hunting for the coffee
mill, found a bag of dried peaches.

"Say, fellows," said Joe, "I'll bet McCann has
hauled this fruit a thousand miles and never knew
he had it amongst all this plunder. I'm going to

stew a saucepan full of it, just to show his royal
nibs that he's been thoughtless of his boarders."

Officer volunteered to cut and fry the meat, for
we were eating stray beef now with great regular-
ity; and the making of the biscuits fell to me.
Honeyman soon had a fire so big that you could
not have got near it without a wet blanket on; and
when my biscuits were ready for the Dutch oven,
Officer threw a bucket of water on the fire, remarking: "Honeyman, if you was *cusi segundo*
under me, and built up such a big fire for the chef,
there would be trouble in camp. You may be a
good enough horse wrangler for a through Texas
outfit, but when it comes to playing second fiddle to a cook of my accomplishments — well, you
simply don't know salt from wild honey. A man
might as well try to cook on a burning haystack
as on a fire of your building."

When the fire had burned down sufficiently,
the cooks got their respective utensils upon the
fire; I had an ample supply of live coals for the
Dutch oven, and dinner was shortly afterwards
announced as ready. After dinner, Officer and I
relieved the men on herd, but over an hour passed
before we caught sight of the first and second
guards returning from the Ford. They were men
who could stay in town all day and enjoy themselves; but, as Flood had reminded them, there
were others who were entitled to a holiday. When
Bob Blades and Fox Quarternight came to our

relief on herd, they attempted to detain us with a description of Frenchman's Ford, but we cut all conversation short by riding away to camp.

" We 'll just save them the trouble, and go in and see it for ourselves," said Officer to me, as we galloped along. We had left word with Honey- man what horses we wanted to ride that after- noon, and lost little time in changing mounts; then we all set out to pay our respects to the mushroom village on the Yellowstone. Most of us had money; and those of the outfit who had returned were clean shaven and brought the report that a shave was two-bits and a drink the same price. The town struck me as something new and novel, two thirds of the habitations being of canvas. Immense quantities of buffalo hides were drying or already baled, and waiting transporta- tion as we afterward learned to navigable points on the Missouri. Large bull trains were encamped on the outskirts of the village, while many such outfits were in town, receiving cargoes or dis- charging freight. The drivers of these ox trains lounged in the streets and thronged the saloons and gambling resorts. The population was extremely mixed, and almost every language could be heard spoken on the streets. The men were fine types of the pioneer, — buffalo hunters, freighters, and other plainsmen, though hardly as picturesque in figure and costume as a modern artist would paint them. For native coloring, there were typical specimens of northern Indians, grunting their jargon amid the babel of other tongues; and groups of squaws wandered through the irregular streets in gaudy blankets and red calico. The only civilizing element to be seen was the camp of engineers, running the survey of the Northern Pacific railroad.

Tying our horses in a group to a hitch-rack in the rear of a saloon called The Buffalo Bull, we entered by a rear door and lined up at the bar for our first drink since leaving Ogalalla. Games of chance were running in the rear for those who felt inclined to try their luck, while in front of the bar, against the farther wall, were a number of small tables, around which were seated the patrons of the place, playing for the drinks. One couldn't help being impressed with the unrestrained freedom of the village, whose sole product seemed to be buffalo hides. Every man in the place wore the regulation six-shooter in his belt, and quite a number wore two. The primitive law of nature known as self-preservation, was very evident in August of '82 at Frenchman's Ford. It reminded me of the early days at home in Texas, where, on arising in the morning, one buckled on his six-shooter as though it were part of his dress. After a second round of drinks, we strolled out into the front street to look up Flood and McCann, and incidentally get a shave. We soon located McCann, who had a hunk of dried buffalo meat, and was

chipping it off and feeding it to some Indian children whose acquaintance he seemed to be culti-
vating.   On sighting us, he gave the children the
remainder of the jerked buffalo, and at once placed
himself at our disposal as guide to Frenchman's
Ford.   He had been all over the town that morning; knew the name of every saloon and those of
several barkeepers as well; pointed out the bullet
holes in a log building where the last shooting
scrape occurred, and otherwise showed us the sights
in the village which we might have overlooked.
A barber shop?   Why, certainly; and he led the
way, informing us that the wagon wheel would be
filled by evening, that the mules were already shod,
and that Flood had ridden down to the crossing to
look at the ford.

Two barbers turned us out rapidly, and as we
left we continued to take in the town, strolling by
pairs and drinking moderately as we went.   Flood
had returned in the mean time, and seemed rather
convivial and quite willing to enjoy the enforced
lay-over with us.   While taking a drink in Yellowstone Bob's place, the foreman took occasion to
call the attention of The Rebel to a cheap litho-
graph of General Grant which hung behind the
bar.   The two discussed the merits of the picture,
and Priest, who was an admirer of the magnanim-
ity as well as the military genius of Grant, spoke
in reserved yet favorable terms of the general,
when Flood flippantly chided him on his eulogistic

remarks over an officer to whom he had once been surrendered. The Rebel took the chaffing in all good humor, and when our glasses were filled, Flood suggested to Priest that since he was such an admirer of Grant, possibly he wished to propose a toast to the general's health.

"You're young, Jim," said The Rebel, "and if you'd gone through what I have, your views of things might be different. My admiration for the generals on our side survived wounds, prisons, and changes of fortune; but time has tempered my views on some things, and now I don't enthuse over generals when the men of the ranks who made them famous are forgotten. Through the fortunes of war, I saluted Grant when we were surrendered, but I would n't propose a toast or take off my hat now to any man that lives."

During the comments of The Rebel, a stranger, who evidently overheard them, rose from one of the tables in the place and sauntered over to the end of the bar, an attentive listener to the succeeding conversation. He was a younger man than Priest, — with a head of heavy black hair reaching his shoulders, while his dress was largely of buckskin, profusely ornamented with beadwork and fringes. He was armed, as was every one else, and from his languid demeanor as well as from his smart appearance, one would classify him at a passing glance as a frontier gambler. As we turned away from the bar to an unoccupied table, Priest waited

for his change, when the stranger accosted him
with an inquiry as to where he was from. In the
conversation that ensued, the stranger, who had
noticed the good-humored manner in which The
Rebel had taken the chiding of our foreman, pretended to take him to task for some of his remarks.
But in this he made a mistake. What his friends
might safely say to Priest would be treated as an
insult from a stranger. Seeing that he would not
stand his chiding, the other attempted to mollify
him by proposing they have a drink together and
part friendly, to which The Rebel assented. I
was pleased with the favorable turn of affairs, for
my bunkie had used some rather severe language
in resenting the remarks of the stranger, which
now had the promise of being dropped amicably.

I knew the temper of Priest, and so did Flood
and Honeyman, and we were all anxious to get him
away from the stranger. So I asked our foreman
as soon as they had drunk together, to go over and
tell Priest we were waiting for him to make up a
game of cards. The two were standing at the bar
in a most friendly attitude, but as they raised their
glasses to drink, the stranger, holding his at arm's
length, said: "Here's a toast for you: To General
Grant, the ablest " —

But the toast was never finished, for Priest
dashed the contents of his glass in the stranger's
face, and calmly replacing the glass on the bar,
backed across the room towards us. When half-

way across, a sudden movement on the part of the
stranger caused him to halt. But it seemed the
picturesque gentleman beside the bar was only
searching his pockets for a handkerchief.

"Don't get your hand on that gun you wear,"
said The Rebel, whose blood was up, "unless you
intend to use it. But you can't shoot a minute
too quick to suit me. What do you wear a gun
for, anyhow? Let's see how straight you can
shoot."

As the stranger made no reply, Priest continued, "The next time you have anything to rub
in, pick your man better. The man who insults
me'll get all that's due him for his trouble."
Still eliciting no response, The Rebel taunted him
further, saying, "Go on and finish your toast, you
patriotic beauty. I'll give you another: Jeff
Davis and the Southern Confederacy."

We all rose from the table, and Flood, going
over to Priest, said, "Come along, Paul we don't
want to have any trouble here. Let's go across
the street and have a game of California Jack."

But The Rebel stood like a chiseled statue, ignor-
ing the friendly counsel of our foreman, while the
stranger, after wiping the liquor from his face and
person, walked across the room and seated himself
at the table from which he had risen. A stillness
as of death pervaded the room, which was only
broken by our foreman repeating his request to
Priest to come away, but the latter replied, "No;

when I leave this place it will not be done in fear of any one. When any man goes out of his way to insult me he must take the consequences, and he can always find me if he wants satisfaction. We 'll take another drink before we go. Everybody in the house, come up and take a drink with Paul Priest."

The inmates of the place, to the number of possibly twenty, who had been witness to what had occurred, accepted the invitation, quitting their games and gathering around the bar. Priest took a position at the end of the bar, where he could notice any movement on the part of his adversary as well as the faces of his guests, and smiling on them, said in true hospitality, "What will you have, gentlemen?" There was a forced effort on the part of the drinkers to appear indifferent to the situation, but with the stranger sitting sullenly in their rear and an iron-gray man standing at the farther end of the line, hungering for an opportunity to settle differences with six-shooters, their indifference was an empty mockery. Some of the players returned to their games, while others sauntered into the street, yet Priest showed no disposition to go. After a while the stranger walked over to the bar and called for a glass of whiskey.

The Rebel stood at the end of the bar, calmly rolling a cigarette, and as the stranger seemed not to notice him, Priest attracted his attention and said, "I 'm just passing through here, and shall only be in town this afternoon; so if there's anything between us that demands settlement, don't hesitate to ask for it."

The stranger drained his glass at a single gulp, and with admirable composure replied, "If there's anything between us, we'll settle it in due time, and as men usually settle such differences in this country. I have a friend or two in town, and as soon as I see them, you will receive notice, or you may consider the matter dropped. That's all I care to say at present."

He walked away to the rear of the room, Priest joined us, and we strolled out of the place. In the street, a grizzled, gray-bearded man, who had drunk with him inside, approached my bunkie and said, "You want to watch that fellow. He claims to be from the Gallatin country, but he isn't, for I live there. There's a pal with him, and they've got some good horses, but I know every brand on the headwaters of the Missouri, and their horses were never bred on any of its three forks. Don't give him any the best of you. Keep an eye on him, comrade." After this warning, the old man turned into the first open door, and we crossed over to the wheelwright's shop; and as the wheel would not be finished for several hours yet, we continued our survey of the town, and our next landing was at The Buffalo Bull. On entering we found four of our men in a game of cards at the very first table, while Officer was reported as being in the gambling room in the rear. The only vacant table in the bar-room was the last one in the far corner, and calling for a deck of cards, we occupied it. I sat with my back to the log wall of the low one-story room, while on my left and fronting the door, Priest took a seat with Flood for his pardner, while Honeyman fell to me. After playing a few hands, Flood suggested that Billy go forward and exchange seats with some of our outfit, so as to be near the door, where he could see any one that entered, while from his position the rear door would be similarly guarded. Under this change, Rod Wheat came back to our table and took Honeyman's place. We had been playing along for an hour, with people passing in and out of the gambling room, and expected shortly to start for camp, when Priest's long-haired adversary came in at the front door, and, walking through the room, passed into the gambling department.

John Officer, after winning a few dollars in the card room, was standing alongside watching our game; and as the stranger passed by, Priest gave him the wink, on which Officer followed the stranger and a heavy set companion who was with him into the rear room. We had played only a few hands when the heavy-set man came back to the bar, took a drink, and walked over to watch a game of cards at the second table from the front door. Officer came back shortly afterward, and whispered to us that there were four of them to look out for, as he had seen them conferring together. Priest seemed the least concerned of any of us, but I noticed he eased the holster on his belt forward, where it would be ready to his hand. We had called for a round of drinks, Officer taking one with us, when two men came out of the gambling hell, and halting at the bar, pretended to divide some money which they wished to have it appear they had won in the card room. Their conversation was loud and intended to attract attention, but Officer gave us the wink, and their ruse was perfectly understood. After taking a drink and attracting as much attention as possible over the division of the money, they separated, but remained in the room.

I was dealing the cards a few minutes later, when the long-haired man emerged from the gambling hell, and imitating the maudlin, sauntered up to the bar and asked for a drink. After being served, he walked about halfway to the door, then whirling suddenly, stepped to the end of the bar, placed his hands upon it, sprang up and stood upright on it. He whipped out two six-shooters, let loose a yell which caused a commotion throughout the room, and walked very deliberately the length of the counter, his attention centred upon the occupants of our table. Not attracting the notice he expected in our quarter, he turned, and slowly repaced the bar, hurling anathemas on Texas and Texans in general.

I saw The Rebel's eyes, steeled to intensity, meet Flood's across the table, and in that glance of our foreman he evidently read approval, for he rose rigidly with the stealth of a tiger, and for the first time that day his hand went to the handle of his six-shooter. One of the two pretended winners at cards saw the movement in our quarter, and sang out as a warning, "Cuidado, mucho." The man on the bar whirled on the word of warning, and blazed away with his two guns into our corner. I had risen at the word and was pinned against the wall, where on the first fire a rain of dirt fell from the chinking in the wall over my head. As soon as the others sprang away from the table, I kicked it over in clearing myself, and came to my feet just as The Rebel fired his second shot. I had the satisfaction of seeing his long-haired adversary reel backwards, firing his guns into the ceiling as he went, and in falling crash heavily into the glassware on the back bar.

The smoke which filled the room left nothing visible for a few moments. Meantime Priest, satisfied that his aim had gone true, turned, passed through the rear room, gained his horse, and was galloping away to the herd before any semblance of order was restored. As the smoke cleared away and we passed forward through the room, John Officer had one of the three pardners standing with his hands to the wall, while his six-shooter lay on the floor under Officer's foot. He had made but one shot into our corner, when the muzzle of a gun was pushed against his ear with an imperative order to drop his arms, which he had promptly done. The two others, who had been under the surveillance of our men at the forward table, never made a move or offered to bring a gun into action, and after the killing of their picturesque pardner passed together out of the house. There had been five or six shots fired into our corner, but the first double shot, fired when three of us were still sitting, went too high for effect, while the remainder were scattering, though Rod Wheat got a bullet through his coat, close enough to burn the skin on his shoulder.

The dead man was laid out on the floor of the saloon; and through curiosity, for it could hardly have been much of a novelty to the inhabitants of Frenchman's Ford, hundreds came to gaze on the corpse and examine the wounds, one above the other through his vitals, either of which would have been fatal. Officer's prisoner admitted that the dead man was his pardner, and offered to remove the corpse if released. On turning his six-shooter over to the proprietor of the place, he was given his freedom to depart and look up his friends.

As it was after sundown, and our wheel was refilled and ready, we set out for camp, where we found that Priest had taken a fresh horse and started back over the trail. No one felt any uneasiness over his absence, for he had demonstrated his ability to protect himself; and truth compels me to say that the outfit to a man was proud of him. Honeyman was substituted on our guard in The Rebel's place, sleeping with me that night, and after we were in bed, Billy said in his enthusiasm: "If that horse thief had not relied on pot shooting, and had been modest and only used one gun, he might have hurt some of you fellows. But when I saw old Paul raising his gun to a level as he shot, I knew he was cool and steady, and I'd rather died right there than see him fail to get his man."

CHAPTER XXII

By early dawn the next morning we were astir at our last camp on Sweet Grass, and before the horses were brought in, we had put on the wagon box and reloaded our effects. The rainy season having ended in the mountain regions, the stage of water in the Yellowstone would present no difficulties in fording, and our foreman was anxious to make a long drive that day so as to make up for our enforced lay-over. We had breakfasted by the time the horses were corralled, and when we overtook the grazing herd, the cattle were within a mile of the river. Flood had looked over the ford the day before, and took one point of the herd as we went down into the crossing. The water was quite chilly to the cattle, though the horses in the lead paid little attention to it, the water in no place being over three feet deep. A number of spectators had come up from Frenchman's to watch the herd ford, the crossing being about half a mile above the village. No one made any inquiry for Priest, though ample opportunity was given them to see that the gray-haired man was missing. After the herd had crossed, a number of us lent a

rope in assisting the wagon over, and when we
reached the farther bank, we waved our hats to
the group on the south side in farewell to them
and to Frenchman's Ford.

The trail on leaving the river led up Many Ber-
ries, one of the tributaries of the Yellowstone putting in from the north side; and we paralleled it
mile after mile. It was with difficulty that riders
could be kept on the right hand side of the herd,
for along it grew endless quantities of a species of
upland huckleberry, and, breaking off branches,
we feasted as we rode along. The grade up this
creek was quite pronounced, for before night the
channel of the creek had narrowed to several yards
in width. On the second day out the wild fruit
disappeared early in the morning, and after a continued gradual climb, we made camp that night on
the summit of the divide within plain sight of the
Musselshell River. From this divide there was a
splendid view of the surrounding country as far
as eye could see. To our right, as we neared the
summit, we could see in that rarefied atmosphere
the buttes, like sentinels on duty, as they dotted the
immense tableland between the Yellowstone and
the mother Missouri, while on our left lay a thousand hills, untenanted save by the deer, elk, and
a remnant of buffalo. Another half day's drive
brought us to the shoals on the Musselshell, about
twelve miles above the entrance of Flatwillow
Creek. It was one of the easiest crossings we had

encountered in many a day, considering the size of the river and the flow of water. Long before the advent of the white man, these shoals had been in use for generations by the immense herds of buffalo and elk migrating back and forth between their summer ranges and winter pasturage, as the converging game trails on either side indicated. It was also an old Indian ford. After crossing and resuming our afternoon drive, the cattle trail ran within a mile of the river, and had it not been for the herd of northern wintered cattle, and possibly others, which had passed along a month or more in advance of us, it would have been hard to determine which were cattle and which were game trails, the country being literally cut up with these pathways.

When within a few miles of the Flatwillow, the trail bore off to the northwest, and we camped that night some distance below the junction of the former creek with the Big Box Elder. Before our watch had been on guard twenty minutes that night, we heard some one whistling in the distance; and as whoever it was refused to come any nearer the herd, a thought struck me, and I rode out into the darkness and hailed him.

"Is that you, Tom?" came the question to my challenge, and the next minute I was wringing the hand of my old bunkie, The Rebel. I assured him that the coast was clear, and that no inquiry had been even made for him the following morning,

when crossing the Yellowstone, by any of the inhabitants of Frenchman's Ford. He returned
with me to the bed ground, and meeting Honeyman as he circled around, was almost unhorsed by
the latter's warmth of reception, and Officer's
delight on meeting my bunkie was none the less
demonstrative. For nearly half an hour he rode
around with one or the other of us, and as we knew
he had had little if any sleep for the last three
nights, all of us begged him to go on into camp
and go to sleep. But the old rascal loafed around
with us on guard, seemingly delighted with our
company and reluctant to leave. Finally Honeyman and I prevailed on him to go to the wagon,
but before leaving us he said, "Why, I 've been
in sight of the herd for the last day and night, but
I 'm getting a little tired of lying out with the dry
cattle these cool nights, and living on huckleber-
ries and grouse, so I thought I 'd just ride in and
get a fresh horse and a square meal once more.
But if Flood says stay, you 'll see me at my old
place on the point to-morrow."

Had the owner of the herd suddenly appeared in
camp, he could not have received such an ovation
as was extended Priest the next morning when
his presence became known. From the cook to
the foreman, they gathered around our bed, where
The Rebel sat up in the blankets and held an in-
formal reception; and two hours afterward he was
riding on the right point of the herd as if nothing

had happened. We had a fair trail up Big Box Elder, and for the following few days, or until the source of that creek was reached, met nothing to check our course. Our foreman had been riding in advance of the herd, and after returning to us at noon one day, reported that the trail turned a due northward course towards the Missouri, and all herds had seemingly taken it. As we had to touch at Fort Benton, which was almost due westward, he had concluded to quit the trail and try to intercept the military road running from Fort Maginnis to Benton. Maginnis lay to the south of us, and our foreman hoped to strike the military road at an angle on as near a westward course as possible.

Accordingly after dinner he set out to look out the country, and took me with him. We bore off toward the Missouri, and within half an hour's ride after leaving the trail we saw some loose horses about three miles distant, down in a little valley through which flowed a creek towards the Musselshell. We reined in and watched the horses several minutes, when we both agreed from their movements that they were hobbled. We scouted out some five or six miles, finding the country somewhat rough, but passable for a herd and wagon. Flood was anxious to investigate those hobbled horses, for it bespoke the camp of some one in the immediate vicinity. On our return, the horses were still in view, and with no little diffi-

culty, we descended from the mesa into the valley
and reached them. To our agreeable surprise, one
of them was wearing a bell, while nearly half of
them were hobbled, there being twelve head, the
greater portion of which looked like pack horses.
Supposing the camp, if there was one, must be up
in the hills, we followed a bridle path up stream
in search of it, and soon came upon four men,
placer mining on the banks of the creek.

When we made our errand known, one of these
placer miners, an elderly man who seemed familiar
with the country, expressed some doubts about our
leaving the trail, though he said there was a bridle
path with which he was acquainted across to the
military road. Flood at once offered to pay him
well if he would pilot us across to the road, or
near enough so that we could find our way. The
old placerman hesitated, and after consulting
among his partners, asked how we were fixed for
provision, explaining that they wished to remain a
month or so longer, and that game had been scared
away from the immediate vicinity, until it had become hard to secure meat. But he found Flood
ready in that quarter, for he immediately offered
to kill a beef and load down any two pack horses
they had, if he would consent to pilot us over to
within striking distance of the Fort Benton road.
The offer was immediately accepted, and I was
dispatched to drive in their horses. Two of the
placer miners accompanied us back to the trail,

both riding good saddle horses and leading two others under pack saddles. We overtook the herd within a mile of the point where the trail was to be abandoned, and after sending the wagon ahead, our foreman asked our guests to pick out any cow or steer in the herd. When they declined, he cut out a fat stray cow which had come into the herd down on the North Platte, had her driven in after the wagon, killed and quartered. When we had laid the quarters on convenient rocks to cool and harden during the night, our future pilot timidly inquired what we proposed to do with the hide, and on being informed that he was welcome to it, seemed delighted, remarking, as I helped him to stake it out where it would dry, that "rawhide was mighty handy repairing pack saddles."

Our visitors interested us, for it is probable that not a man in our outfit had ever seen a miner before, though we had read of the life and were deeply interested in everything they did or said. They were very plain men and of simple manners, but we had great difficulty in getting them to talk. After supper, while idling away a couple of hours around our camp-fire, the outfit told stories, in the hope that our guests would become reminiscent and give us some insight into their experiences, Bob Blades leading off.

"I was in a cow town once up on the head of the Chisholm trail at a time when a church fair was being pulled off. There were lots of old long-

horn cowmen living in the town, who owned cattle
in that Cherokee Strip that Officer is always talking about. Well, there's lots of folks up there
that think a nigger is as good as anybody else, and
when you find such people set in their ways, it's
best not to argue matters with them, but lay low
and let on you think that way too. That's the
way those old Texas cowmen acted about it.

"Well, at this church fair there was to be
voted a prize of a nice baby wagon, which had
been donated by some merchant, to the prettiest
baby under a year old. Colonel Bob Zellers was
in town at the time, stopping at a hotel where the
darky cook was a man who had once worked for
him on the trail. ' Frog,' the darky, had married
when he quit the colonel's service, and at the time
of this fair there was a pickaninny in his family
about a year old, and nearly the color of a new
saddle. A few of these old cowmen got funny and
thought it would be a good joke to have Frog enter
his baby at the fair, and Colonel Bob being the
leader in the movement, he had no trouble convin-
cing the darky that that baby wagon was his, if he
would only enter his youngster. Frog thought the
world of the old Colonel, and the latter assured him
that he would vote for his baby while he had a
dollar or a cow left. The result was, Frog gave
his enthusiastic consent, and the Colonel agreed to
enter the pickaninny in the contest.

"Well, the Colonel attended to the entering of

the baby's name, and then on the dead quiet went
around and rustled up every cowman and puncher
in town, and had them promise to be on hand, to
vote for the prettiest baby at ten cents a throw.
The fair was being held in the largest hall in town,
and at the appointed hour we were all on hand, as
well as Frog and his wife and baby.   There were
about a dozen entries, and only one blackbird in
the covey.   The list of contestants was read by the
minister, and as each name was announced, there
was a vigorous clapping of hands all over the house
by the friends of each baby.   But when the name
of Miss Precilla June Jones was announced, the
Texas contingent made their presence known by
such a deafening outburst of applause that old
Frog grinned from ear to ear — he saw himself
right then pushing that baby wagon.

"Well, on the first heat we voted sparingly, and
as the vote was read out about every quarter hour,
Precilla June Jones on the first turn was fourth in
the race.   On the second report, our favorite had
moved up to third place, after which the weaker
ones were deserted, and all the voting blood was
centered on the two white leaders, with our blackbird a close third.   We were behaving ourselves
nicely, and our money was welcome if we were n't.
When the third vote was announced, Frog's pickaninny was second in the race, with her nose lapped
on the flank of the leader.   Then those who thought
a darky was as good as any one else got on the

prod in a mild form, and you could hear them voicing their opinions all over the hall. We heard it all, but sat as nice as pie and never said a word.

"When the final vote was called for, we knew it was the home stretch, and every rascal of us got his weasel skin out and sweetened the voting on Miss Precilla June Jones. Some of those old longhorns didn't think any more of a twenty-dollar gold piece than I do of a white chip, especially when there was a chance to give those good people a dose of their own medicine. I don't know how many votes we cast on the last whirl, but we swamped all opposition, and our favorite cantered under the wire an easy winner. Then you should have heard the kicking, but we kept still and inwardly chuckled. The minister announced the winner, and some of those good people didn't have any better manners than to hiss and cut up ugly. We stayed until Frog got the new baby wagon in his clutches, when we dropped out casually and met at the Ranch saloon, where Colonel Zellers had taken possession behind the bar and was dispensing hospitality in proper celebration of his victory."

Much to our disappointment, our guests remained silent and showed no disposition to talk, except to answer civil questions which Flood asked regarding the trail crossing on the Missouri, and what that river was like in the vicinity of old Fort Benton. When the questions had been answered, they again relapsed into silence. The fire was replenished, and after the conversation had touched on several subjects, Joe Stallings took his turn with a yarn.

"When my folks first came to Texas," said Joe, "they settled in Ellis County, near Waxahachie. My father was one of the pioneers in that county at a time when his nearest neighbor lived ten miles from his front gate. But after the war, when the country had settled up, these old pioneers naturally hung together and visited and chummed with one another in preference to the new settlers. One spring when I was about fifteen years old, one of those old pioneer neighbors of ours died, and my father decided that he would go to the funeral or burst a hame string. If any of you know anything about that black-waxy, hog-wallow land in Ellis County, you know that when it gets muddy in the spring a wagon wheel will fill solid with waxy mud. So at the time of this funeral it was impossible to go on the road with any kind of a vehicle, and my father had to go on horseback. He was an old man at the time and didn't like the idea, but it was either go on horseback or stay at home, and go he would.

"They raise good horses in Ellis County, and my father had raised some of the best of them — brought the stock from Tennessee. He liked good blood in a horse, and was always opposed to racing, but he raised some boys who weren't. I had a number of brothers older than myself, and they took a special pride in trying every colt we raised, to see what he amounted to in speed. Of course this had to be done away from home; but that was easy, for these older brothers thought nothing of riding twenty miles to a tournament, barbecue, or round-up, and when away from home they always tried their horses with the best in the country. At the time of this funeral, we had a crackerjack five year old chestnut sorrel gelding that could show his heels to any horse in the country. He was a peach, — you could turn him on a saddle blanket and jump him fifteen feet, and that cow never lived that he could n't cut.

"So the day of the funeral my father was in a quandary as to which horse to ride, but when he appealed to his boys, they recommended the best on the ranch, which was the chestnut gelding. My old man had some doubts as to his ability to ride the horse, for he had n't been on a horse's back for years; but my brothers assured him that the chestnut was as obedient as a kitten, and that before he had been on the road an hour the mud would take all the frisk and frolic out of him. There was nearly fifteen miles to go, and they assured him that he would never get there if he rode any other horse. Well, at last he consented to ride the gelding, and the horse was made ready, properly groomed, his tail tied up, and saddled and led up to the block. It took every member of the family to get my father rigged to start, but at last he announced himself as ready. Two of my brothers held the horse until he found the off stirrup, and then they turned him loose. The chestnut danced off a few rods, and settled down into a steady clip that was good for five or six miles an hour.

"My father reached the house in good time for the funeral services, but when the procession started for the burial ground, the horse was somewhat restless and impatient from the cold. There was quite a string of wagons and other vehicles from the immediate neighborhood which had braved the mud, and the line was nearly half a mile in length between the house and the graveyard. There were also possibly a hundred men on horseback bringing up the rear of the procession; and the chestnut, not understanding the solemnity of the occasion, was right on his mettle. Surrounded as he was by other horses, he kept his weather eye open for a race, for in coming home from dances and picnics with my brothers, he had often been tried in short dashes of half a mile or so. In order to get him out of the crowd of horses, my father dropped back with another pioneer to the extreme rear of the funeral line.

"When the procession was nearing the cemetery, a number of horsemen, who were late, galloped up in the rear. The chestnut, supposing a race was on, took the bit in his teeth and tore

down past the procession as though it was a free-
for-all Texas sweepstakes, the old man's white
beard whipping the breeze in his endeavor to hold
in the horse. Nor did he check him until the head
of the procession had been passed. When my father returned home that night, there was a family
round-up, for he was smoking under the collar.
Of course, my brothers denied having ever run the
horse, and my mother took their part; but the old
gent knew a thing or two about horses, and shortly
afterwards he got even with his boys by selling
the chestnut, which broke their hearts properly."

The elder of the two placer miners, a long-whiskered, pock-marked man, arose, and after walking
out from the fire some distance returned and called
our attention to signs in the sky, which he assured
us were a sure indication of a change in the
weather. But we were more anxious that he should
talk about something else, for we were in the habit
of taking the weather just as it came. When
neither one showed any disposition to talk, Flood
said to them, —

"It's bedtime with us, and one of you can sleep
with me, while I've fixed up an extra bed for the
other. I generally get out about daybreak, but if
that's too early for you, don't let my getting up
disturb you. And you fourth guard men, let the
cattle off the bed ground on a due westerly course
and point them up the divide. Now get to bed,
everybody, for we want to make a big drive to-
morrow."

CHAPTER XXIII

DELIVERY

I SHALL never forget the next morning, — August 26, 1882. As we of the third guard were relieved, about two hours before dawn, the wind veered around to the northwest, and a mist which had been falling during the fore part of our watch changed to soft flakes of snow. As soon as we were relieved, we skurried back to our blankets, drew the tarpaulin over our heads, and slept until dawn, when on being awakened by the foreman, we found a wet, slushy snow some two inches in depth on the ground. Several of the boys in the outfit declared it was the first snowfall they had ever seen, and I had but a slight recollection of having witnessed one in early boyhood in our old Georgia home. We gathered around the fire like a lot of frozen children, and our only solace was that our drive was nearing an end. The two placermen paid little heed to the raw morning, and our pilot assured us that this was but the squaw winter which always preceded Indian summer.

We made our customary early start, and while saddling up that morning, Flood and the two placer miners packed the beef on their two pack horses, first cutting off enough to last us several days. The cattle, when we overtook them, presented a sorry spectacle, apparently being as cold as we were, although we had our last stitch of clothing on, including our slickers, belted with a horse hobble. But when Flood and our guide rode past the herd, I noticed our pilot's coat was not even buttoned, nor was the thin cotton shirt which he wore, but his chest was exposed to that raw morning air which chilled the very marrow in our bones. Our foreman and guide kept in sight in the lead, the herd traveling briskly up the long mountain divide, and about the middle of the forenoon the sun came out warm and the snow began to melt. Within an hour after starting that morning, Quince Forrest, who was riding in front of me in the swing, dismounted, and picking out of the snow a brave little flower which looked something like a pansy, dropped back to me and said, "My weather gauge says it's eighty-eight degrees below freezo. But I want you to smell this posy, Quirk, and tell me on the dead thieving, do you ever expect to see your sunny southern home again? And did you notice the pock-marked colonel, baring his brisket to the morning breeze?"

Two hours after the sun came out, the snow had disappeared, and the cattle fell to and grazed until long after the noon hour. Our pilot led us up the divide between the Missouri and the headwaters of the Musselshell during the afternoon, weaving in and out around the heads of creeks putting into either river; and towards evening we crossed quite a creek running towards the Missouri, where we secured ample water for the herd. We made a late camp that night, and our guide assured us that another half day's drive would put us on the Judith River, where we would intercept the Fort Benton road.

The following morning our guide led us for several hours up a gradual ascent to the plateau, till we reached the tableland, when he left us to return to his own camp. Flood again took the lead, and within a mile we turned on our regular course, which by early noon had descended into the valley of the Judith River, and entered the Fort Maginnis and Benton military road. Our route was now clearly defined, and about noon on the last day of the month we sighted, beyond the Missouri River, the flag floating over Fort Benton. We made a crossing that afternoon below the Fort, and Flood went into the post, expecting either to meet Lovell or to receive our final instructions regarding the delivery.

After crossing the Missouri, we grazed the herd over to the Teton River, a stream which paralleled the former watercourse, — the military post being located between the two. We had encamped for the night when Flood returned with word of a letter he had received from our employer and an interview he had had with the commanding officer

of Fort Benton, who, it seemed, was to have a hand
in the delivery of the herd. Lovell had been detained in the final settlement of my brother Bob's
herd at the Crow Agency by some differences regarding weights. Under our present instructions,
we were to proceed slowly to the Blackfoot Agency,
and immediately on the arrival of Lovell at Benton, he and the commandant would follow by ambulance and overtake us. The distance from Fort
Benton to the agency was variously reported to be
from one hundred and twenty to one hundred and
thirty miles, six or seven days' travel for the herd
at the farthest, and then good-by, Circle Dots!

A number of officers and troopers from the post
overtook us the next morning and spent several
hours with us as the herd trailed out up the Teton.
They were riding fine horses, which made our
through saddle stock look insignificant in comparison, though had they covered twenty-four hundred
miles and lived on grass as had our mounts, some
of the lustre of their glossy coats would have been
absent. They looked well, but it would have been
impossible to use them or any domestic bred horses
in trail work like ours, unless a supply of grain
could be carried with us. The range country produced a horse suitable to range needs, hardy and
a good forager, which, when not overworked under
the saddle, met every requirement of his calling,
as well as being self-sustaining. Our horses, in
fact, were in better flesh when we crossed the

Missouri than they were the day we received the herd on the Rio Grande. The spectators from the fort quitted us near the middle of the forenoon, and we snailed on westward at our leisurely gait.

There was a fair road up the Teton, which we followed for several days without incident, to the forks of that river, where we turned up Muddy Creek, the north fork of the Teton. That noon, while catching saddle horses, dinner not being quite ready, we noticed a flurry amongst the cattle, then almost a mile in our rear. Two men were on herd with them as usual, grazing them forward up the creek and watering as they came, when suddenly the cattle in the lead came tearing out of the creek, and on reaching open ground turned at bay. After several bunches had seemingly taken fright at the same object, we noticed Bull Durham, who was on herd, ride through the cattle to the scene of disturbance. We saw him, on nearing the spot, lie down on the neck of his horse, watch intently for several minutes, then quietly drop back to the rear, circle the herd, and ride for the wagon. We had been observing the proceedings closely, though from a distance, for some time. Daylight was evidently all that saved us from a stampede, and as Bull Durham galloped up he was almost breathless. He informed us that an old cinnamon bear and two cubs were berrying along the creek, and had taken the right of way. Then there was a hustling and borrowing of cartridges, while saddles were cinched on to horses as though human life depended on alacrity. We were all feeling quite gala anyhow, and this looked like a chance for some sport. It was hard to hold the impulsive ones in check until the others were ready. The cattle pointed us to the location of the quarry as we rode forward. When within a quarter of a mile, we separated into two squads, in order to gain the rear of the bears, cut them off from the creek, and force them into the open. The cattle held the attention of the bears until we had gained their rear, and as we came up between them and the creek, the old one reared up on her haunches and took a most astonished and innocent look at us.

A single "woof" brought one of the cubs to her side, and she dropped on all fours and lumbered off, a half dozen shots hastening her pace in an effort to circle the horsemen who were gradually closing in. In making this circle to gain the protection of some thickets which skirted the creek, she was compelled to cross quite an open space, and before she had covered the distance of fifty yards, a rain of ropes came down on her, and she was thrown backward with no less than four lariats fastened over her neck and fore parts. Then ensued a lively scene, for the horses snorted and in spite of rowels refused to face the bear. But ropes securely snubbed to pommels held them to the quarry. Two minor circuses were meantime in pro-

gress with the two cubs, but pressure of duty held
those of us who had fastened on to the old cinnamon. The ropes were taut and several of them
were about her throat; the horses were pulling in
as many different directions, yet the strain of all
the lariats failed to choke her as we expected. At
this juncture, four of the loose men came to our
rescue, and proposed shooting the brute. We
were willing enough, for though we had better
than a tail hold, we were very ready to let go.
But while there were plenty of good shots among
us, our horses had now become wary, and could
not, when free from ropes, be induced to approach
within twenty yards of the bear, and they were so
fidgety that accurate aim was impossible. We who
had ropes on the old bear begged the boys to get
down and take it afoot, but they were not disposed
to listen to our reasons, and blazed away from
rearing horses, not one shot in ten taking effect.
There was no telling how long this random shooting would have lasted; but one shot cut my rope
two feet from the noose, and with one rope less on
her the old bear made some ugly surges, and had
not Joe Stallings had a wheeler of a horse on the
rope, she would have done somebody damage.

The Rebel was on the opposite side from Stallings and myself, and as soon as I was freed, he
called me around to him, and shifting his rope to
me, borrowed my six-shooter and joined those who
were shooting. Dismounting, he gave the reins of

his horse to Flood, walked up to within fifteen steps of mother bruin, and kneeling, emptied both six-shooters with telling accuracy. The old bear winced at nearly every shot, and once she made an ugly surge on the ropes, but the three guy lines held her up to Priest's deliberate aim. The vitality of that cinnamon almost staggers belief, for after both six-shooters had been emptied into her body, she floundered on the ropes with all her former strength, although the blood was dripping and gushing from her numerous wounds. Borrowing a third gun, Priest returned to the fight, and as we slacked the ropes slightly, the old bear reared, facing her antagonist. The Rebel emptied his third gun into her before she sank, choked, bleeding, and exhausted, to the ground; and even then no one dared to approach her, for she struck out wildly with all fours as she slowly succumbed to the inevitable.

One of the cubs had been roped and afterwards shot at close quarters, while the other had reached the creek and climbed a sapling which grew on the bank, when a few shots brought him to the ground. The two cubs were about the size of a small black bear, though the mother was a large specimen of her species. The cubs had nice coats of soft fur, and their hides were taken as trophies of the fight, but the robe of the mother was a summer one and worthless. While we were skinning the cubs, the foreman called our attention to the fact that the herd had drifted up the creek nearly opposite the wagon. During the encounter with the bears he was the most excited one in the outfit, and was the man who cut my rope with his random shooting from horseback. But now the herd recovered his attention, and he dispatched some of us to ride around the cattle. When we met at the wagon for dinner, the excitement was still on us, and the hunt was unanimously voted the most exciting bit of sport and powder burning we had experienced on our trip.

Late that afternoon a forage wagon from Fort Benton passed us with four loose ambulance mules in charge of five troopers, who were going on ahead to establish a relay station in anticipation of the trip of the post commandant to the Blackfoot Agency. There were to be two relay stations between the post and the agency, and this detachment expected to go into camp that night within forty miles of our destination, there to await the arrival of the commanding officer and the owner of the herd at Benton. These soldiers were out two days from the post when they passed us, and they assured us that the ambulance would go through from Benton to Blackfoot without a halt, except for the changing of relay teams. The next forenoon we passed the last relay camp, well up the Muddy, and shortly afterwards the road left that creek, turning north by a little west, and we entered on the last tack of our long drive. On the even-

ing of the 6th of September, as we were going into
camp on Two Medicine Creek, within ten miles
of the agency, the ambulance overtook us, under
escort of the troopers whom we had passed at the
last relay station. We had not seen Don Lovell
since June, when we passed Dodge, and it goes
without saying that we were glad to meet him
again. On the arrival of the party, the cattle had
not yet been bedded, so Lovell borrowed a horse,
and with Flood took a look over the herd before
darkness set in, having previously prevailed on the
commanding officer to rest an hour and have supper before proceeding to the agency.

When they returned from inspecting the cattle,
the commandant and Lovell agreed to make the
final delivery on the 8th, if it were agreeable to
the agent, and with this understanding continued
their journey. The next morning Flood rode into
the agency, borrowing McCann's saddle and taking an extra horse with him, having left us instructions to graze the herd all day and have them in
good shape with grass and water, in case they were
inspected that evening on their condition. Near
the middle of the afternoon quite a cavalcade
rode out from the agency, including part of a company of cavalry temporarily encamped there. The
Indian agent and the commanding officer from
Benton were the authorized representatives of the
government, it seemed, as Lovell took extra pains
in showing them over the herd, frequently consult-

ing the contract which he held, regarding sex, age, and flesh of the cattle.

The only hitch in the inspection was over a number of sore-footed cattle, which was unavoidable after such a long journey. But the condition of these tender-footed animals being otherwise satisfactory, Lovell urged the agent and commandant to call up the men for explanations. The agent was no doubt a very nice man, and there may have been other things that he understood better than cattle, for he did ask a great many simple, innocent questions. Our replies, however, might have been condensed into a few simple statements. We had, we related, been over five months on the trail; after the first month, tender-footed cattle began to appear from time to time in the herd, as stony or gravelly portions of the trail were encountered, — the number so affected at any one time varying from ten to forty head. Frequently well-known lead cattle became tender in their feet and would drop back to the rear, and on striking soft or sandy footing recover and resume their position in the lead; that since starting, it was safe to say, fully ten per cent of the entire herd had been so affected, yet we had not lost a single head from this cause; that the general health of the animal was never affected, and that during enforced lay-overs nearly all so affected recovered. As there were not over twenty-five sore-footed animals in the herd on our arrival, our explanation was suffi-

cient and the herd was accepted. There yet remained the counting and classification, but as this
would require time, it went over until the following day. The cows had been contracted for by
the head, while the steers went on their estimated
weight in dressed beef, the contract calling for a
million pounds with a ten per cent leeway over
that amount.

I was amongst the first to be interviewed by the
Indian agent, and on being excused, I made the
acquaintance of one of two priests who were with
the party. He was a rosy-cheeked, well-fed old
padre, who informed me that he had been stationed
among the Blackfeet for over twenty years, and
that he had labored long with the government to
assist these Indians. The cows in our herd, which
were to be distributed amongst the Indian families
for domestic purposes, were there at his earnest
solicitation. I asked him if these cows would not
perish during the long winter — my recollection
was still vivid of the touch of squaw winter we had
experienced some two weeks previous. But he
assured me that the winters were dry, if cold, and
his people had made some progress in the ways of
civilization, and had provided shelter and forage
against the wintry weather. He informed me that
previous to his labors amongst the Blackfeet their
ponies wintered without loss on the native grasses,
though he had since taught them to make hay, and
in anticipation of receiving these cows, such fami-

lies as were entitled to share in the division had amply provided for the animals' sustenance.

Lovell returned with the party to the agency, and we were to bring up the herd for classification early in the morning. Flood informed us that a beef pasture had been built that summer for the steers, while the cows would be held under herd by the military, pending their distribution. We spent our last night with the herd singing songs, until the first guard called the relief, when realizing the lateness of the hour, we burrowed into our blankets.

"I don't know how you fellows feel about it," said Quince Forrest, when the first guard were relieved and they had returned to camp, "but I bade those cows good-by on their beds to-night without a regret or a tear. The novelty of night-herding loses its charm with me when it's drawn out over five months. I might be fool enough to make another such trip, but I'd rather be the Indian and let the other fellow drive the cows to me — there's a heap more comfort in it."

The next morning, before we reached the agency, a number of gaudily bedecked bucks and squaws rode out to meet us. The arrival of the herd had been expected for several weeks, and our approach was a delight to the Indians, who were flocking to the agency from the nearest villages. Physically, they were fine specimens of the aborigines. But our Spanish, which Quarternight and I tried on

them, was as unintelligible to them as their guttural gibberish was to us.

Lovell and the agent, with a detachment of the
cavalry, met us about a mile from the agency buildings, and we were ordered to cut out the cows.
The herd had been grazed to contentment, and
were accordingly rounded in, and the task begun
at once. Our entire outfit were turned into the
herd to do the work, while an abundance of troopers held the herd and looked after the cut. It
took about an hour and a half, during which time
we worked like Trojans. Cavalrymen several times
attempted to assist us, but their horses were no
match for ours in the work. A cow can turn on
much less space than a cavalry horse, and except
for the amusement they afforded, the military were
of very little effect.

After we had retrimmed the cut, the beeves
were started for their pasture, and nothing now
remained but the counting to complete the receiving. Four of us remained behind with the cows,
but for over two hours the steers were in plain
sight, while the two parties were endeavoring to
make a count. How many times they recounted
them before agreeing on the numbers I do not
know, for the four of us left with the cows became occupied by a controversy over the sex of a
young Indian — a Blackfoot — riding a cream-col-
ored pony. The controversy originated between
Fox Quarternight and Bob Blades, who had dis-

covered this swell among a band who had just ridden in from the west, and John Officer and myself
were appealed to for our opinions. The Indian
was pointed out to us across the herd, easily distinguished by beads and beaver fur trimmings in
the hair, so we rode around to pass our judgment
as experts on the beauty. The young Indian was
not over sixteen years of age, with remarkable
features, from which every trace of the aborigine
seemed to be eliminated. Officer and myself were
in a quandary, for we felt perfectly competent
when appealed to for our opinions on such a deli-
cate subject, and we made every endeavor to open
a conversation by signs and speech. But the young
Blackfoot paid no attention to us, being intent
upon watching the cows. The neatly moccasined
feet and the shapely hand, however, indicated the
feminine, and when Blades and Quarternight rode
up, we rendered our decision accordingly. Blades
took exception to the decision and rode alongside
the young Indian, pretending to admire the long
plaits of hair, toyed with the beads, pinched and
patted the young Blackfoot, and finally, although
the rest of us, for fear the Indian might take of-
fense and raise trouble, pleaded with him to desist,
he called the youth his "squaw," when the young
blood, evidently understanding the appellation, relaxed into a broad smile, and in fair English said,
"Me buck."

Blades burst into a loud laugh at his success, at

which the Indian smiled but accepted a cigarette,
and the two cronied together, while we rode away
to look after our cows. The outfit returned shortly
afterward, when The Rebel rode up to me and
expressed himself rather profanely at the inability
of the government's representatives to count cattle
in Texas fashion. On the arrival of the agent and
others, the cows were brought around; and these
being much more gentle, and being under Lovell's
instruction fed between the counters in the nar-
rowest file possible, a satisfactory count was agreed
upon at the first trial. The troopers took charge
of the cows after counting, and, our work over,
we galloped away to the wagon, hilarious and care
free.

McCann had camped on the nearest water to the
agency, and after dinner we caught out the top
horses, and, dressed in our best, rode into the
agency proper. There was quite a group of houses
for the attachés, one large general warehouse, and
several school and chapel buildings. I again met
the old padre, who showed us over the place. One
could not help being favorably impressed with the
general neatness and cleanliness of the place. In
answer to our questions, the priest informed us
that he had mastered the Indian language early in
his work, and had adopted it in his ministry, the
better to effect the object of his mission. There
was something touching in the zeal of this devoted

padre in his work amongst the tribe, and the recognition of the government had come as a fitting climax to his work and devotion.

As we rode away from the agency, the cows being in sight under herd of a dozen soldiers, several of us rode out to them, and learned that they intended to corral the cows at night, and within a week distribute them to Indian families, when the troop expected to return to Fort Benton. Lovell and Flood appeared at the camp about dusk — Lovell in high spirits. This, he said, was the easiest delivery of the three herds which he had driven that year. He was justified in feeling well over the year's drive, for he had in his possession a voucher for our Circle Dots which would crowd six figures closely. It was a gay night with us, for man and horse were free, and as we made down our beds, old man Don insisted that Flood and he should make theirs down alongside ours. He and The Rebel had been joking each other during the evening, and as we went to bed were taking an occasional fling at one another as opportunity offered.

"It's a strange thing to me," said Lovell, as he was pulling off his boots, "that this herd counted out a hundred and twelve head more than we started with, while Bob Quirk's herd was only eighty-one long at the final count."

"Well, you see," replied The Rebel, "Quirk's

was a steer herd, while ours had over a thousand cows in it, and you must make allowance for some of them to calve on the way. That ought to be easy figuring for a foxy, long-headed Yank like you."

CHAPTER XXIV

BACK TO TEXAS

THE nearest railroad point from the Blackfoot Agency was Silver Bow, about a hundred and seventy-five miles due south, and at that time the terminal of the Utah Northern Railroad. Everything connected with the delivery having been completed the previous day, our camp was astir with the dawn in preparation for departure on our last ride together. As we expected to make not less than forty miles a day on the way to the railroad, our wagon was lightened to the least possible weight. The chuck-box, water kegs, and such superfluities were dropped, and the supplies reduced to one week's allowance, while beds were overhauled and extra wearing apparel of the outfit was discarded. Who cared if we did sleep cold and hadn't a change to our backs? We were going home and would have money in our pockets.

"The first thing I do when we strike that town of Silver Bow," said Bull Durham, as he was putting on his last shirt, "is to discard to the skin and get me new togs to a finish. I'll commence on my little pattering feet, which will require fifteen-dollar moccasins, and then about a six-dollar checked cottonade suit, and top off with a seven-dollar brown Stetson. Then with a few drinks under my belt and a rim-fire cigar in my mouth, I'd admire to meet the governor of Montana if convenient."

Before the sun was an hour high, we bade farewell to the Blackfoot Agency and were doubling back over the trail, with Lovell in our company. Our first night's camp was on the Muddy and the second on the Sun River. We were sweeping across the tablelands adjoining the main divide of the Rocky Mountains like the chinook winds which sweep that majestic range on its western slope. We were a free outfit; even the cook and wrangler were relieved; their little duties were divided among the crowd and almost disappeared. There was a keen rivalry over driving the wagon, and McCann was transferred to the hurricane deck of a cow horse, which he sat with ease and grace, having served an apprenticeship in the saddle in other days. There were always half a dozen wranglers available in the morning, and we traveled as if under forced marching orders. The third night we camped in the narrows between the Missouri River and the Rocky Mountains, and on the evening of the fourth day camped several miles to the eastward of Helena, the capital of the territory.

Don Lovell had taken the stage for the capital the night before; and on making camp that evening, Flood took a fresh horse and rode into town. The next morning he and Lovell returned with the superintendent of the cattle company which had contracted for our horses and outfit on the Republican. We corralled the horses for him, and after roping out about a dozen which, as having sore backs or being lame, he proposed to treat as damaged and take at half price, the *remuda* was counted out, a hundred and forty saddle horses, four mules, and a wagon constituting the transfer. Even with the loss of two horses and the concessions on a dozen others, there was a nice profit on the entire outfit over its cost in the lower country, due to the foresight of Don Lovell in mounting us well. Two of our fellows who had borrowed from the superintendent money to redeem their six-shooters after the horse race on the Republican, authorized Lovell to return him the loans and thanked him for the favor. Everything being satisfactory between buyer and seller, they returned to town together for a settlement, while we moved on south towards Silver Bow, where the outfit was to be delivered.

Another day's easy travel brought us to within a mile of the railroad terminus; but it also brought us to one of the hardest experiences of our trip, for each of us knew, as we unsaddled our horses, that we were doing it for the last time. Although we were in the best of spirits over the successful conclusion of the drive; although we were glad to

be free from herd duty and looked forward eagerly
to the journey home, there was still a feeling of
regret in our hearts which we could not dispel. In
the days of my boyhood I have shed tears when a
favorite horse was sold from our little ranch on
the San Antonio, and have frequently witnessed
Mexican children unable to hide their grief when
need of bread had compelled the sale of some favorite horse to a passing drover. But at no time in
my life, before or since, have I felt so keenly the
parting between man and horse as I did that September evening in Montana. For on the trail an
affection springs up between a man and his mount
which is almost human. Every privation which
he endures his horse endures with him, — carrying
him through falling weather, swimming rivers by
day and riding in the lead of stampedes by night,
always faithful, always willing, and always patiently enduring every hardship, from exhausting
hours under saddle to the sufferings of a dry drive.
And on this drive, covering nearly three thousand
miles, all the ties which can exist between man
and beast had not only become cemented, but our
remuda as a whole had won the affection of both
men and employer for carrying without serious
mishap a valuable herd all the way from the Rio
Grande to the Blackfoot Agency. Their bones
may be bleaching in some coulee by now, but the
men who knew them then can never forget them
or the part they played in that long drive.

Three men from the ranch rode into our camp that evening, and the next morning we counted over our horses to them and they passed into strangers' hands. That there might be no delay, Flood had ridden into town the evening before and secured a wagon and gunny bags in which to sack our saddles; for while we willingly discarded all other effects, our saddles were of sufficient value to return and could be checked home as baggage. Our foreman reported that Lovell had arrived by stage and was awaiting us in town, having already arranged for our transportation as far as Omaha, and would accompany us to that city, where other transportation would have to be secured to our destination. In our impatience to get into town, we were trudging in by twos and threes before the wagon arrived for our saddles, and had not Flood remained behind to look after them, they might have been abandoned.

There was something about Silver Bow that reminded me of Frenchman's Ford on the Yellowstone. Being the terminal of the first railroad into Montana, it became the distributing point for all the western portion of that territory, and immense ox trains were in sight for the transportation of goods to remoter points in the north and west. The population too was very much the same as at Frenchman's, though the town in general was an improvement over the former, there being some stability to its buildings. As we were to leave on an eleven o'clock train, we had little opportunity to see the town, and for the short time at our disposal, barber shops and clothing stores claimed our first attention. Most of us had some remnants of money, while my bunkie was positively rich, and Lovell advanced us fifty dollars apiece, pending a final settlement on reaching our destination.

Within an hour after receiving the money, we blossomed out in new suits from head to heel. Our guard hung together as if we were still on night herd, and in the selection of clothing the opinion of the trio was equal to a purchase. The Rebel was very easily pleased in his selection, but John Officer and myself were rather fastidious. Officer was so tall it was with some little difficulty that a suit could be found to fit him, and when he had stuffed his pants in his boots and thrown away the vest, for he never wore either vest or suspenders, he emerged looking like an Alpine tourist, with his new pink shirt and nappy brown beaver slouch hat jauntily cocked over one ear. As we sauntered out into the street, Priest was dressed as became his years and mature good sense, while my costume rivaled Officer's in gaudiness, and it is safe to assert two thirds of our outlay had gone for boots and hats.

Flood overtook us in the street, and warned us to be on hand at the depot at least half an hour in advance of train time, informing us that he had checked our saddles and did n't want any of us to get left at the final moment. We all took a drink together, and Officer assured our foreman that he would be responsible for our appearance at the proper time, "sober and sorry for it." So we sauntered about the straggling village, drinking occasionally, and on the suggestion of The Rebel, made a cow by putting in five apiece and had Officer play it on faro, he claiming to be an expert on the game. Taking the purse thus made up, John sat into a game, while Priest and myself, after watching the play some minutes, strolled out again and met others of our outfit in the street, scarcely recognizable in their killing rigs. The Rebel was itching for a monte game, but this not being a cow town there was none, and we strolled next into a saloon, where a piano was being played by a venerable-looking individual, — who proved quite amiable, taking a drink with us and favoring us with a number of selections of our choosing. We were enjoying this musical treat when our foreman came in and asked us to get the boys together. Priest and I at once started for Officer, whom we found quite a winner, but succeeded in choking him off on our employer's order, and after the checks had been cashed, took a parting drink, which made us the last in reaching the depot. When we were all assembled, our employer informed us that he only wished to keep us together until embarking, and invited us to accompany him across the street to Tom Robbins's saloon.

On entering the saloon, Lovell inquired of the young fellow behind the bar, "Son, what will you take for the privilege of my entertaining this outfit for fifteen minutes?"

"The ranch is yours, sir, and you can name your own figures," smilingly and somewhat shrewdly replied the young fellow, and promptly vacated his position.

"Now, two or three of you rascals get in behind there," said old man Don, as a quartet of the boys picked him up and set him on one end of the bar, "and let's see what this ranch has in the way of refreshment."

McCann, Quarternight, and myself obeyed the order, but the fastidious tastes of the line in front soon compelled us to call to our assistance both Robbins and the young man who had just vacated the bar in our favor.

"That's right, fellows," roared Lovell from his commanding position, as he jingled a handful of gold coins, "turn to and help wait on these thirsty Texans; and remember that nothing's too rich for our blood to-day. This outfit has made one of the longest cattle drives on record, and the best is none too good for them. So set out your best, for they can't cut much hole in the profits in the short time we have to stay. The train leaves in twenty minutes, and see that every rascal is provided with an extra bottle for the journey. And drop down this

way when you get time, as I want a couple of
boxes of your best cigars to smoke on the way.
Montana has treated us well, and we want to leave
some of our coin with you.''